M.I.T.H.™

MAGICAL INTELLIGENCE TACTICAL HEADQUARTERS

"Everything you can imagine is real."

-- **Pablo Picasso**

M.I.T.H.™

M.I.T.H. Written and Created By:
Jennifer Brandes Hepler and **Chris Hepler**

Executive Produced by:
John Frank Rosenblum and **Cindi Rice**
for Epic Level Entertainment

Art by:
Stephen Segovia

Colors by:
Mike Kelleher

Letters by:
Simon Bowland

For the cover
Art by: **Tyler Kirkham**
Colors by: **John Starr**

Special Thanks to: **Lawrence Brandes**

For this edition
Book design and Layout by: Phil Smith

for Top Cow Productions
Marc Silvestri_chief executive officer
Matt Hawkins_president / chief operating officer
Jim McLauchlin_editor in chief
Renae Geerlings_vp of publishing / managing editor
Scott Tucker_editor
Chaz Riggs_production manager
Annie Pham_marketing director
Peter Lam_webmaster
Phil Smith_trades and submissions
Rob Levin, Zach Matheny_production assistants
Scott Newman_intern

for Spacedog, Inc.
Roger Mincheff_chief executive officer
Hal Burg_director of business development
and marketing
Joe Berry_production designer
Justin Bain_marketing manager

What did you think of this book?
We love to hear from our readers.

write us at:
M.I.T.H. Letters
c/o Top Cow Productions, Inc.
10350 Santa Monica Blvd., Suite #100
Los Angeles, CA 90025

To find the comics shop
nearest you call
1-888-COMICBOOK

ISBN # 1-58240-515-8
Published by Image Comics®
M.I.T.H.: Operation Smoking Jaguar **November 2005 First Printing.**
Office of Publication: 1942 University Ave., Suite 305, Berkeley, CA 94704. M.I.T.H. is © 2005 M.I.T.H. Entertainment.
"M.I.T.H.," the M.I.T.H. logo, the M.I.T.H. characters, and their distinctive likenesses thereof are trademarks owned by M.I.T.H.
Entertainment, and are used herein under license. All rights reserved. Any similarities to persons living or dead are purely coin-
cidental. "Left Jab Entertainment," and the Left Jab Logo are trademarks of Left Jab Entertainment. "Spacedog," and the Space-
dog logo are registered trademarks of Spacedog, Inc. "Top Cow" and the Top Cow logo are registered trademarks of Top Cow
Productions, Inc. The entire contents of this book are © 2005 Top Cow Productions, Inc. and Spacedog Inc. With the exception of
art used for review purposes, none of the contents of this book may be reprinted in any form without the express written consent of
Top Cow Productions, Inc.
Printed in Canada

for Image Comics
publisher Erik Larsen

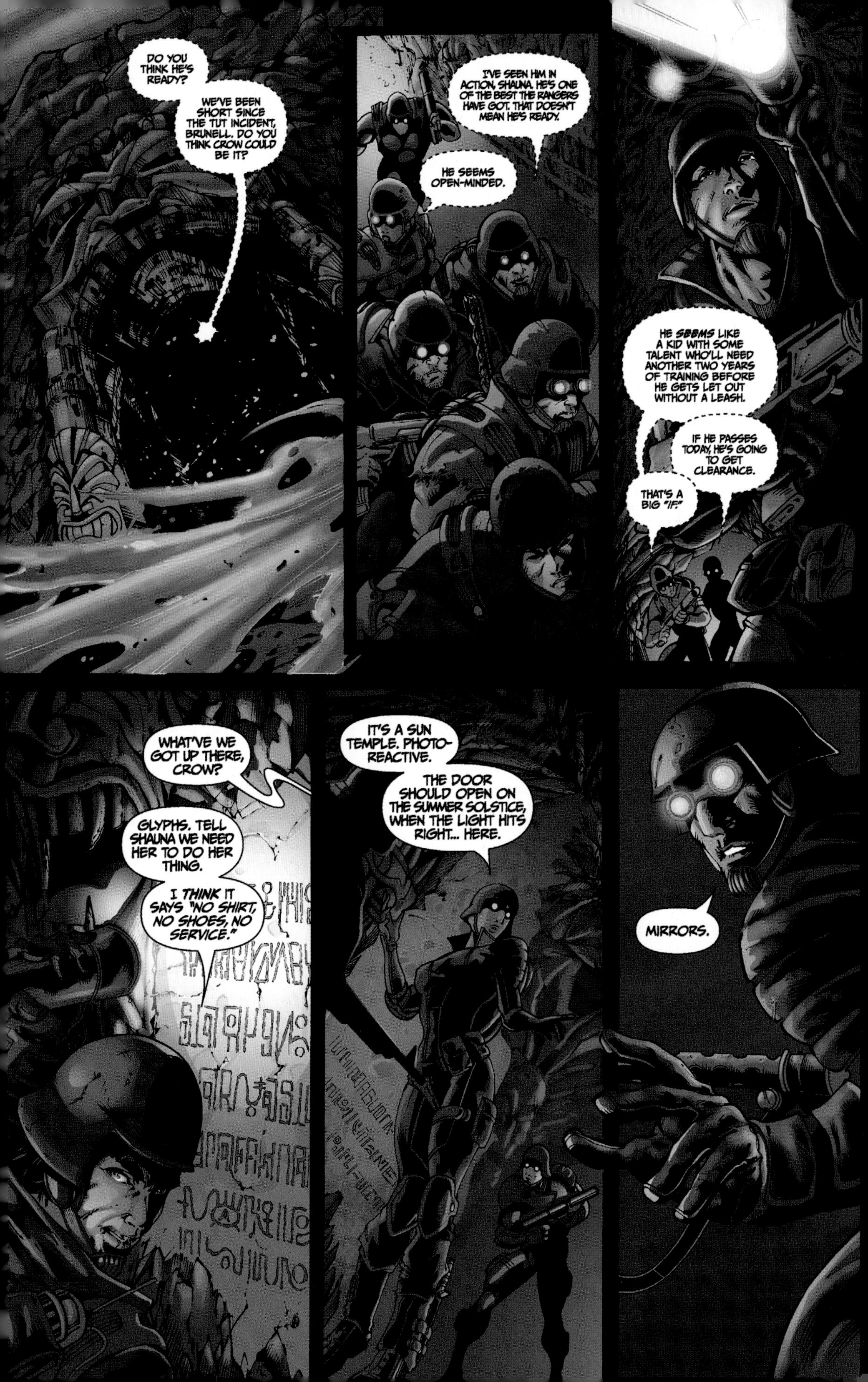
DO YOU THINK HE'S READY?
WE'VE BEEN SHORT SINCE THE TUT INCIDENT, BRUNELL. DO YOU THINK CROW COULD BE IT?
I'VE SEEN HIM IN ACTION, SHAUNA. HE'S ONE OF THE BEST THE RANGERS HAVE GOT. THAT DOESN'T MEAN HE'S READY.
HE SEEMS OPEN-MINDED.
HE SEEMS LIKE A KID WITH SOME TALENT WHO'LL NEED ANOTHER TWO YEARS OF TRAINING BEFORE HE GETS LET OUT WITHOUT A LEASH.
IF HE PASSES TODAY, HE'S GOING TO GET CLEARANCE.
THAT'S A BIG "IF."
WHAT'VE WE GOT UP THERE, CROW?
GLYPHS. TELL SHAUNA WE NEED HER TO DO HER THING.
I THINK IT SAYS "NO SHIRT, NO SHOES, NO SERVICE."
IT'S A SUN TEMPLE. PHOTO-REACTIVE.
THE DOOR SHOULD OPEN ON THE SUMMER SOLSTICE, WHEN THE LIGHT HITS RIGHT... HERE.
MIRRORS.

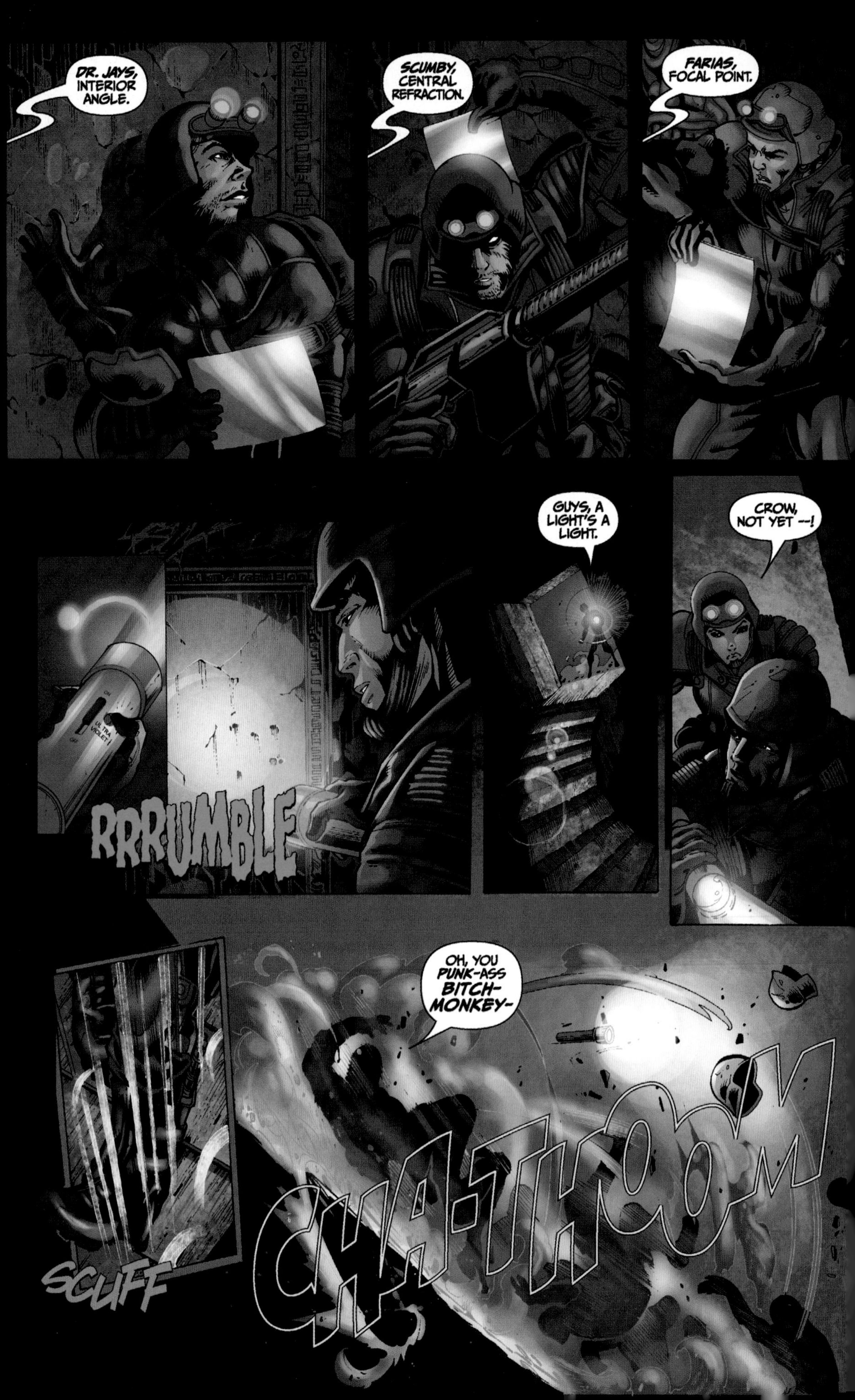
DR. JAYS, INTERIOR ANGLE.
SCUMBY, CENTRAL REFRACTION.
FARIAS, FOCAL POINT.
ON
ULTRA VIOLET
OFF
RRRUMBLE
GUYS, A LIGHT'S A LIGHT.
CROW, NOT YET --!
SCUFF
OH, YOU PUNK-ASS BITCH-MONKEY-
CHA-THOOM

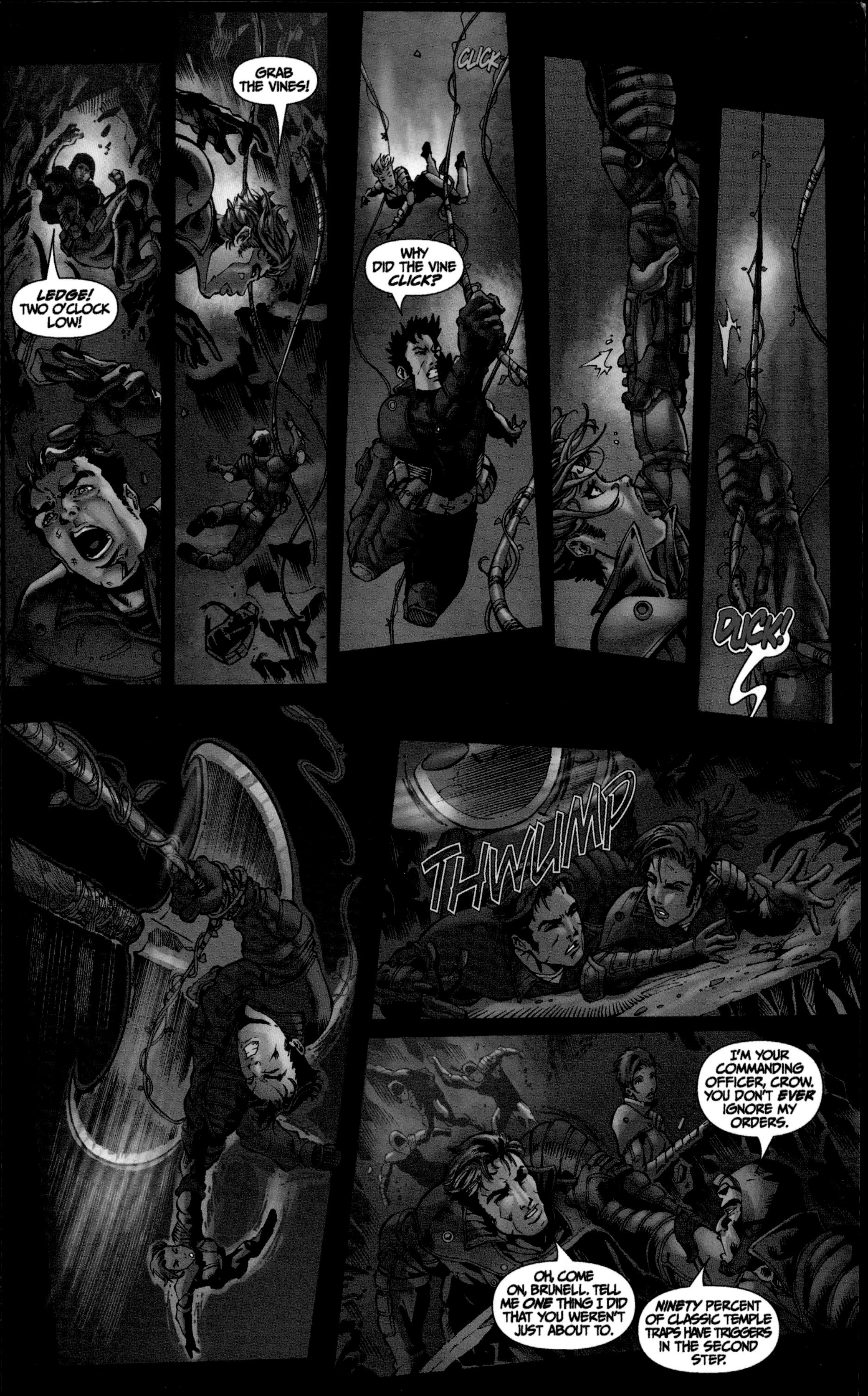
LEDGE! TWO O'CLOCK LOW!
GRAB THE VINES!
CLICK
WHY DID THE VINE CLICK?
DUCK!
THWUMP
I'M YOUR COMMANDING OFFICER, CROW. YOU DON'T EVER IGNORE MY ORDERS.
OH, COME ON, BRUNELL. TELL ME ONE THING I DID THAT YOU WEREN'T JUST ABOUT TO.
NINETY PERCENT OF CLASSIC TEMPLE TRAPS HAVE TRIGGERS IN THE SECOND STEP.

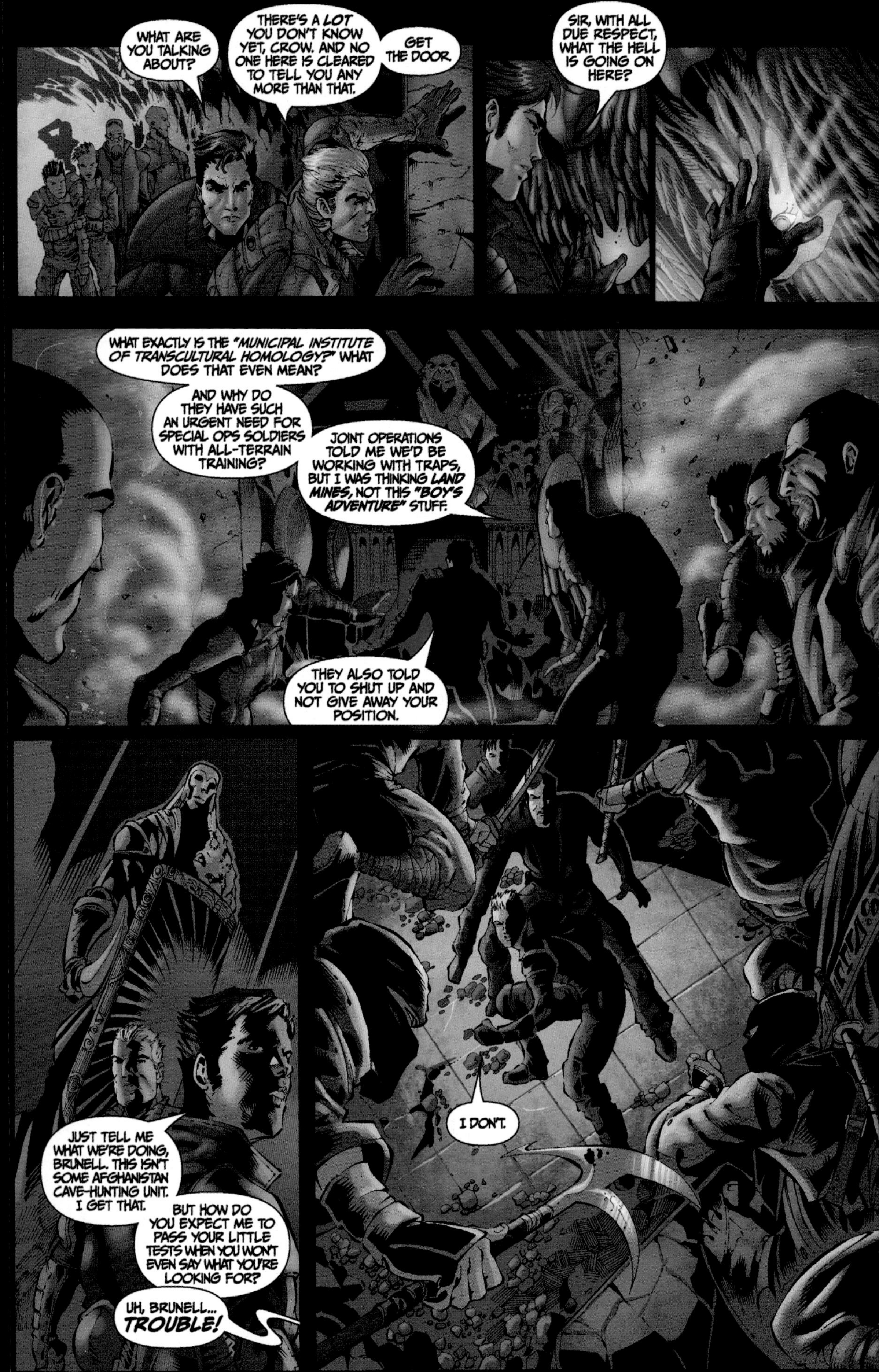
WHAT ARE YOU TALKING ABOUT?
THERE'S A LOT YOU DON'T KNOW YET, CROW. AND NO ONE HERE IS CLEARED TO TELL YOU ANY MORE THAN THAT.
GET THE DOOR.
SIR, WITH ALL DUE RESPECT, WHAT THE HELL IS GOING ON HERE?
WHAT EXACTLY IS THE "MUNICIPAL INSTITUTE OF TRANSCULTURAL HOMOLOGY?" WHAT DOES THAT EVEN MEAN?
AND WHY DO THEY HAVE SUCH AN URGENT NEED FOR SPECIAL OPS SOLDIERS WITH ALL-TERRAIN TRAINING?
JOINT OPERATIONS TOLD ME WE'D BE WORKING WITH TRAPS, BUT I WAS THINKING LAND MINES, NOT THIS "BOY'S ADVENTURE" STUFF.
THEY ALSO TOLD YOU TO SHUT UP AND NOT GIVE AWAY YOUR POSITION.
JUST TELL ME WHAT WE'RE DOING, BRUNELL. THIS ISN'T SOME AFGHANISTAN CAVE-HUNTING UNIT. I GET THAT.
BUT HOW DO YOU EXPECT ME TO PASS YOUR LITTLE TESTS WHEN YOU WON'T EVEN SAY WHAT YOU'RE LOOKING FOR?
I DON'T.
UH, BRUNELL... TROUBLE!

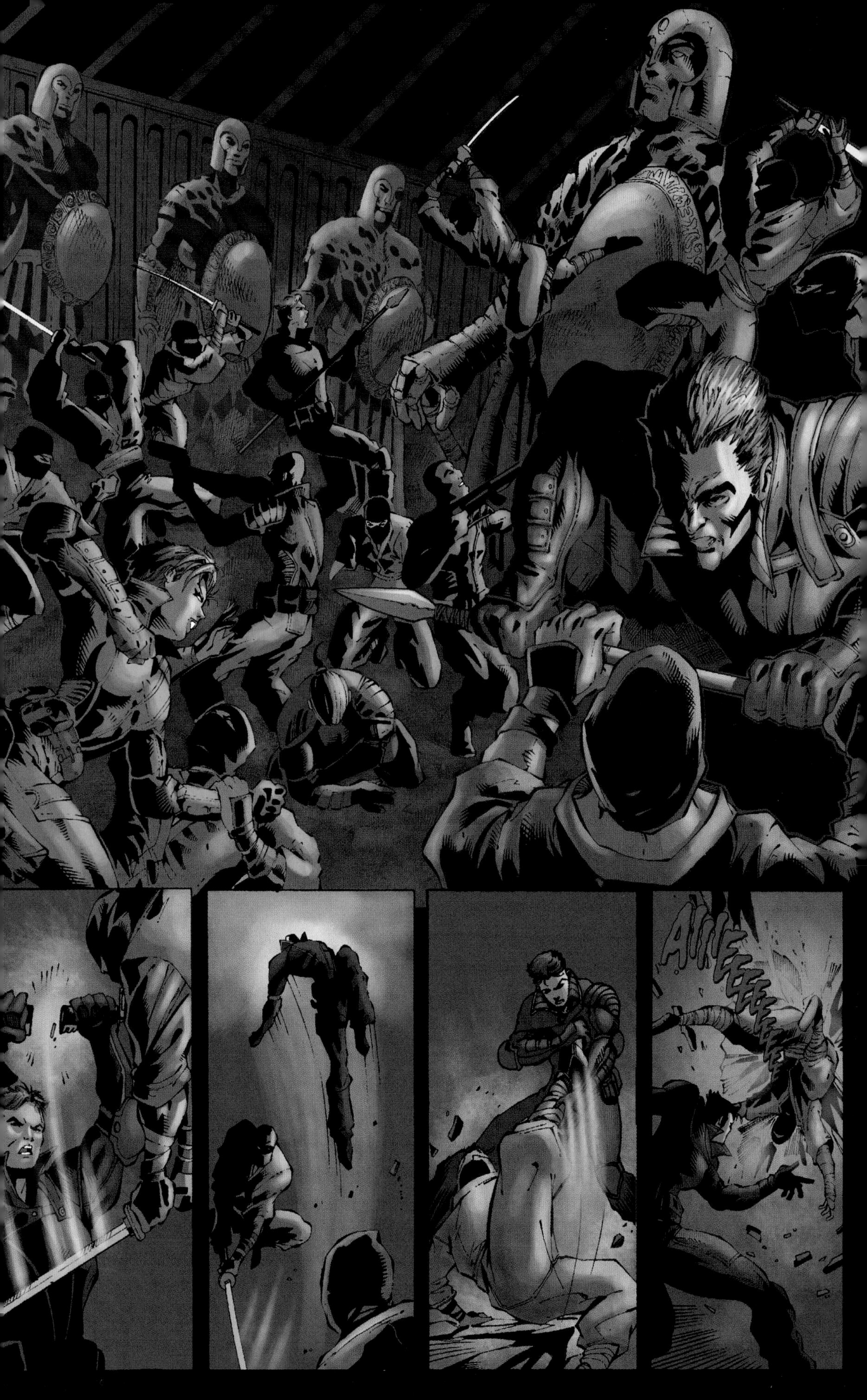
AIIEEEEEEE

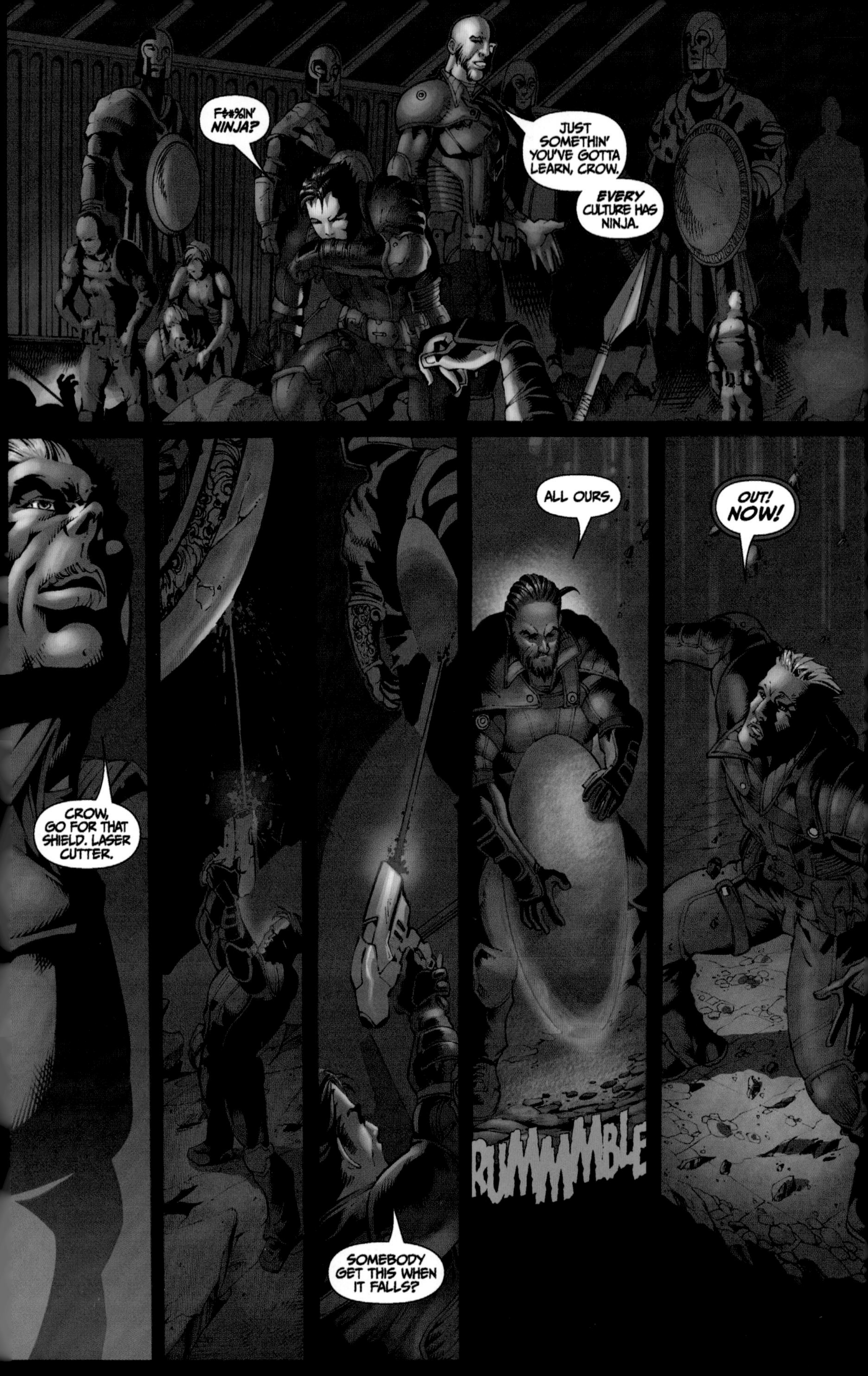
F#%$IN' NINJA?
JUST SOMETHIN' YOU'VE GOTTA LEARN, CROW.
EVERY CULTURE HAS NINJA.
CROW, GO FOR THAT SHIELD. LASER CUTTER.
SOMEBODY GET THIS WHEN IT FALLS?
ALL OURS.
RUMMMBLE
OUT! NOW!

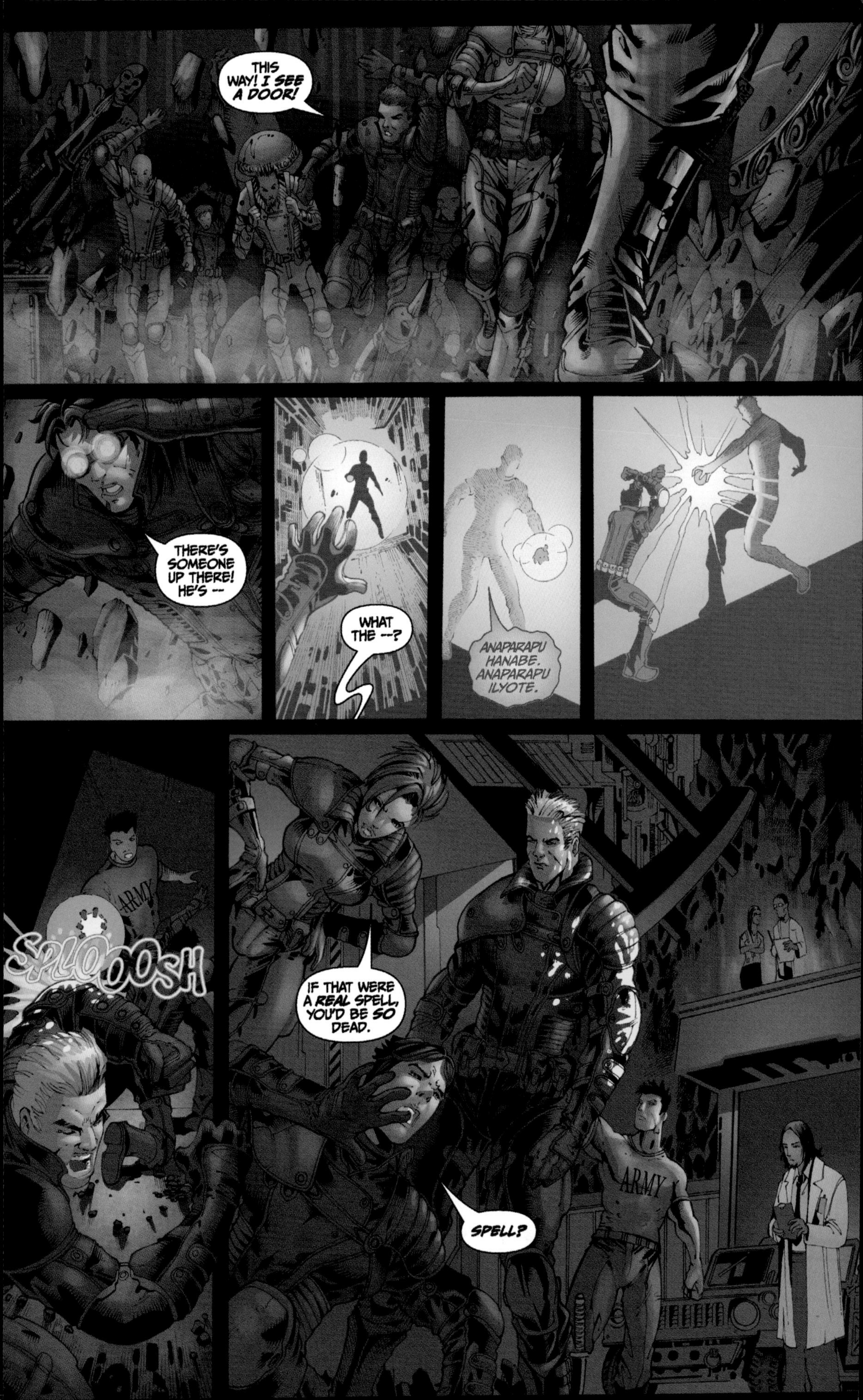
THIS WAY! I SEE A DOOR!
THERE'S SOMEONE UP THERE! HE'S --
WHAT THE --?
ANAPARAPU HANABE. ANAPARAPU ILYOTE.
SPLOOOSH
IF THAT WERE A REAL SPELL, YOU'D BE SO DEAD.
SPELL?

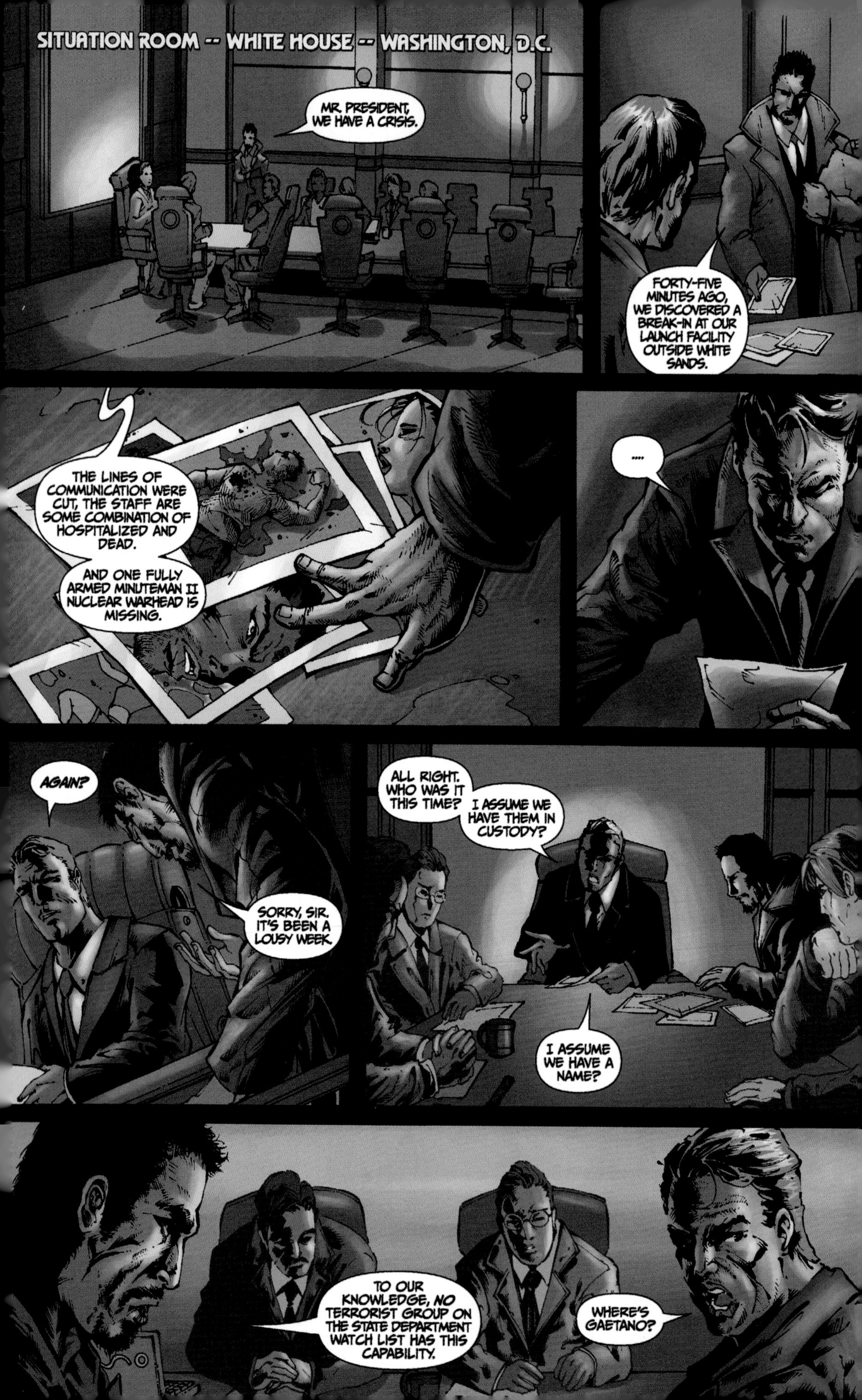
SITUATION ROOM -- WHITE HOUSE -- WASHINGTON, D.C.
MR. PRESIDENT, WE HAVE A CRISIS.
FORTY-FIVE MINUTES AGO, WE DISCOVERED A BREAK-IN AT OUR LAUNCH FACILITY OUTSIDE WHITE SANDS.
THE LINES OF COMMUNICATION WERE CUT, THE STAFF ARE SOME COMBINATION OF HOSPITALIZED AND DEAD.
AND ONE FULLY ARMED MINUTEMAN II NUCLEAR WARHEAD IS MISSING.
....
AGAIN?
SORRY, SIR. IT'S BEEN A LOUSY WEEK.
ALL RIGHT. WHO WAS IT THIS TIME?
I ASSUME WE HAVE THEM IN CUSTODY?
I ASSUME WE HAVE A NAME?
TO OUR KNOWLEDGE, NO TERRORIST GROUP ON THE STATE DEPARTMENT WATCH LIST HAS THIS CAPABILITY.
WHERE'S GAETANO?

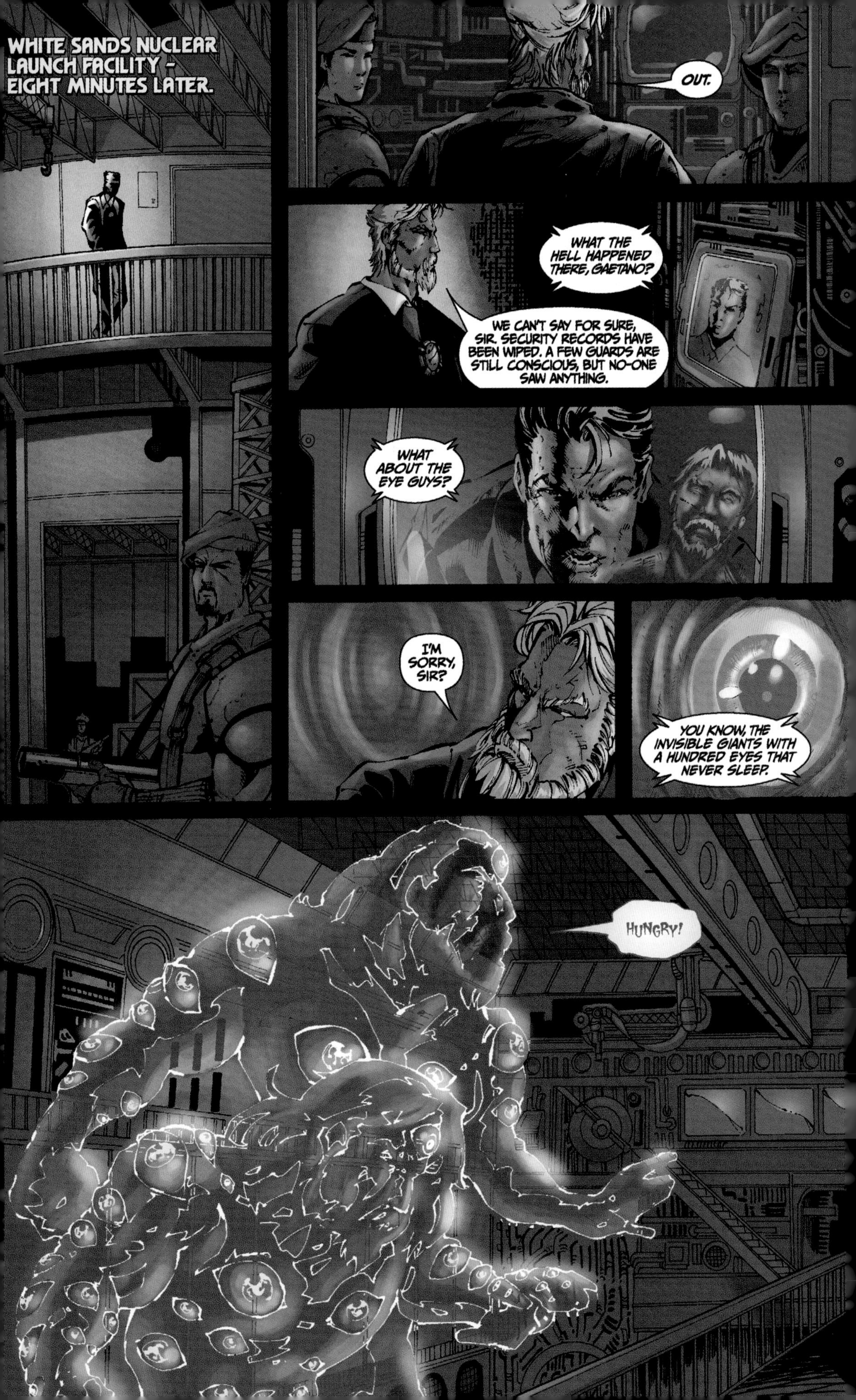
WHITE SANDS NUCLEAR LAUNCH FACILITY - EIGHT MINUTES LATER.
OUT.
WHAT THE HELL HAPPENED THERE, GAETANO?
WE CAN'T SAY FOR SURE, SIR. SECURITY RECORDS HAVE BEEN WIPED. A FEW GUARDS ARE STILL CONSCIOUS, BUT NO-ONE SAW ANYTHING.
WHAT ABOUT THE EYE GUYS?
I'M SORRY, SIR?
YOU KNOW, THE INVISIBLE GIANTS WITH A HUNDRED EYES THAT NEVER SLEEP.
HUNGRY!

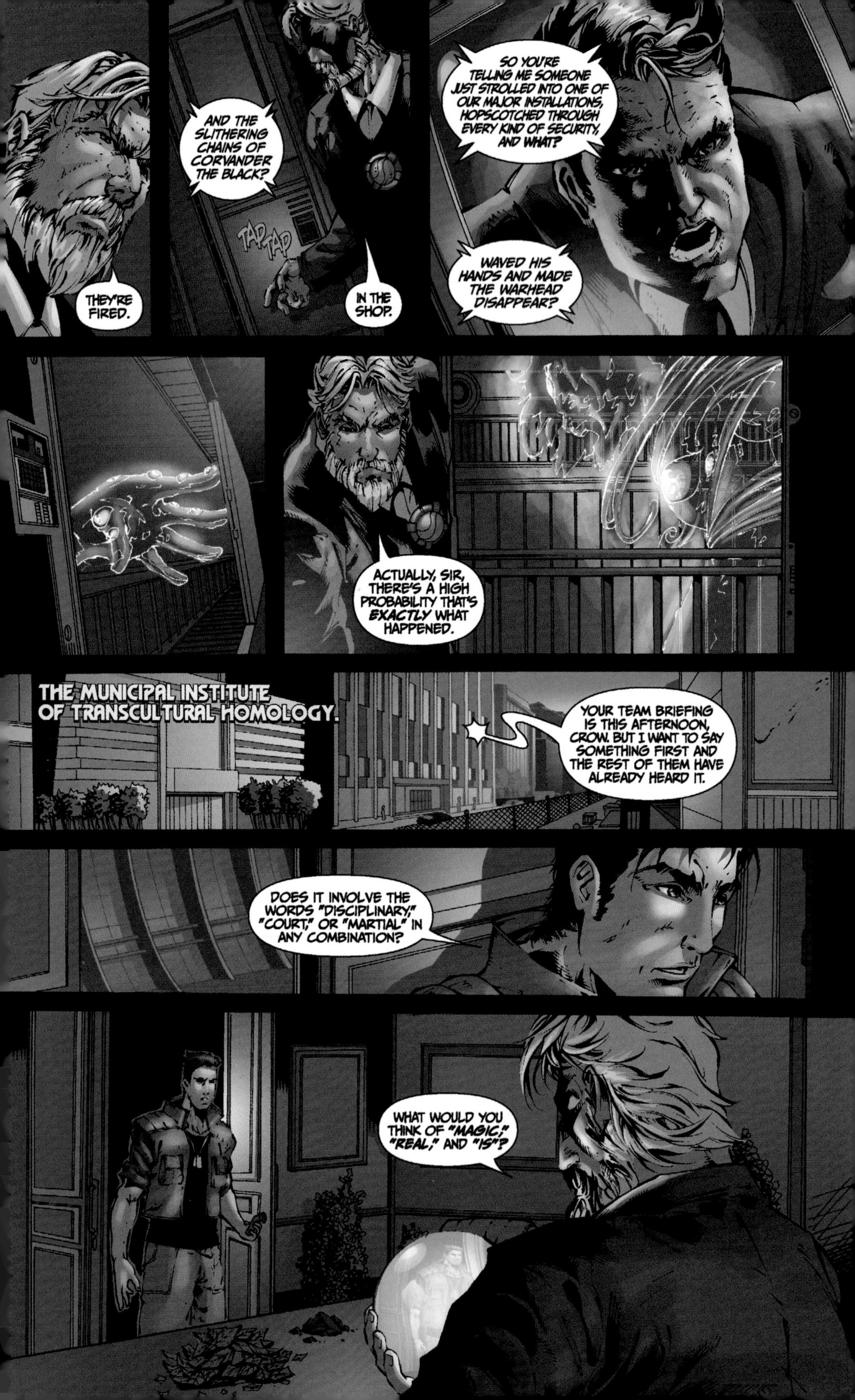
THEY'RE FIRED.
AND THE SLITHERING CHAINS OF CORVANDER THE BLACK?
TAP TAP
IN THE SHOP.
SO YOU'RE TELLING ME SOMEONE JUST STROLLED INTO ONE OF OUR MAJOR INSTALLATIONS, HOPSCOTCHED THROUGH EVERY KIND OF SECURITY, AND WHAT?
WAVED HIS HANDS AND MADE THE WARHEAD DISAPPEAR?
ACTUALLY, SIR, THERE'S A HIGH PROBABILITY THAT'S EXACTLY WHAT HAPPENED.
THE MUNICIPAL INSTITUTE OF TRANSCULTURAL HOMOLOGY.
YOUR TEAM BRIEFING IS THIS AFTERNOON, CROW. BUT I WANT TO SAY SOMETHING FIRST AND THE REST OF THEM HAVE ALREADY HEARD IT.
DOES IT INVOLVE THE WORDS "DISCIPLINARY," "COURT," OR "MARTIAL" IN ANY COMBINATION?
WHAT WOULD YOU THINK OF "MAGIC," "REAL," AND "IS"?

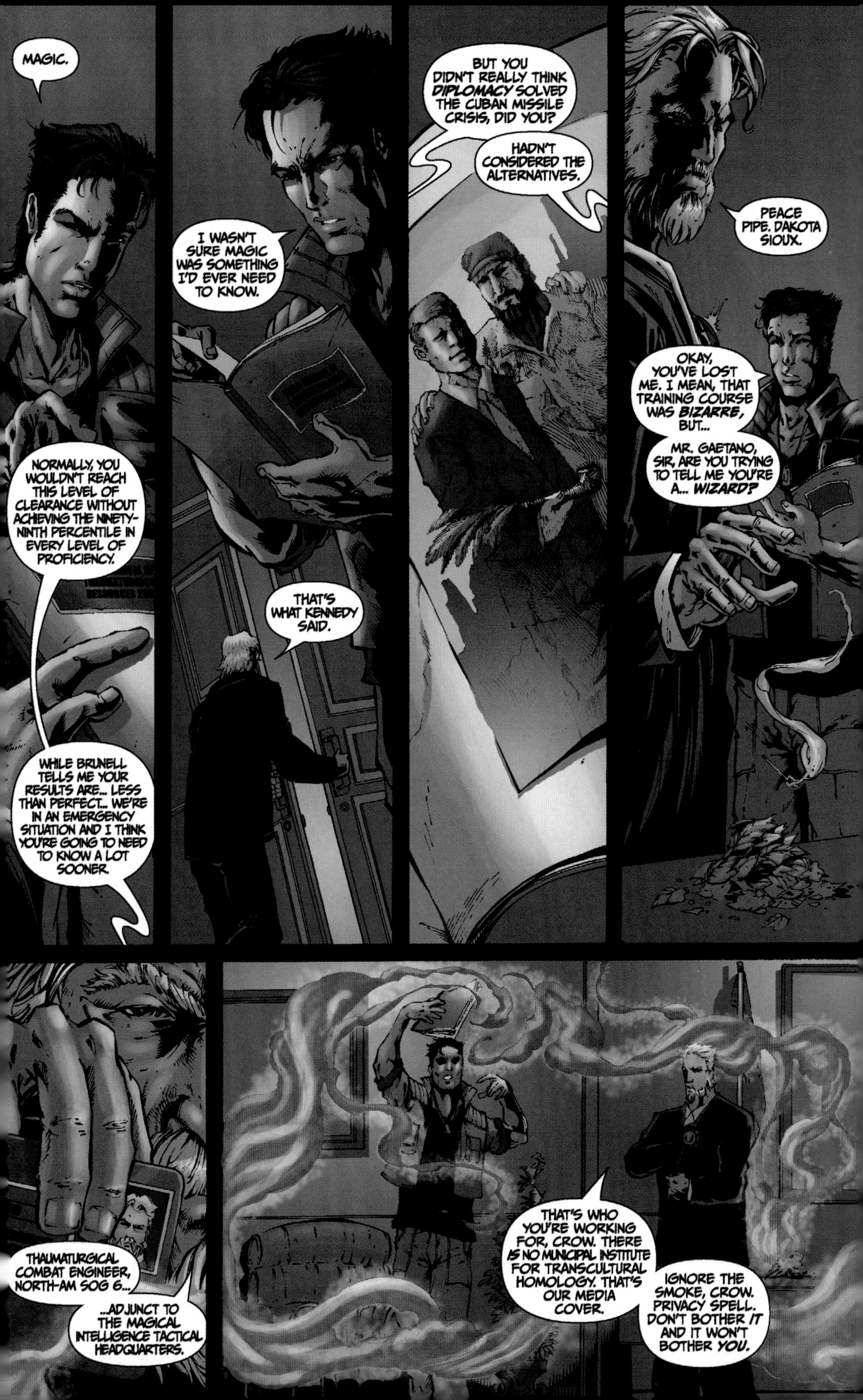
MAGIC.
NORMALLY, YOU WOULDN'T REACH THIS LEVEL OF CLEARANCE WITHOUT ACHIEVING THE NINETY-NINTH PERCENTILE IN EVERY LEVEL OF PROFICIENCY.
WHILE BRUNELL TELLS ME YOUR RESULTS ARE... LESS THAN PERFECT... WE'RE IN AN EMERGENCY SITUATION AND I THINK YOU'RE GOING TO NEED TO KNOW A LOT SOONER.
I WASN'T SURE MAGIC WAS SOMETHING I'D EVER NEED TO KNOW.
THAT'S WHAT KENNEDY SAID.
BUT YOU DIDN'T REALLY THINK *DIPLOMACY* SOLVED THE CUBAN MISSILE CRISIS, DID YOU?
HADN'T CONSIDERED THE ALTERNATIVES.
PEACE PIPE. DAKOTA SIOUX.
OKAY, YOU'VE LOST ME. I MEAN, THAT TRAINING COURSE WAS *BIZARRE*, BUT...
MR. GAETANO, SIR, ARE YOU TRYING TO TELL ME YOU'RE A... *WIZARD?*
THAUMATURGICAL COMBAT ENGINEER, NORTH-AM SOG 6...
...ADJUNCT TO THE MAGICAL INTELLIGENCE TACTICAL HEADQUARTERS.
THAT'S WHO YOU'RE WORKING FOR, CROW. THERE *IS* NO MUNICIPAL INSTITUTE FOR TRANSCULTURAL HOMOLOGY. THAT'S OUR MEDIA COVER.
IGNORE THE SMOKE, CROW. PRIVACY SPELL. DON'T BOTHER *IT* AND IT WON'T BOTHER *YOU*.

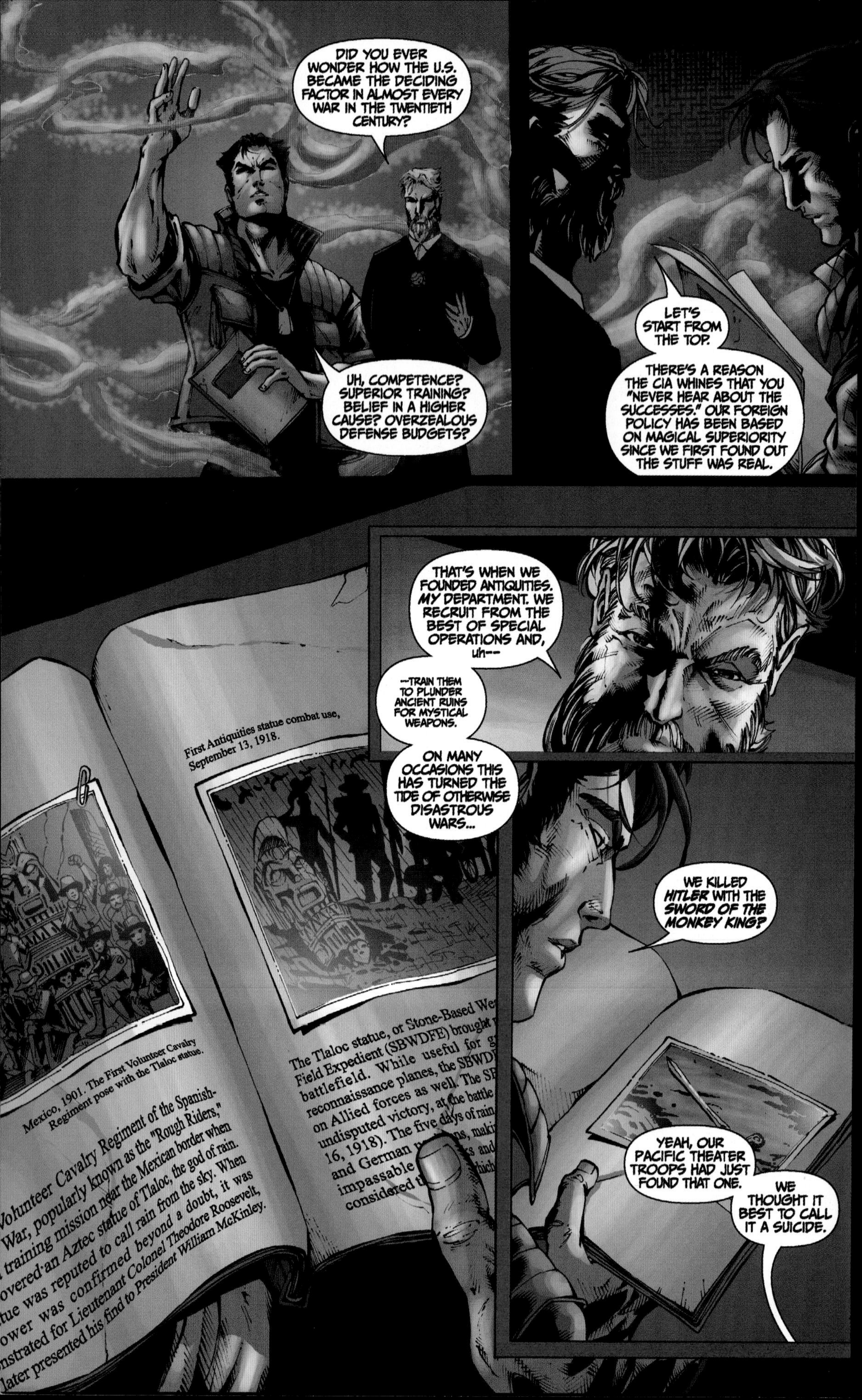
DID YOU EVER WONDER HOW THE U.S. BECAME THE DECIDING FACTOR IN ALMOST EVERY WAR IN THE TWENTIETH CENTURY?
UH, COMPETENCE? SUPERIOR TRAINING? BELIEF IN A HIGHER CAUSE? OVERZEALOUS DEFENSE BUDGETS?
LET'S START FROM THE TOP.
THERE'S A REASON THE CIA WHINES THAT YOU "NEVER HEAR ABOUT THE SUCCESSES." OUR FOREIGN POLICY HAS BEEN BASED ON MAGICAL SUPERIORITY SINCE WE FIRST FOUND OUT THE STUFF WAS REAL.
THAT'S WHEN WE FOUNDED ANTIQUITIES. MY DEPARTMENT. WE RECRUIT FROM THE BEST OF SPECIAL OPERATIONS AND, uh--
--TRAIN THEM TO PLUNDER ANCIENT RUINS FOR MYSTICAL WEAPONS.
ON MANY OCCASIONS THIS HAS TURNED THE TIDE OF OTHERWISE DISASTROUS WARS...
Mexico, 1901. The First Volunteer Cavalry Regiment pose with the Tlaloc statue.
Volunteer Cavalry Regiment of the Spanish-
War, popularly known as the "Rough Riders,"
training mission near the Mexican border when
overed an Aztec statue of Tlaloc, the god of rain.
ue was reputed to call rain from the sky. When
ower was confirmed beyond a doubt, it was
nstrated for Lieutenant Colonel Theodore Roosevelt,
later presented his find to President William McKinley.
First Antiquities statue combat use, September 13, 1918.
The Tlaloc statue, or Stone-Based We
Field Expedient (SBWDFE) brought
battlefield. While useful for g
reconnaissance planes, the SBWDF
on Allied forces as well. The SB
undisputed victory, at the battle
16, 1918). The five days of rain
WE KILLED HITLER WITH THE SWORD OF THE MONKEY KING?
YEAH, OUR PACIFIC THEATER TROOPS HAD JUST FOUND THAT ONE.
WE THOUGHT IT BEST TO CALL IT A SUICIDE.

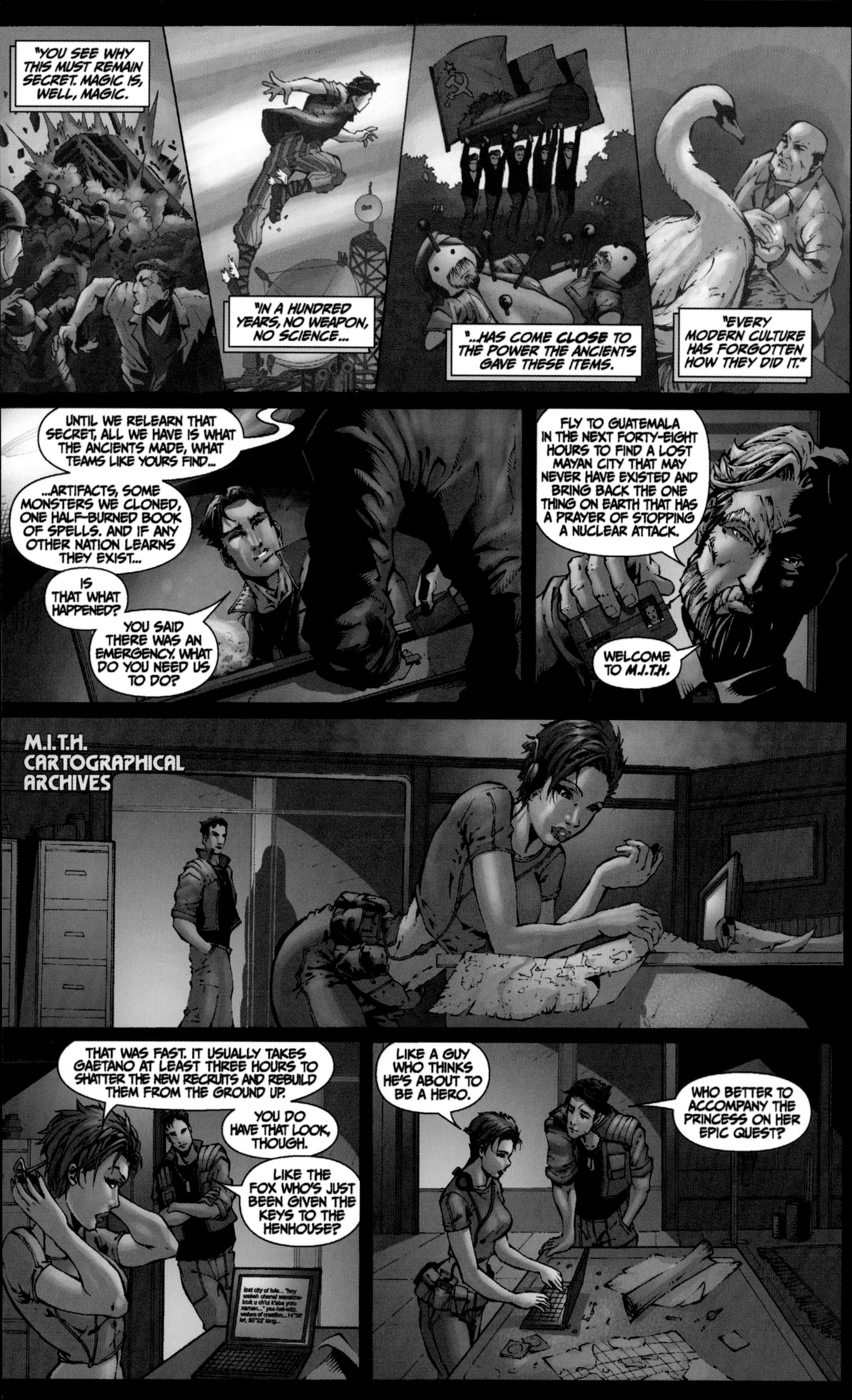

"YOU SEE WHY THIS MUST REMAIN SECRET. MAGIC IS, WELL, MAGIC.
"IN A HUNDRED YEARS, NO WEAPON, NO SCIENCE...
"...HAS COME CLOSE TO THE POWER THE ANCIENTS GAVE THESE ITEMS.
"EVERY MODERN CULTURE HAS FORGOTTEN HOW THEY DID IT."
UNTIL WE RELEARN THAT SECRET, ALL WE HAVE IS WHAT THE ANCIENTS MADE, WHAT TEAMS LIKE YOURS FIND...
...ARTIFACTS, SOME MONSTERS WE CLONED, ONE HALF-BURNED BOOK OF SPELLS. AND IF ANY OTHER NATION LEARNS THEY EXIST...
IS THAT WHAT HAPPENED?
YOU SAID THERE WAS AN EMERGENCY. WHAT DO YOU NEED US TO DO?
FLY TO GUATEMALA IN THE NEXT FORTY-EIGHT HOURS TO FIND A LOST MAYAN CITY THAT MAY NEVER HAVE EXISTED AND BRING BACK THE ONE THING ON EARTH THAT HAS A PRAYER OF STOPPING A NUCLEAR ATTACK.
WELCOME TO M.I.T.H.
M.I.T.H. CARTOGRAPHICAL ARCHIVES
THAT WAS FAST. IT USUALLY TAKES GAETANO AT LEAST THREE HOURS TO SHATTER THE NEW RECRUITS AND REBUILD THEM FROM THE GROUND UP.
YOU DO HAVE THAT LOOK, THOUGH.
LIKE THE FOX WHO'S JUST BEEN GIVEN THE KEYS TO THE HENHOUSE?
LIKE A GUY WHO THINKS HE'S ABOUT TO BE A HERO.
WHO BETTER TO ACCOMPANY THE PRINCESS ON HER EPIC QUEST?

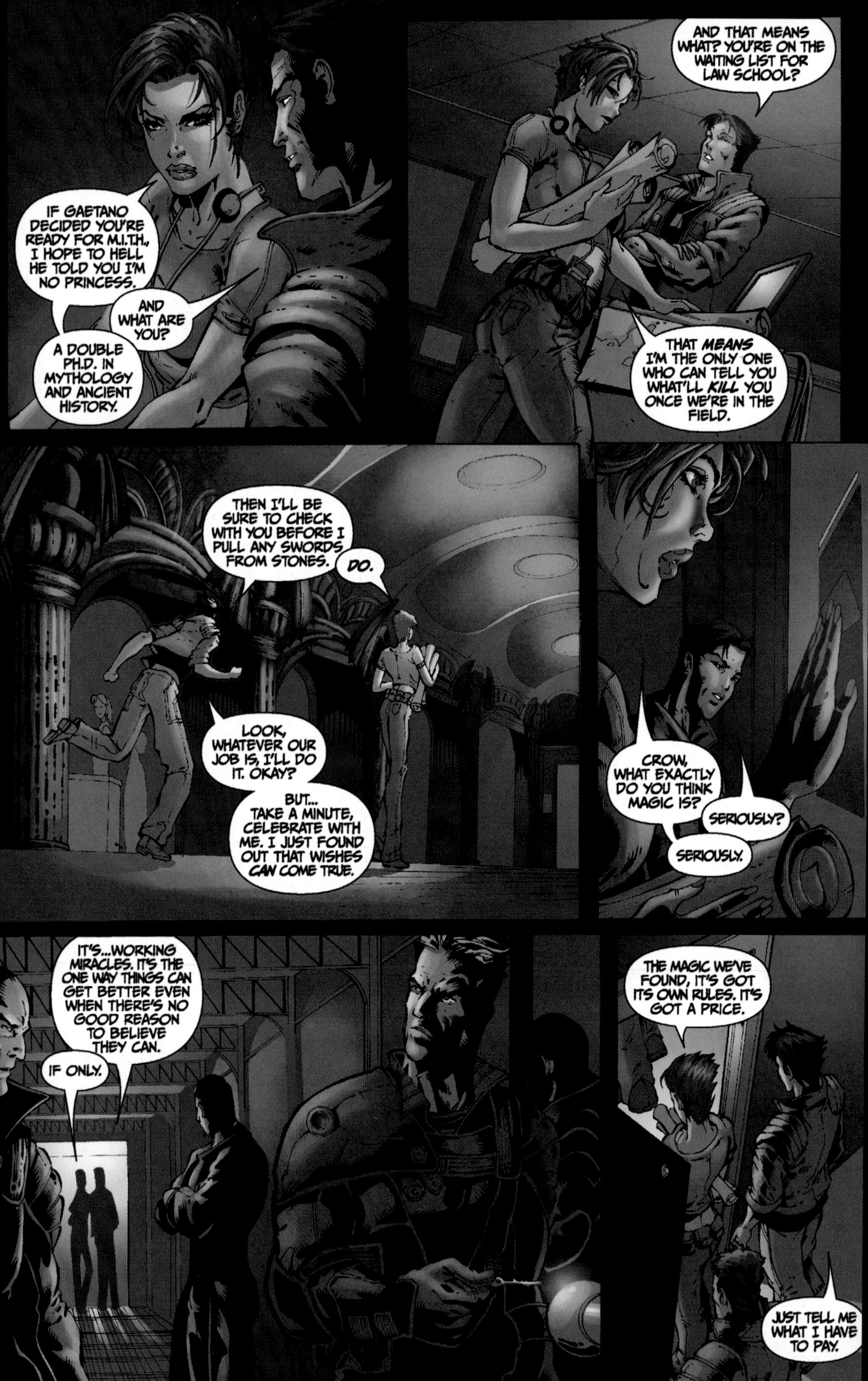
IF GAETANO DECIDED YOU'RE READY FOR M.I.T.H., I HOPE TO HELL HE TOLD YOU I'M NO PRINCESS.
AND WHAT ARE YOU?
A DOUBLE PH.D. IN MYTHOLOGY AND ANCIENT HISTORY.
AND THAT MEANS WHAT? YOU'RE ON THE WAITING LIST FOR LAW SCHOOL?
THAT MEANS I'M THE ONLY ONE WHO CAN TELL YOU WHAT'LL KILL YOU ONCE WE'RE IN THE FIELD.
THEN I'LL BE SURE TO CHECK WITH YOU BEFORE I PULL ANY SWORDS FROM STONES.
DO.
LOOK, WHATEVER OUR JOB IS, I'LL DO IT. OKAY?
BUT... TAKE A MINUTE, CELEBRATE WITH ME. I JUST FOUND OUT THAT WISHES CAN COME TRUE.
CROW, WHAT EXACTLY DO YOU THINK MAGIC IS?
SERIOUSLY?
SERIOUSLY.
IT'S...WORKING MIRACLES. IT'S THE ONE WAY THINGS CAN GET BETTER EVEN WHEN THERE'S NO GOOD REASON TO BELIEVE THEY CAN.
IF ONLY.
THE MAGIC WE'VE FOUND, IT'S GOT ITS OWN RULES. IT'S GOT A PRICE.
JUST TELL ME WHAT I HAVE TO PAY.

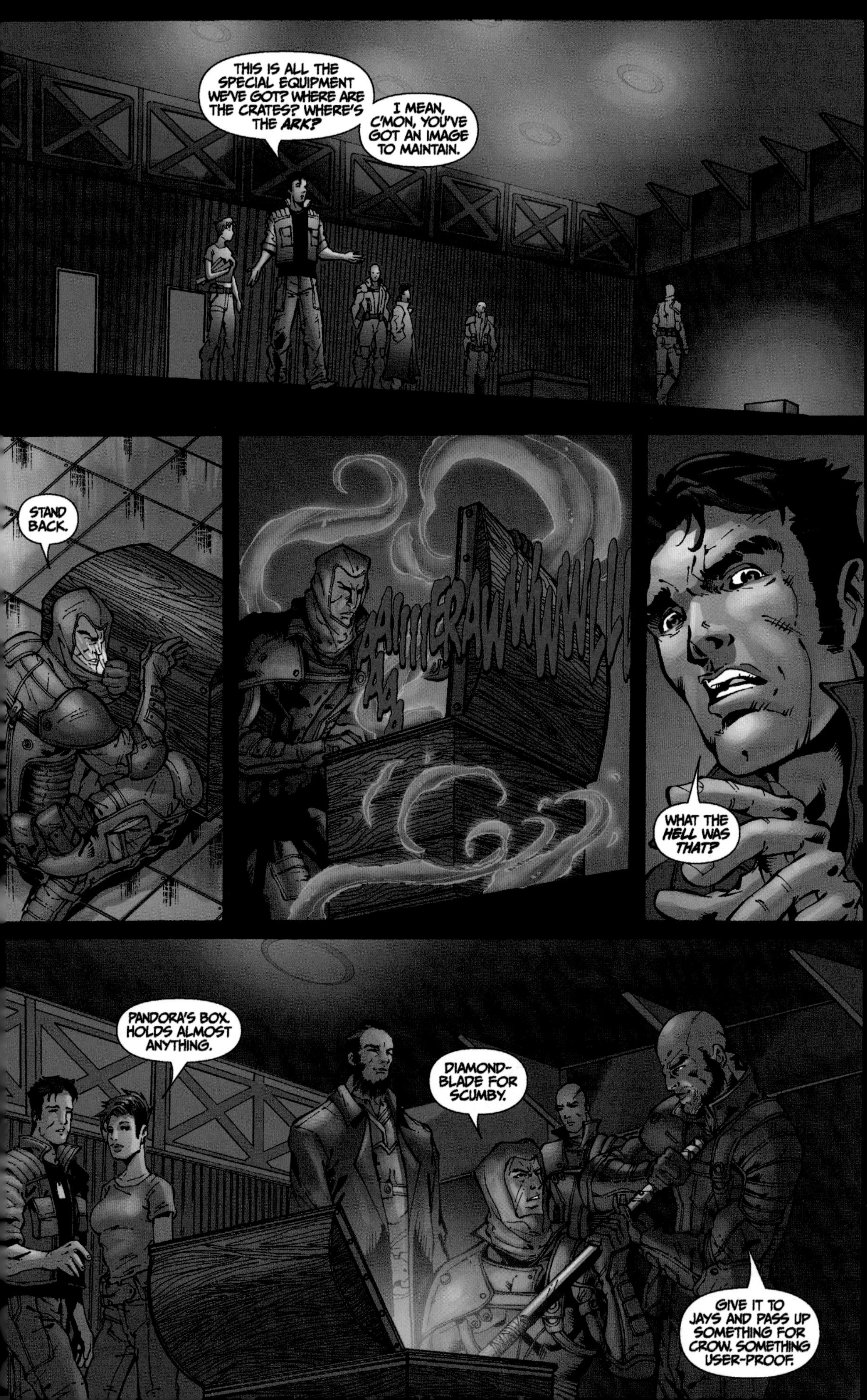
THIS IS ALL THE SPECIAL EQUIPMENT WE'VE GOT? WHERE ARE THE CRATES? WHERE'S THE *ARK?*
I MEAN, C'MON, YOU'VE GOT AN IMAGE TO MAINTAIN.
STAND BACK.
WHAT THE *HELL* WAS *THAT?*
PANDORA'S BOX. HOLDS ALMOST ANYTHING.
DIAMOND-BLADE FOR SCUMBY.
GIVE IT TO JAYS AND PASS UP SOMETHING FOR CROW. SOMETHING USER-PROOF.

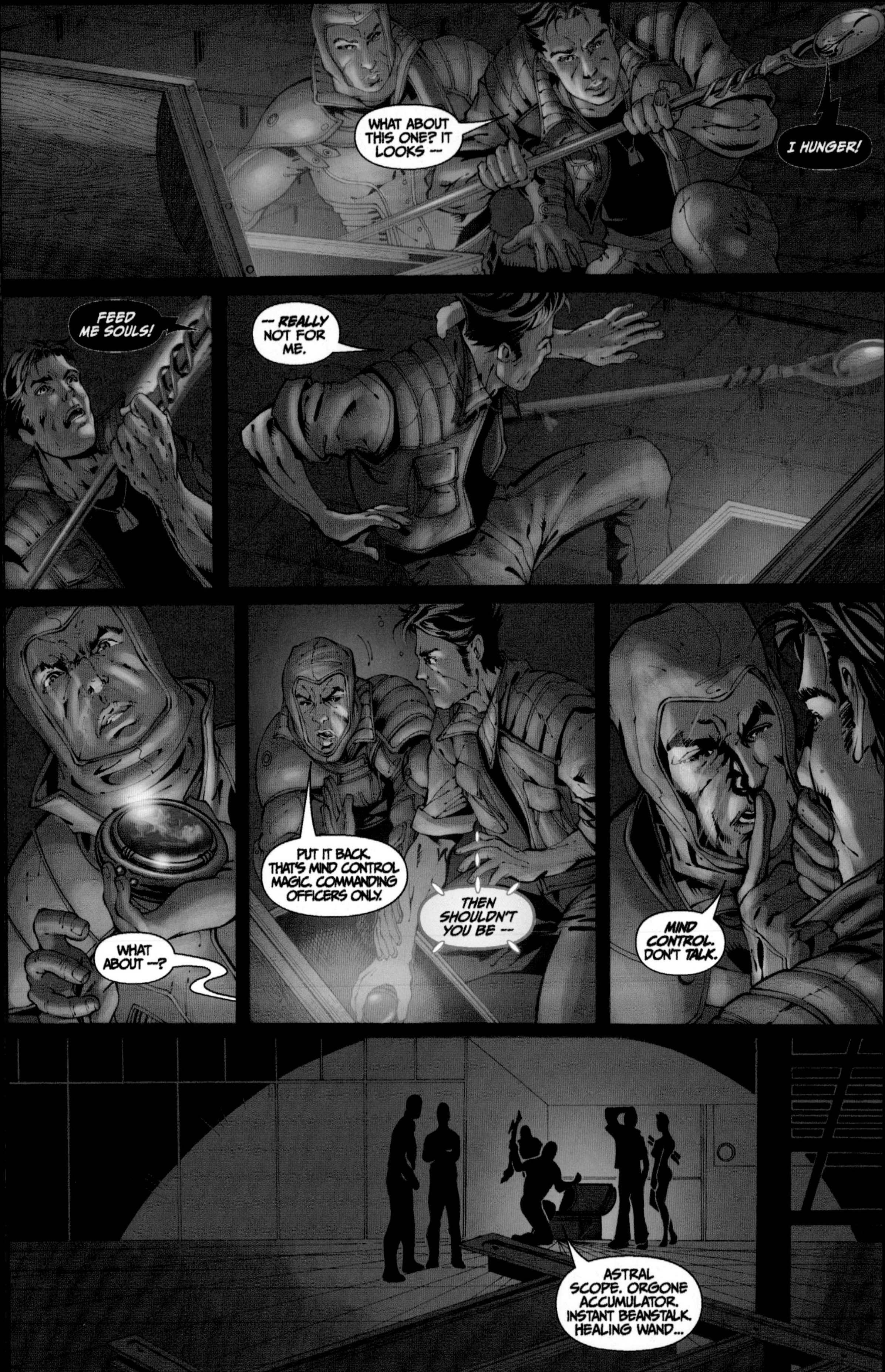
WHAT ABOUT THIS ONE? IT LOOKS --
I HUNGER!
FEED ME SOULS!
-- REALLY NOT FOR ME.
WHAT ABOUT --?
PUT IT BACK. THAT'S MIND CONTROL MAGIC. COMMANDING OFFICERS ONLY.
THEN SHOULDN'T YOU BE --
MIND CONTROL. DON'T TALK.
ASTRAL SCOPE. ORGONE ACCUMULATOR. INSTANT BEANSTALK. HEALING WAND...

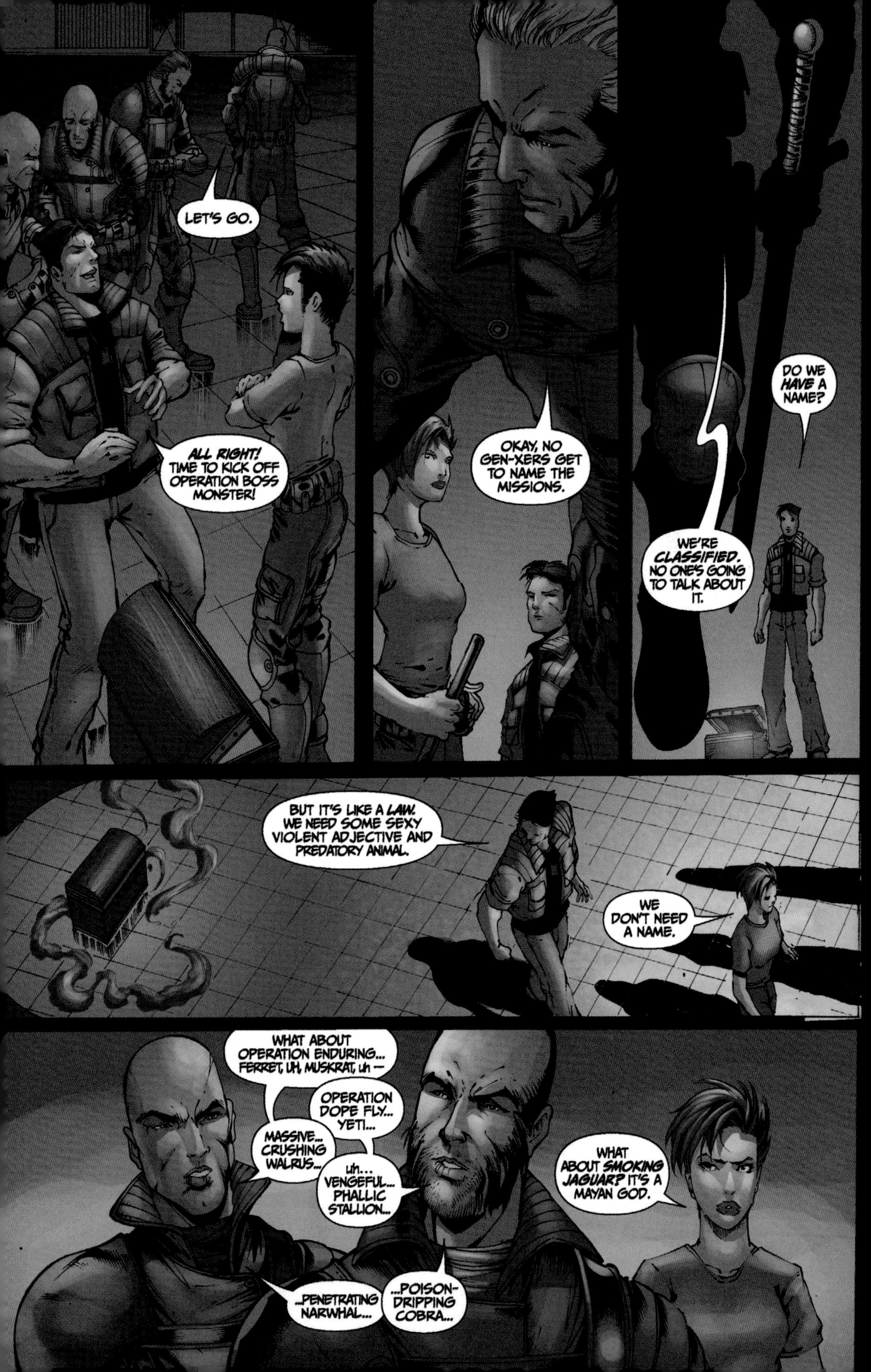
LET'S GO.
ALL RIGHT! TIME TO KICK OFF OPERATION BOSS MONSTER!
OKAY, NO GEN-XERS GET TO NAME THE MISSIONS.
DO WE HAVE A NAME?
WE'RE CLASSIFIED. NO ONE'S GOING TO TALK ABOUT IT.
BUT IT'S LIKE A LAW. WE NEED SOME SEXY VIOLENT ADJECTIVE AND PREDATORY ANIMAL.
WE DON'T NEED A NAME.
WHAT ABOUT OPERATION ENDURING... FERRET, UH, MUSKRAT, uh —
OPERATION DOPE FLY... YETI...
MASSIVE... CRUSHING WALRUS...
uh... VENGEFUL... PHALLIC STALLION...
WHAT ABOUT SMOKING JAGUAR? IT'S A MAYAN GOD.
...PENETRATING NARWHAL...
...POISON-DRIPPING COBRA...

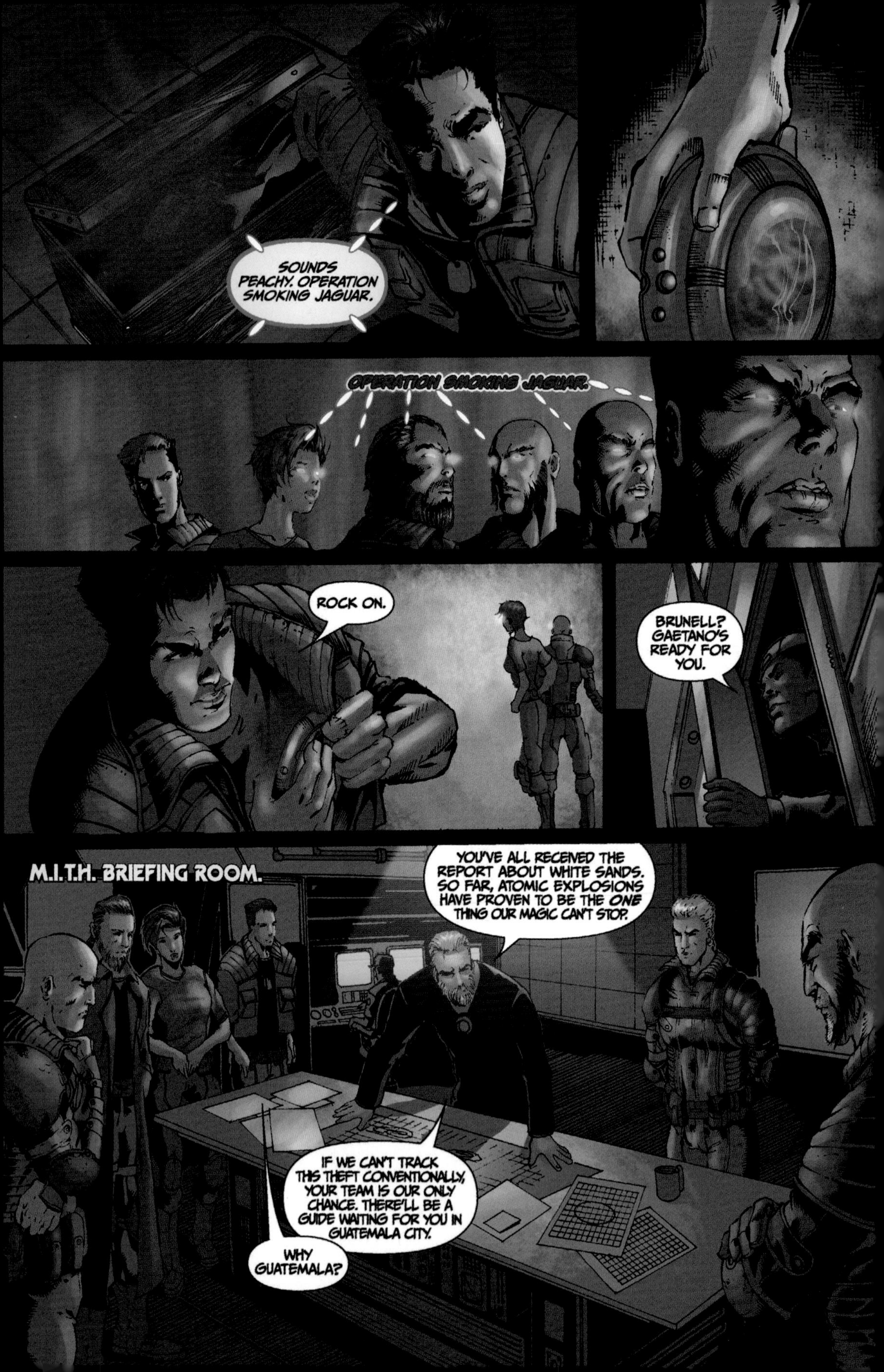
SOUNDS PEACHY. OPERATION SMOKING JAGUAR.
OPERATION SMOKING JAGUAR.
ROCK ON.
BRUNELL? GAETANO'S READY FOR YOU.
M.I.T.H. BRIEFING ROOM.
YOU'VE ALL RECEIVED THE REPORT ABOUT WHITE SANDS. SO FAR, ATOMIC EXPLOSIONS HAVE PROVEN TO BE THE ONE THING OUR MAGIC CAN'T STOP.
IF WE CAN'T TRACK THIS THEFT CONVENTIONALLY, YOUR TEAM IS OUR ONLY CHANCE. THERE'LL BE A GUIDE WAITING FOR YOU IN GUATEMALA CITY.
WHY GUATEMALA?

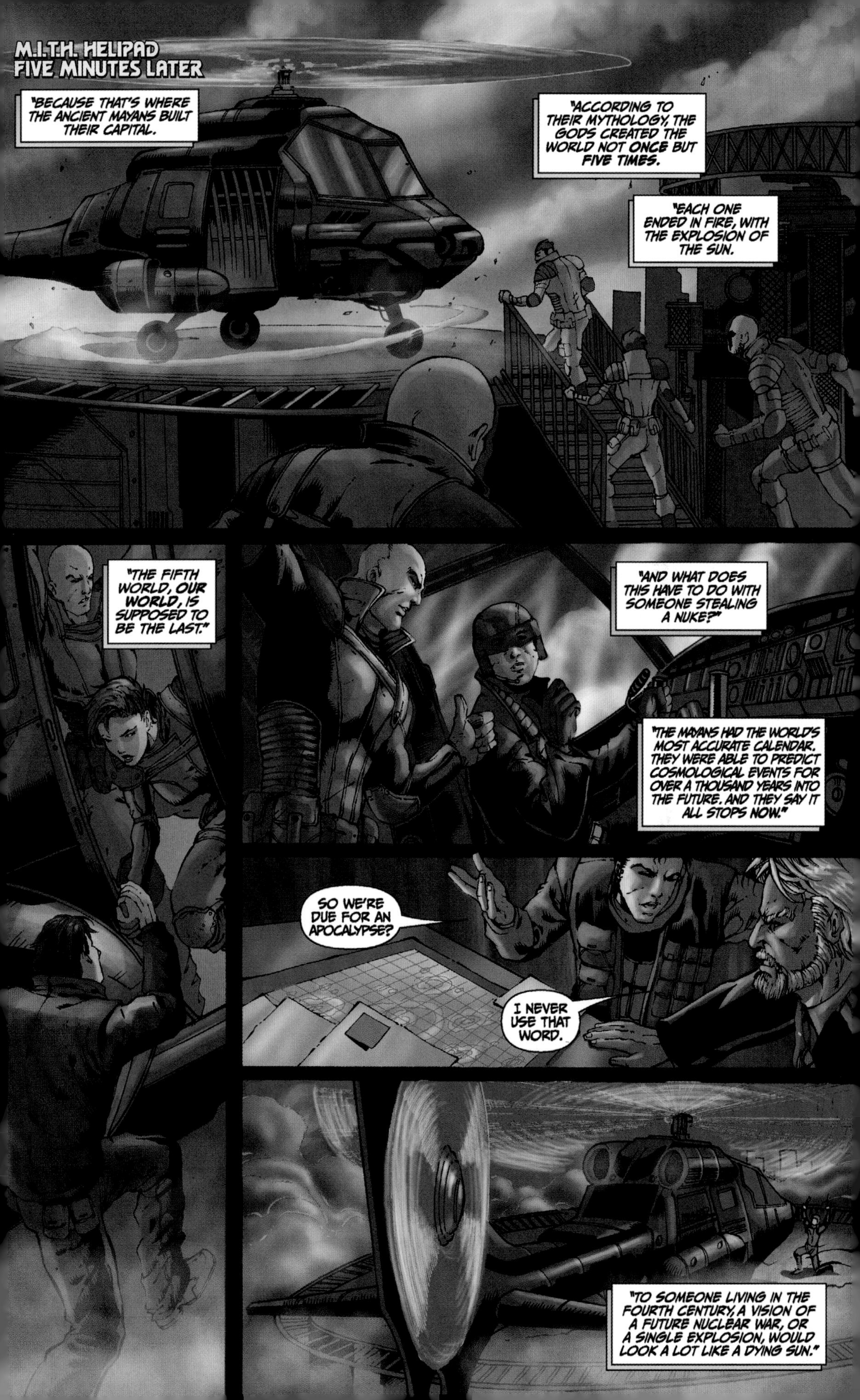
M.I.T.H. HELIPAD
FIVE MINUTES LATER
"BECAUSE THAT'S WHERE THE ANCIENT MAYANS BUILT THEIR CAPITAL.
"ACCORDING TO THEIR MYTHOLOGY, THE GODS CREATED THE WORLD NOT ONCE BUT FIVE TIMES.
"EACH ONE ENDED IN FIRE, WITH THE EXPLOSION OF THE SUN.
"THE FIFTH WORLD, OUR WORLD, IS SUPPOSED TO BE THE LAST."
"AND WHAT DOES THIS HAVE TO DO WITH SOMEONE STEALING A NUKE?"
"THE MAYANS HAD THE WORLD'S MOST ACCURATE CALENDAR. THEY WERE ABLE TO PREDICT COSMOLOGICAL EVENTS FOR OVER A THOUSAND YEARS INTO THE FUTURE. AND THEY SAY IT ALL STOPS NOW."
SO WE'RE DUE FOR AN APOCALYPSE?
I NEVER USE THAT WORD.
"TO SOMEONE LIVING IN THE FOURTH CENTURY, A VISION OF A FUTURE NUCLEAR WAR, OR A SINGLE EXPLOSION, WOULD LOOK A LOT LIKE A DYING SUN."

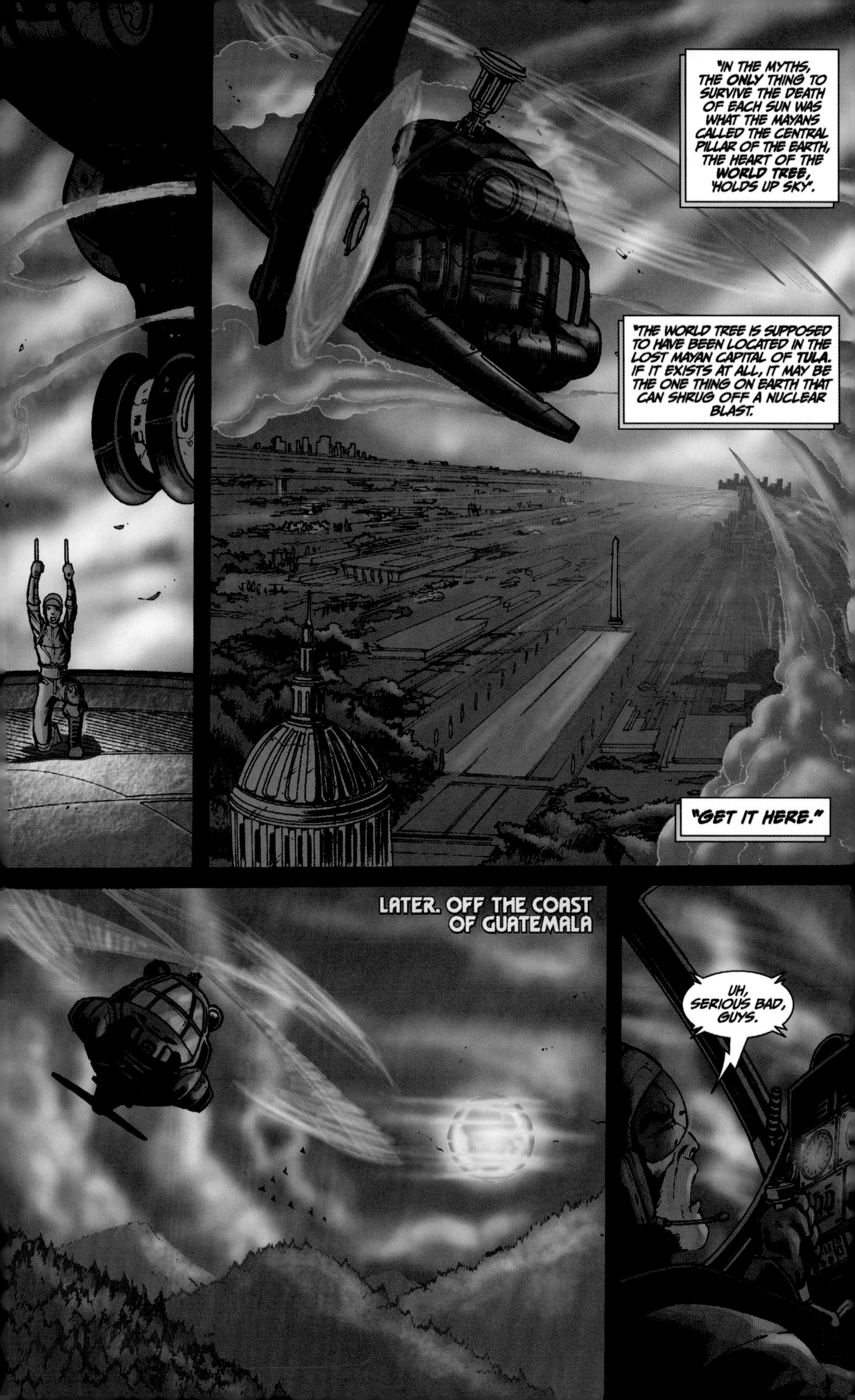
"IN THE MYTHS, THE ONLY THING TO SURVIVE THE DEATH OF EACH SUN WAS WHAT THE MAYANS CALLED THE CENTRAL PILLAR OF THE EARTH, THE HEART OF THE WORLD TREE, 'HOLDS UP SKY'.
"THE WORLD TREE IS SUPPOSED TO HAVE BEEN LOCATED IN THE LOST MAYAN CAPITAL OF TULA. IF IT EXISTS AT ALL, IT MAY BE THE ONE THING ON EARTH THAT CAN SHRUG OFF A NUCLEAR BLAST.
"GET IT HERE."
LATER. OFF THE COAST OF GUATEMALA
UH, SERIOUS BAD, GUYS.

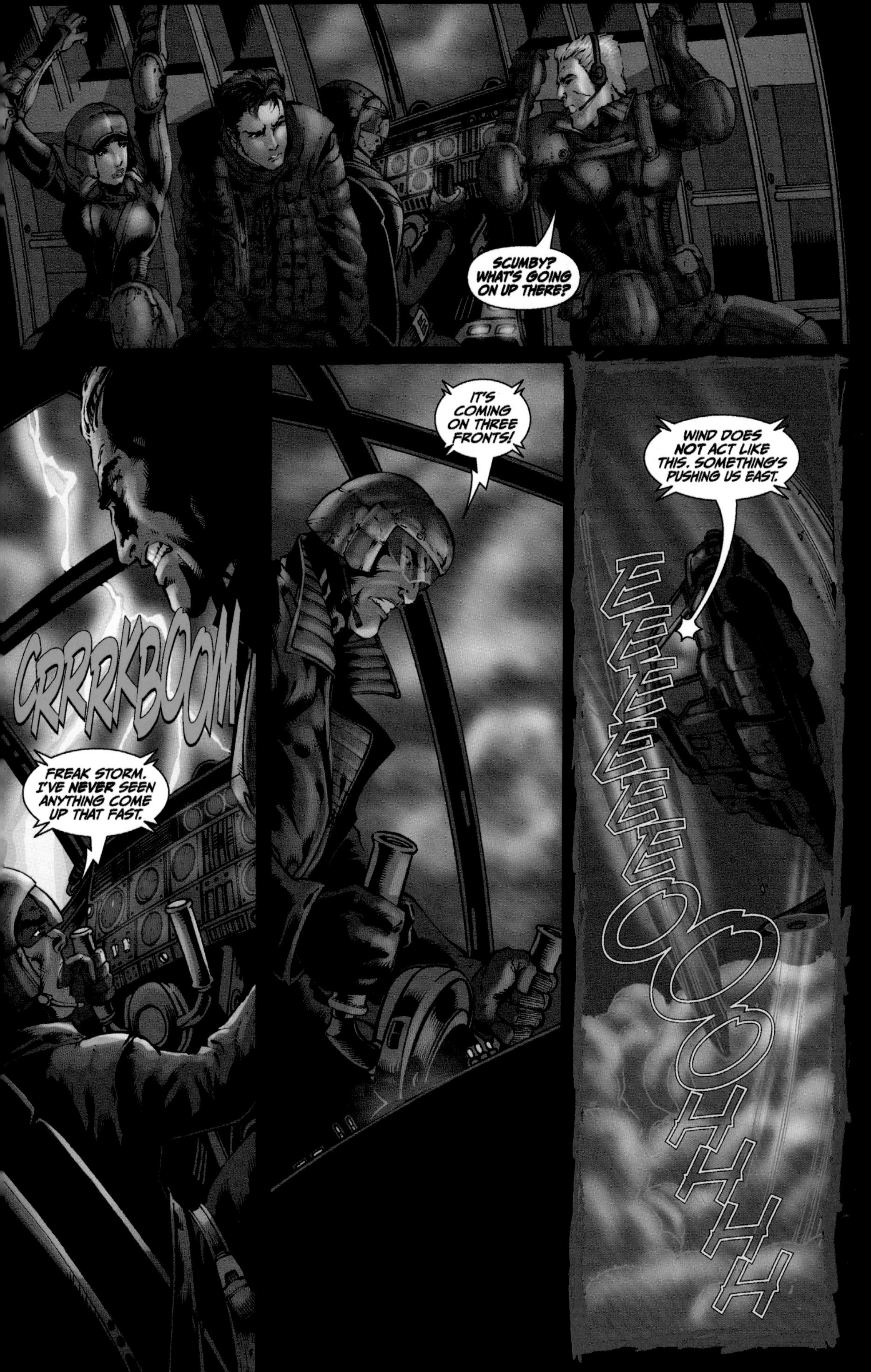
SCUMBY? WHAT'S GOING ON UP THERE?
CRRRKBOOM
FREAK STORM. I'VE NEVER SEEN ANYTHING COME UP THAT FAST.
IT'S COMING ON THREE FRONTS!
WIND DOES NOT ACT LIKE THIS. SOMETHING'S PUSHING US EAST.
EEEEEEEOOOOHHHH

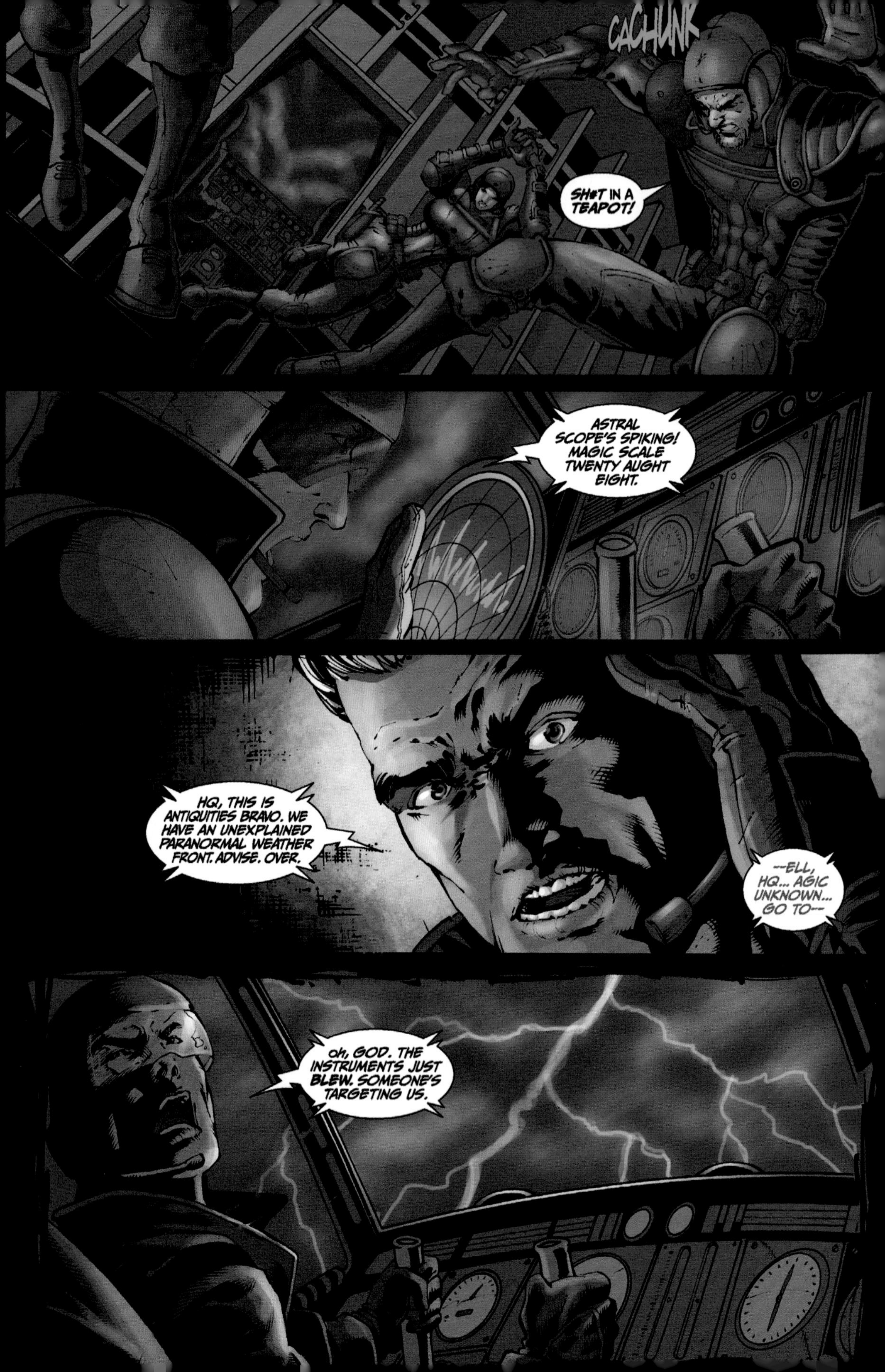
CACHUNK
SH#T IN A TEAPOT!
ASTRAL SCOPE'S SPIKING! MAGIC SCALE TWENTY AUGHT EIGHT.
HQ, THIS IS ANTIQUITIES BRAVO. WE HAVE AN UNEXPLAINED PARANORMAL WEATHER FRONT. ADVISE. OVER.
--ELL, HQ... AGIC UNKNOWN... GO TO--
oh, GOD. THE INSTRUMENTS JUST BLEW. SOMEONE'S TARGETING US.

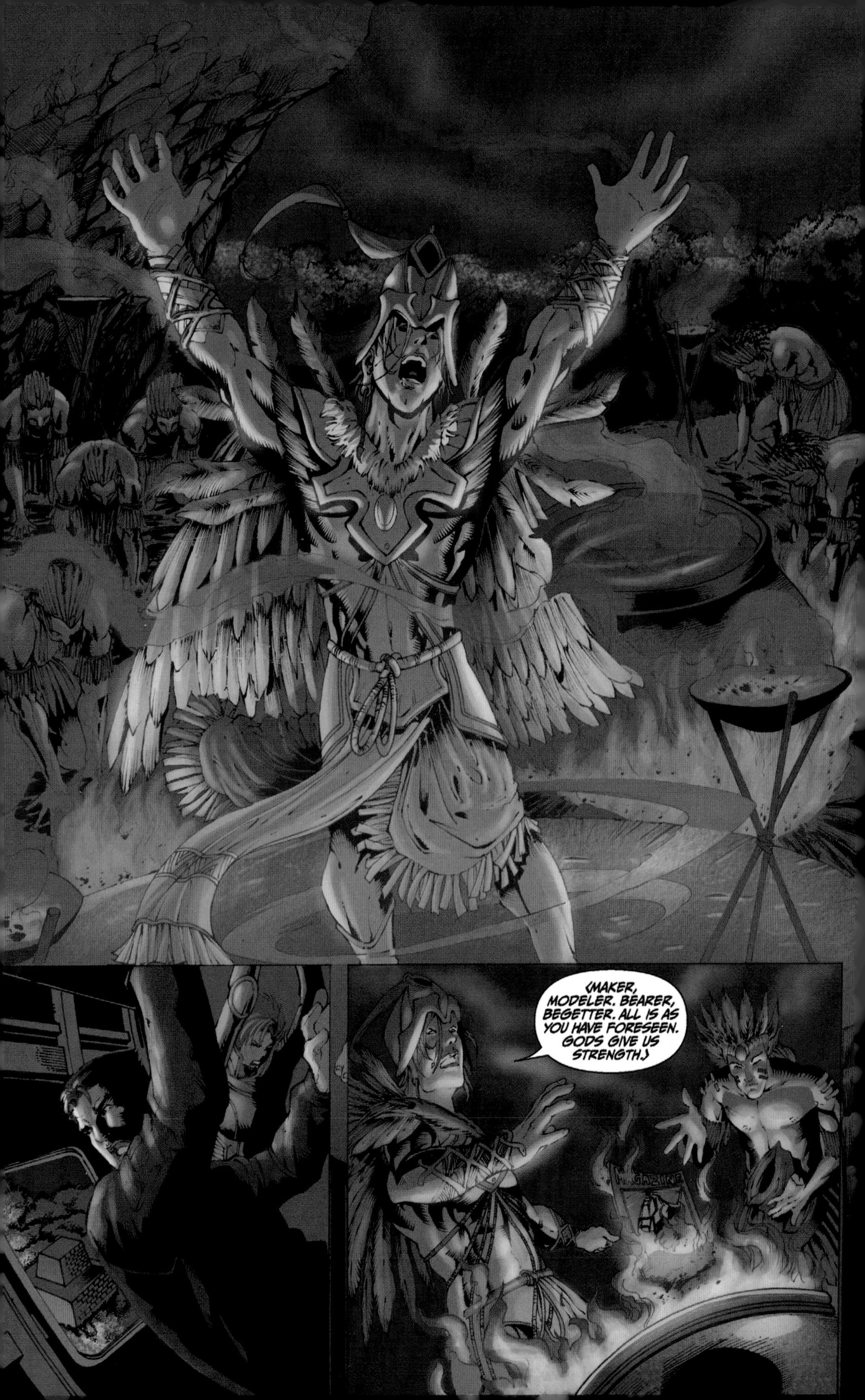
‹MAKER, MODELER. BEARER, BEGETTER. ALL IS AS YOU HAVE FORESEEN. GODS GIVE US STRENGTH.›
MAGAZINE

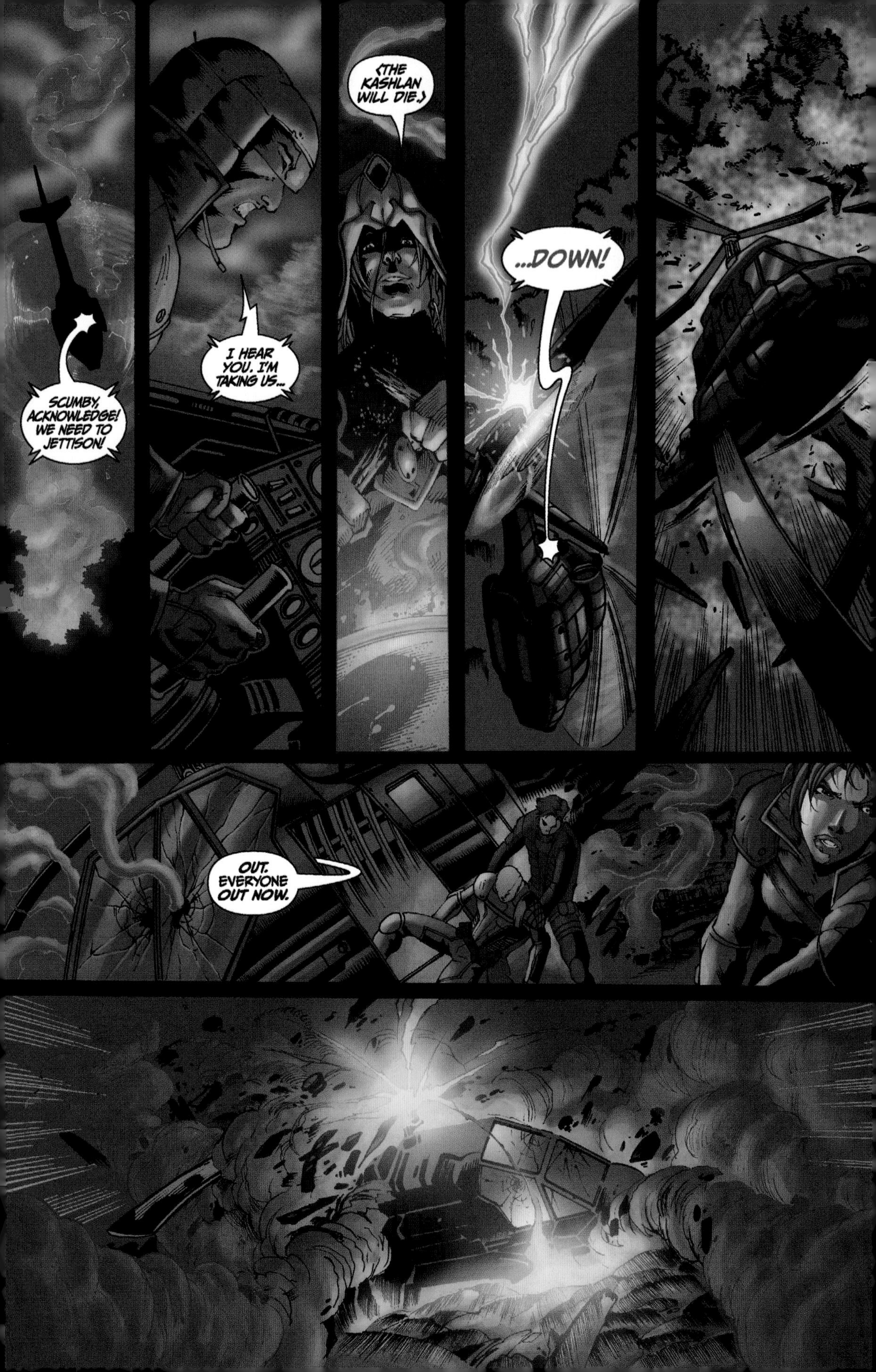
SCUMBY, ACKNOWLEDGE! WE NEED TO JETTISON!
I HEAR YOU. I'M TAKING US...
‹THE KASHLAN WILL DIE.›
...DOWN!
OUT. EVERYONE OUT NOW.

M.I.T.H.

HEADQUARTERS MAGICAL INTELLIGENCE TACTICAL ™

CHAPTER 2

"Disbelief in magic can force a poor soul into believing in government and business."

-- Tom Robbins

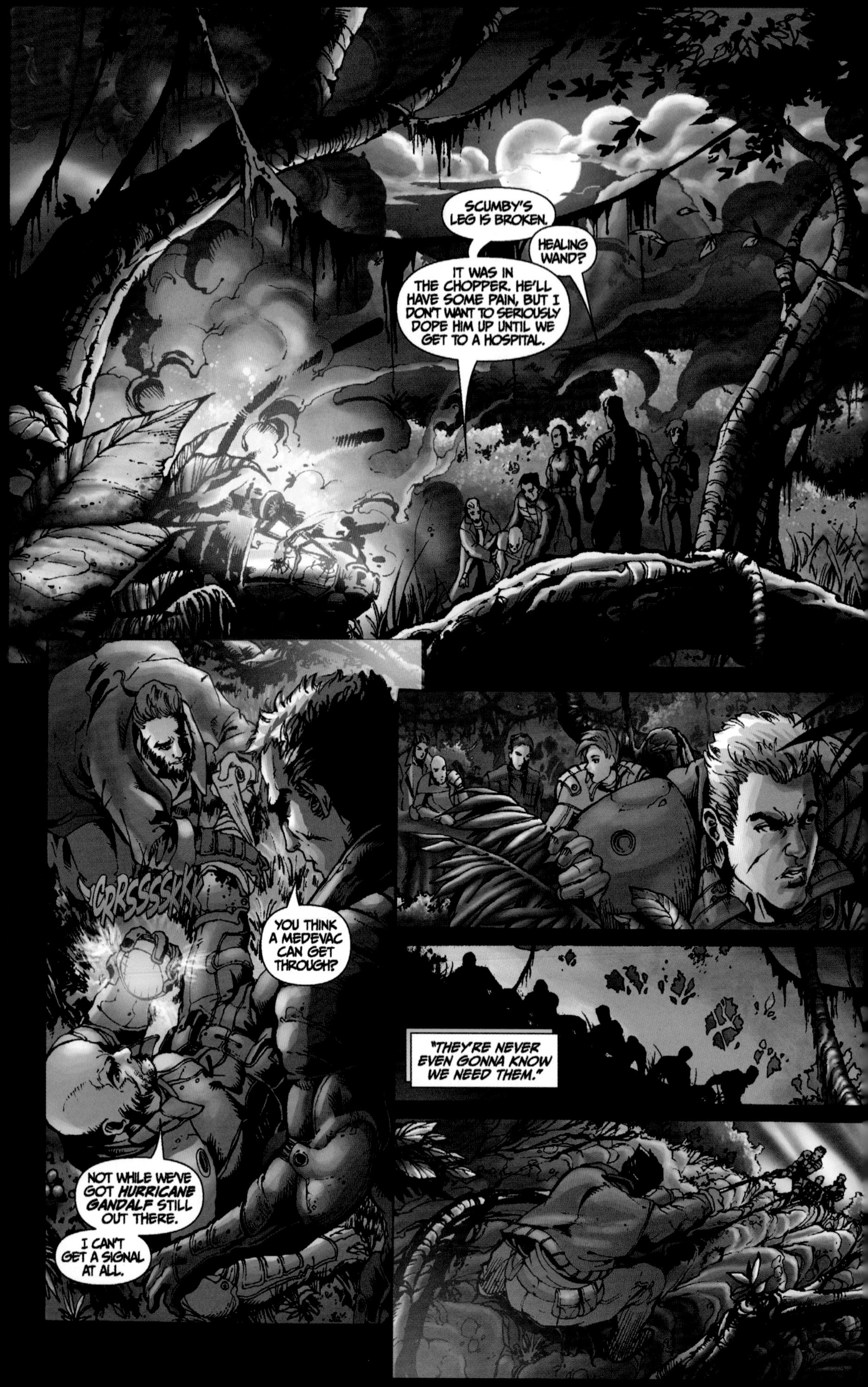
SCUMBY'S LEG IS BROKEN.
HEALING WAND?
IT WAS IN THE CHOPPER. HE'LL HAVE SOME PAIN, BUT I DON'T WANT TO SERIOUSLY DOPE HIM UP UNTIL WE GET TO A HOSPITAL.
KRRSSSSKKK
YOU THINK A MEDEVAC CAN GET THROUGH?
NOT WHILE WE'VE GOT *HURRICANE GANDALF* STILL OUT THERE.
I CAN'T GET A SIGNAL AT ALL.
"THEY'RE NEVER EVEN GONNA KNOW WE NEED THEM."

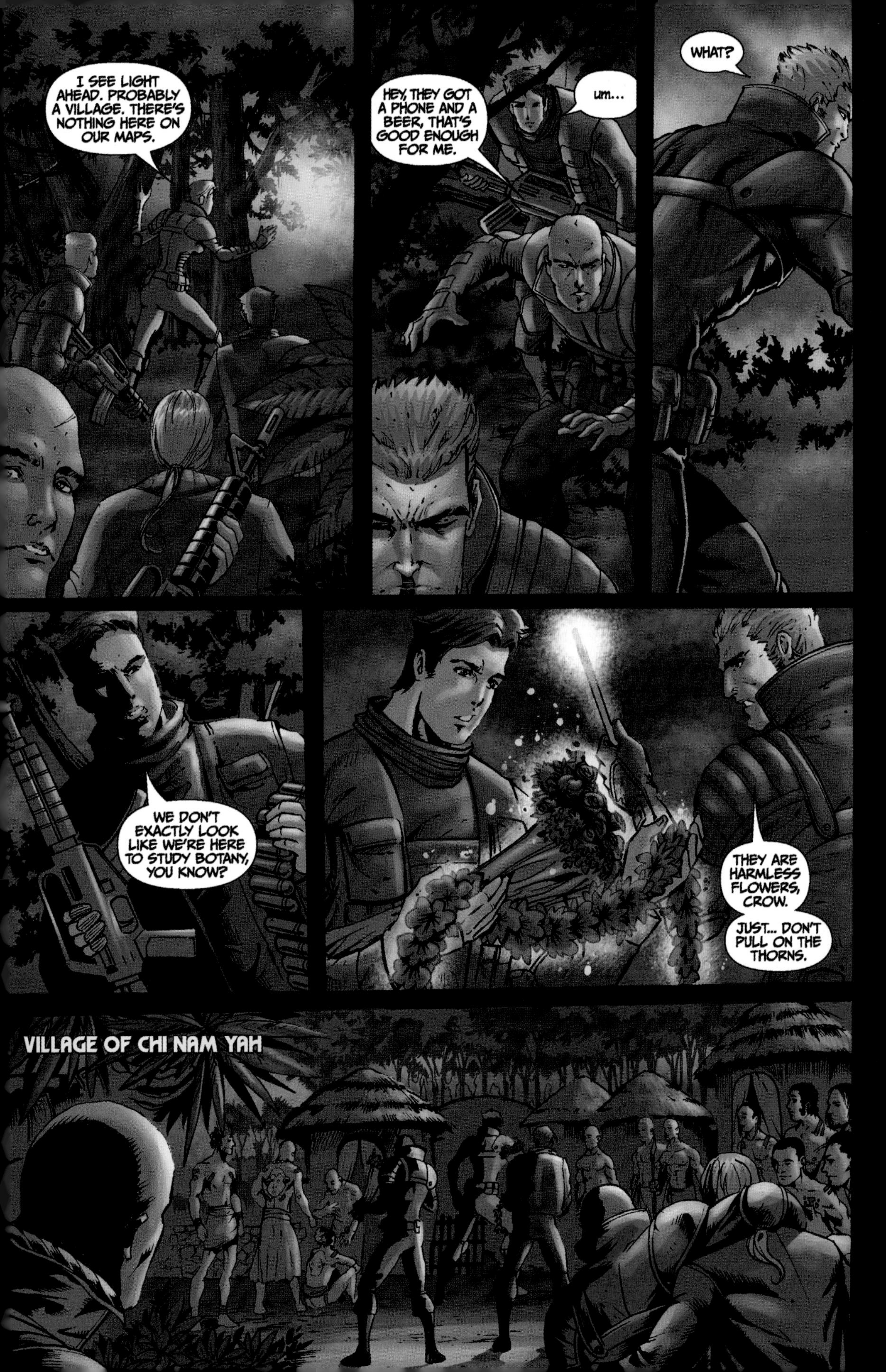
I SEE LIGHT AHEAD. PROBABLY A VILLAGE. THERE'S NOTHING HERE ON OUR MAPS.
HEY, THEY GOT A PHONE AND A BEER, THAT'S GOOD ENOUGH FOR ME.
um...
WHAT?
WE DON'T EXACTLY LOOK LIKE WE'RE HERE TO STUDY BOTANY, YOU KNOW?
THEY ARE HARMLESS FLOWERS, CROW.
JUST... DON'T PULL ON THE THORNS.
VILLAGE OF CHI NAM YAH

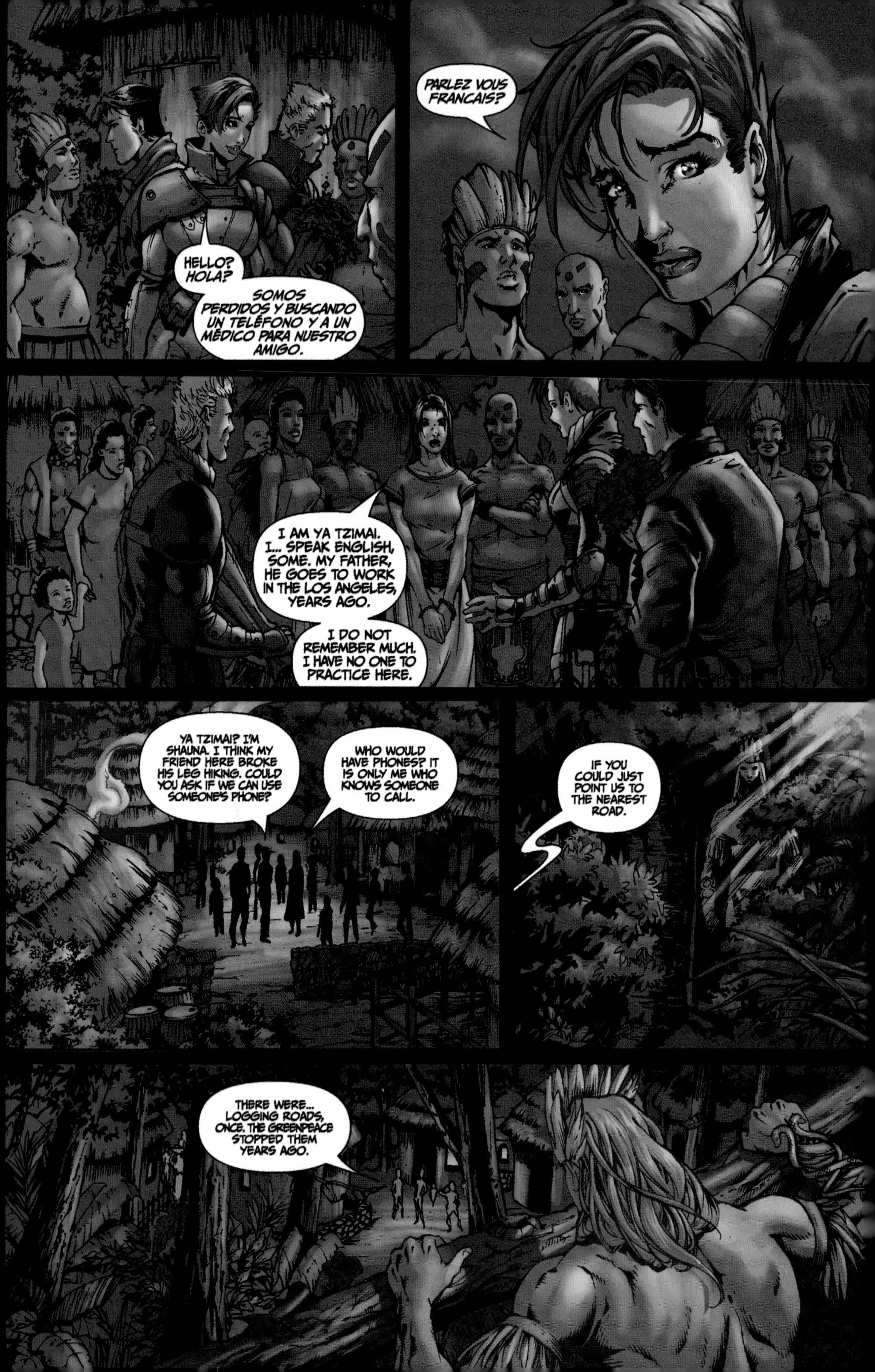
HELLO? HOLA?
SOMOS PERDIDOS Y BUSCANDO UN TELÉFONO Y A UN MÉDICO PARA NUESTRO AMIGO.
PARLEZ VOUS FRANCAIS?
I AM YA TZIMAI. I... SPEAK ENGLISH, SOME. MY FATHER, HE GOES TO WORK IN THE LOS ANGELES, YEARS AGO.
I DO NOT REMEMBER MUCH. I HAVE NO ONE TO PRACTICE HERE.
YA TZIMAI? I'M SHAUNA. I THINK MY FRIEND HERE BROKE HIS LEG HIKING. COULD YOU ASK IF WE CAN USE SOMEONE'S PHONE?
WHO WOULD HAVE PHONES? IT IS ONLY ME WHO KNOWS SOMEONE TO CALL.
IF YOU COULD JUST POINT US TO THE NEAREST ROAD.
THERE WERE... LOGGING ROADS, ONCE. THE GREENPEACE STOPPED THEM YEARS AGO.

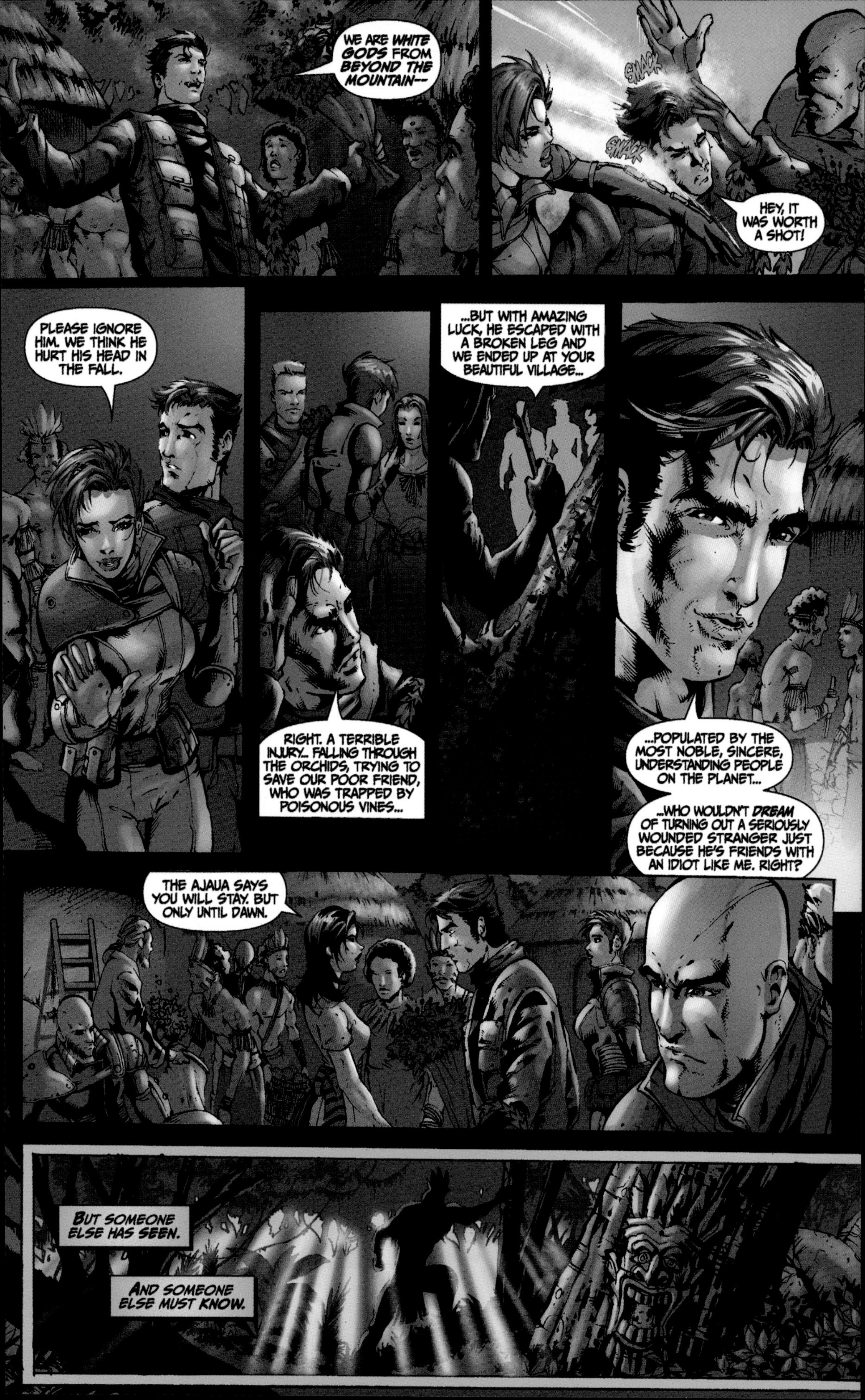
WE ARE WHITE GODS FROM BEYOND THE MOUNTAIN--
SMACK
SMACK
HEY, IT WAS WORTH A SHOT!
PLEASE IGNORE HIM. WE THINK HE HURT HIS HEAD IN THE FALL.
RIGHT. A TERRIBLE INJURY.. FALLING THROUGH THE ORCHIDS, TRYING TO SAVE OUR POOR FRIEND, WHO WAS TRAPPED BY POISONOUS VINES...
...BUT WITH AMAZING LUCK, HE ESCAPED WITH A BROKEN LEG AND WE ENDED UP AT YOUR BEAUTIFUL VILLAGE...
...POPULATED BY THE MOST NOBLE, SINCERE, UNDERSTANDING PEOPLE ON THE PLANET...
...WHO WOULDN'T DREAM OF TURNING OUT A SERIOUSLY WOUNDED STRANGER JUST BECAUSE HE'S FRIENDS WITH AN IDIOT LIKE ME. RIGHT?
THE AJAUA SAYS YOU WILL STAY. BUT ONLY UNTIL DAWN.
BUT SOMEONE ELSE HAS SEEN.
AND SOMEONE ELSE MUST KNOW.

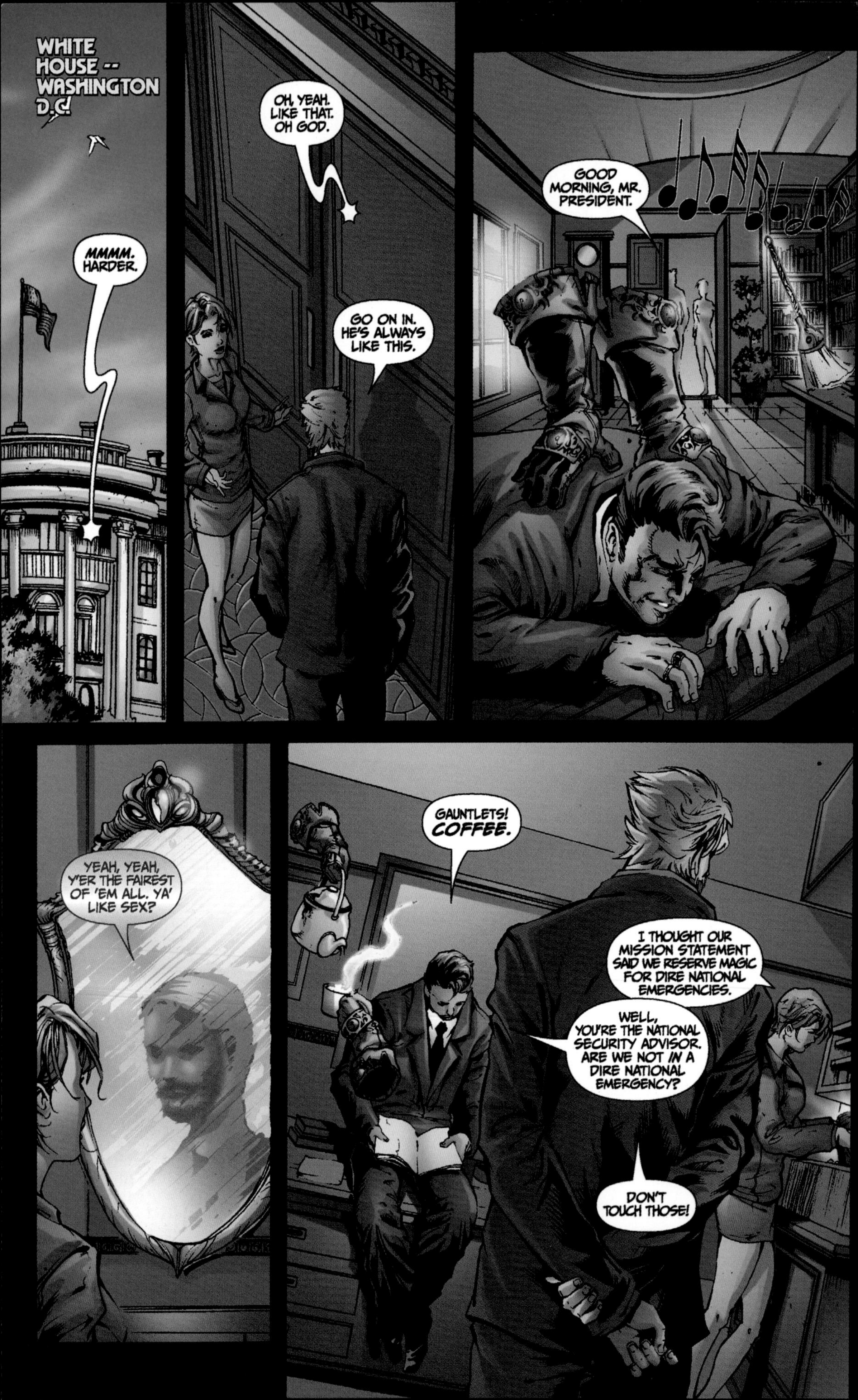
WHITE HOUSE -- WASHINGTON D.C.
MMMM. HARDER.
OH, YEAH. LIKE THAT. OH GOD.
GO ON IN. HE'S ALWAYS LIKE THIS.
GOOD MORNING, MR. PRESIDENT.
YEAH, YEAH, Y'ER THE FAIREST OF 'EM ALL. YA' LIKE SEX?
GAUNTLETS! COFFEE.
I THOUGHT OUR MISSION STATEMENT SAID WE RESERVE MAGIC FOR DIRE NATIONAL EMERGENCIES.
WELL, YOU'RE THE NATIONAL SECURITY ADVISOR. ARE WE NOT IN A DIRE NATIONAL EMERGENCY?
DON'T TOUCH THOSE!

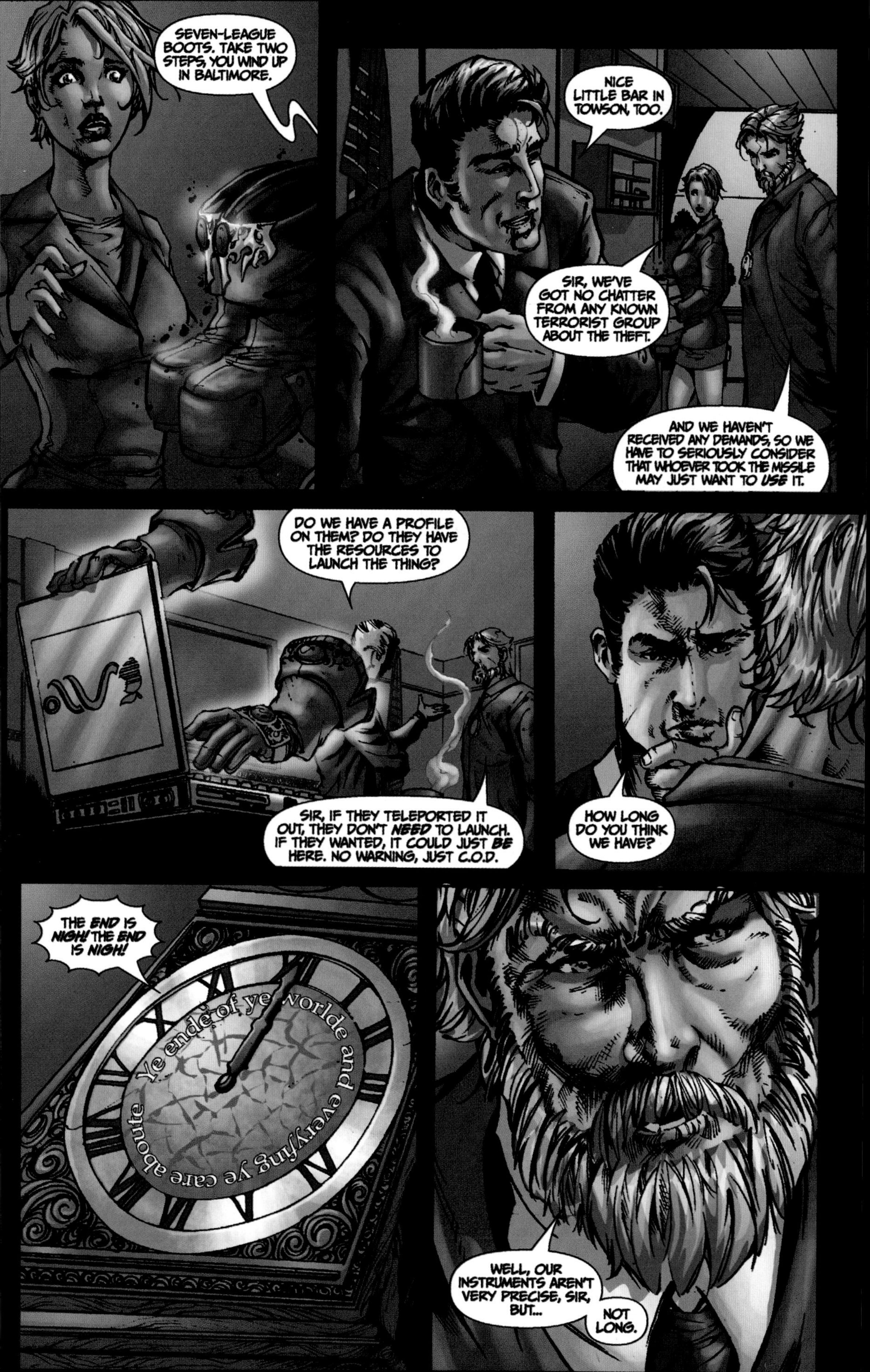
SEVEN-LEAGUE BOOTS. TAKE TWO STEPS, YOU WIND UP IN BALTIMORE.
NICE LITTLE BAR IN TOWSON, TOO.
SIR, WE'VE GOT NO CHATTER FROM ANY KNOWN TERRORIST GROUP ABOUT THE THEFT.
AND WE HAVEN'T RECEIVED ANY DEMANDS, SO WE HAVE TO SERIOUSLY CONSIDER THAT WHOEVER TOOK THE MISSILE MAY JUST WANT TO *USE* IT.
DO WE HAVE A PROFILE ON THEM? DO THEY HAVE THE RESOURCES TO LAUNCH THE THING?
SIR, IF THEY TELEPORTED IT OUT, THEY DON'T *NEED* TO LAUNCH. IF THEY WANTED, IT COULD JUST *BE* HERE. NO WARNING, JUST C.O.D.
HOW LONG DO YOU THINK WE HAVE?
THE *END* IS *NIGH!* THE *END* IS *NIGH!*
Ye ende of ye worlde and everyfing ye care aboute
WELL, OUR INSTRUMENTS AREN'T VERY PRECISE, SIR, BUT...
NOT LONG.

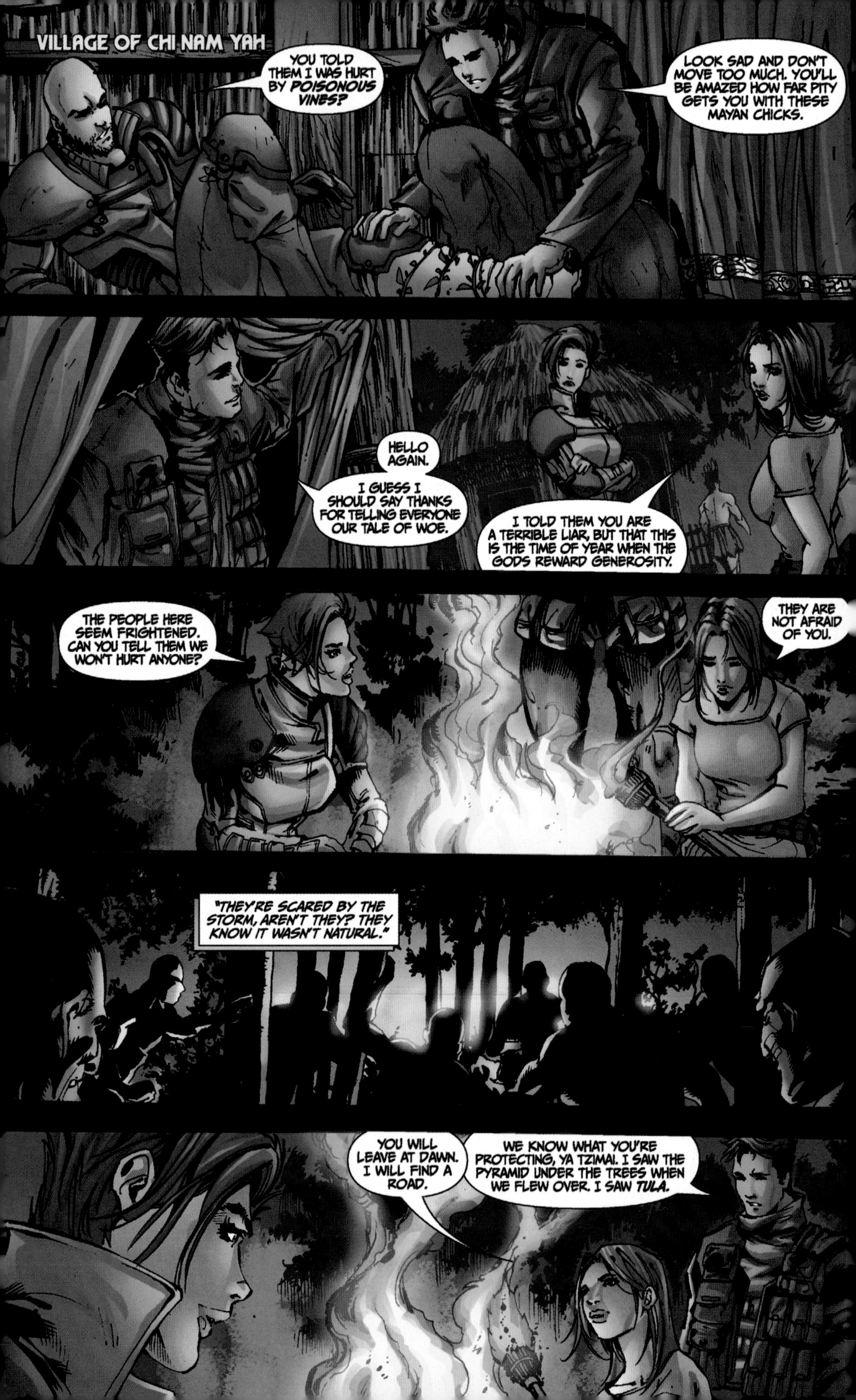
VILLAGE OF CHI NAM YAH
YOU TOLD THEM I WAS HURT BY POISONOUS VINES?
LOOK SAD AND DON'T MOVE TOO MUCH. YOU'LL BE AMAZED HOW FAR PITY GETS YOU WITH THESE MAYAN CHICKS.
HELLO AGAIN.
I GUESS I SHOULD SAY THANKS FOR TELLING EVERYONE OUR TALE OF WOE.
I TOLD THEM YOU ARE A TERRIBLE LIAR, BUT THAT THIS IS THE TIME OF YEAR WHEN THE GODS REWARD GENEROSITY.
THE PEOPLE HERE SEEM FRIGHTENED. CAN YOU TELL THEM WE WON'T HURT ANYONE?
THEY ARE NOT AFRAID OF YOU.
"THEY'RE SCARED BY THE STORM, AREN'T THEY? THEY KNOW IT WASN'T NATURAL."
YOU WILL LEAVE AT DAWN. I WILL FIND A ROAD.
WE KNOW WHAT YOU'RE PROTECTING, YA TZIMAI. I SAW THE PYRAMID UNDER THE TREES WHEN WE FLEW OVER. I SAW TULA.

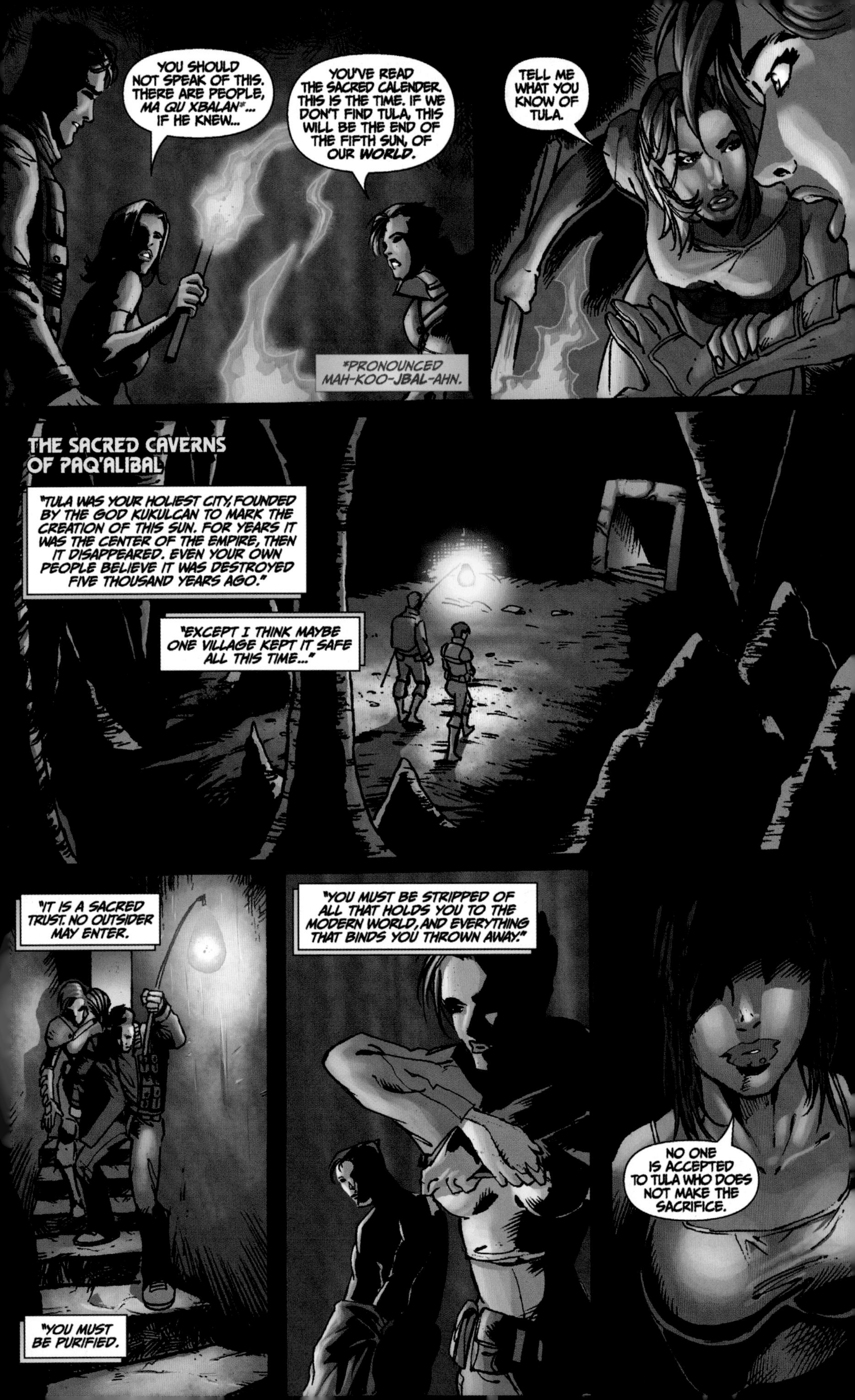
YOU SHOULD NOT SPEAK OF THIS. THERE ARE PEOPLE, MA QU XBALAN*... IF HE KNEW...
YOU'VE READ THE SACRED CALENDER. THIS IS THE TIME. IF WE DON'T FIND TULA, THIS WILL BE THE END OF THE FIFTH SUN, OF OUR WORLD.
*PRONOUNCED MAH-KOO-JBAL-AHN.
TELL ME WHAT YOU KNOW OF TULA.
THE SACRED CAVERNS OF PAQ'ALIBAL
"TULA WAS YOUR HOLIEST CITY, FOUNDED BY THE GOD KUKULCAN TO MARK THE CREATION OF THIS SUN. FOR YEARS IT WAS THE CENTER OF THE EMPIRE, THEN IT DISAPPEARED. EVEN YOUR OWN PEOPLE BELIEVE IT WAS DESTROYED FIVE THOUSAND YEARS AGO."
"EXCEPT I THINK MAYBE ONE VILLAGE KEPT IT SAFE ALL THIS TIME..."
"IT IS A SACRED TRUST. NO OUTSIDER MAY ENTER.
"YOU MUST BE PURIFIED.
"YOU MUST BE STRIPPED OF ALL THAT HOLDS YOU TO THE MODERN WORLD, AND EVERYTHING THAT BINDS YOU THROWN AWAY."
NO ONE IS ACCEPTED TO TULA WHO DOES NOT MAKE THE SACRIFICE.

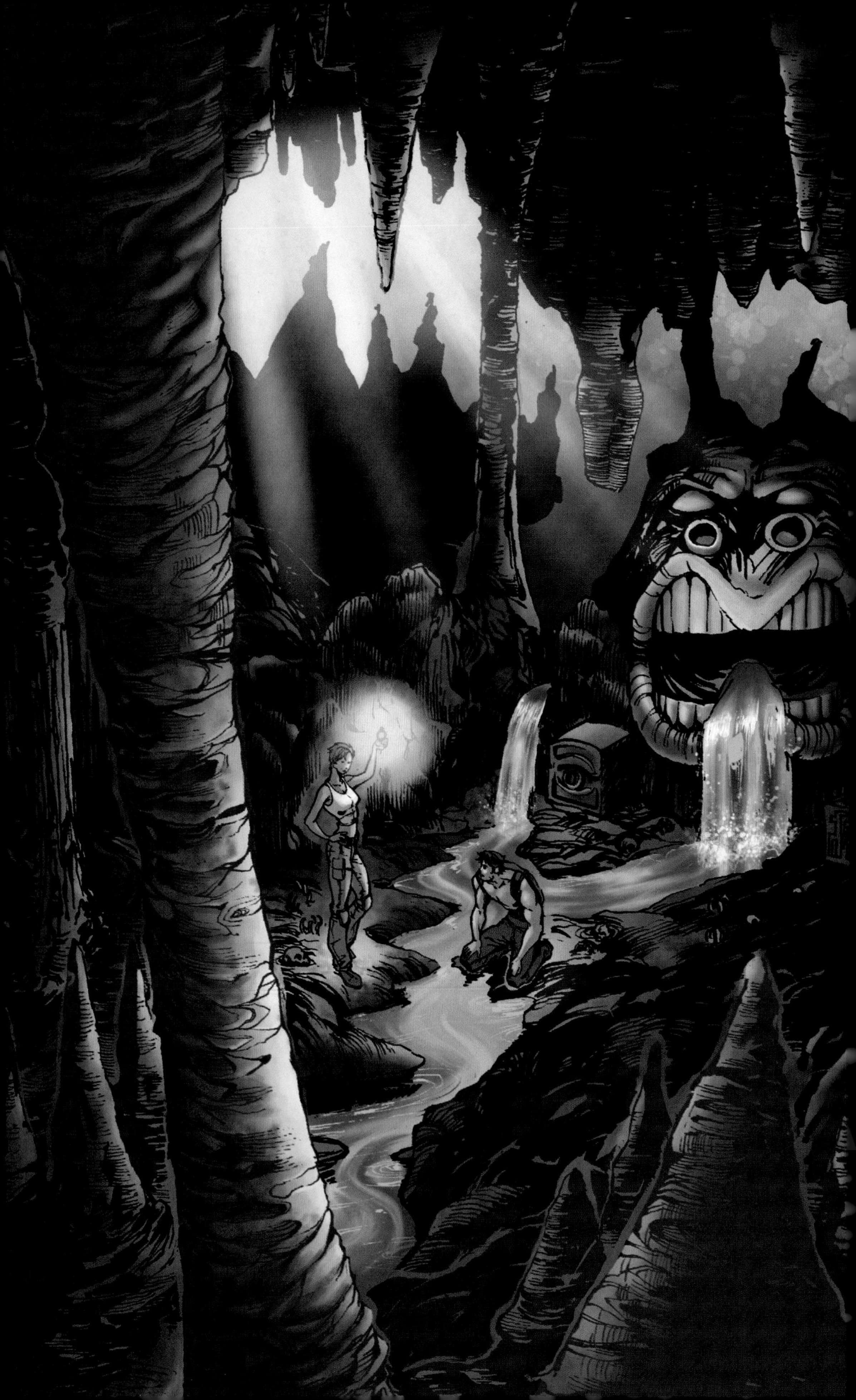

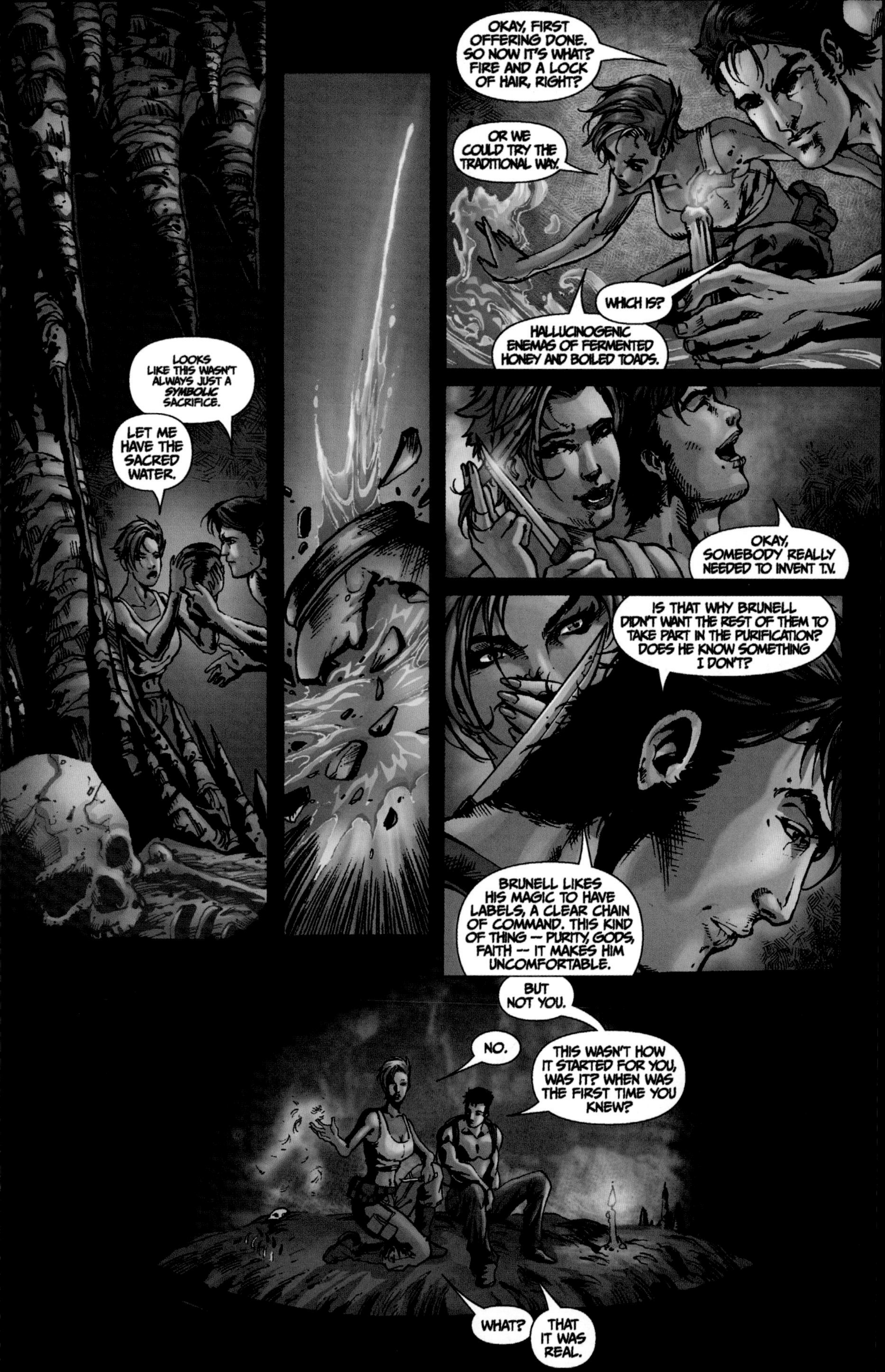
OKAY, FIRST OFFERING DONE. SO NOW IT'S WHAT? FIRE AND A LOCK OF HAIR, RIGHT?
OR WE COULD TRY THE TRADITIONAL WAY.
WHICH IS?
HALLUCINOGENIC ENEMAS OF FERMENTED HONEY AND BOILED TOADS.
OKAY, SOMEBODY REALLY NEEDED TO INVENT T.V.
IS THAT WHY BRUNELL DIDN'T WANT THE REST OF THEM TO TAKE PART IN THE PURIFICATION? DOES HE KNOW SOMETHING I DON'T?
BRUNELL LIKES HIS MAGIC TO HAVE LABELS, A CLEAR CHAIN OF COMMAND. THIS KIND OF THING -- PURITY, GODS, FAITH -- IT MAKES HIM UNCOMFORTABLE.
LOOKS LIKE THIS WASN'T ALWAYS JUST A SYMBOLIC SACRIFICE.
LET ME HAVE THE SACRED WATER.
BUT NOT YOU.
NO.
THIS WASN'T HOW IT STARTED FOR YOU, WAS IT? WHEN WAS THE FIRST TIME YOU KNEW?
WHAT?
THAT IT WAS REAL.

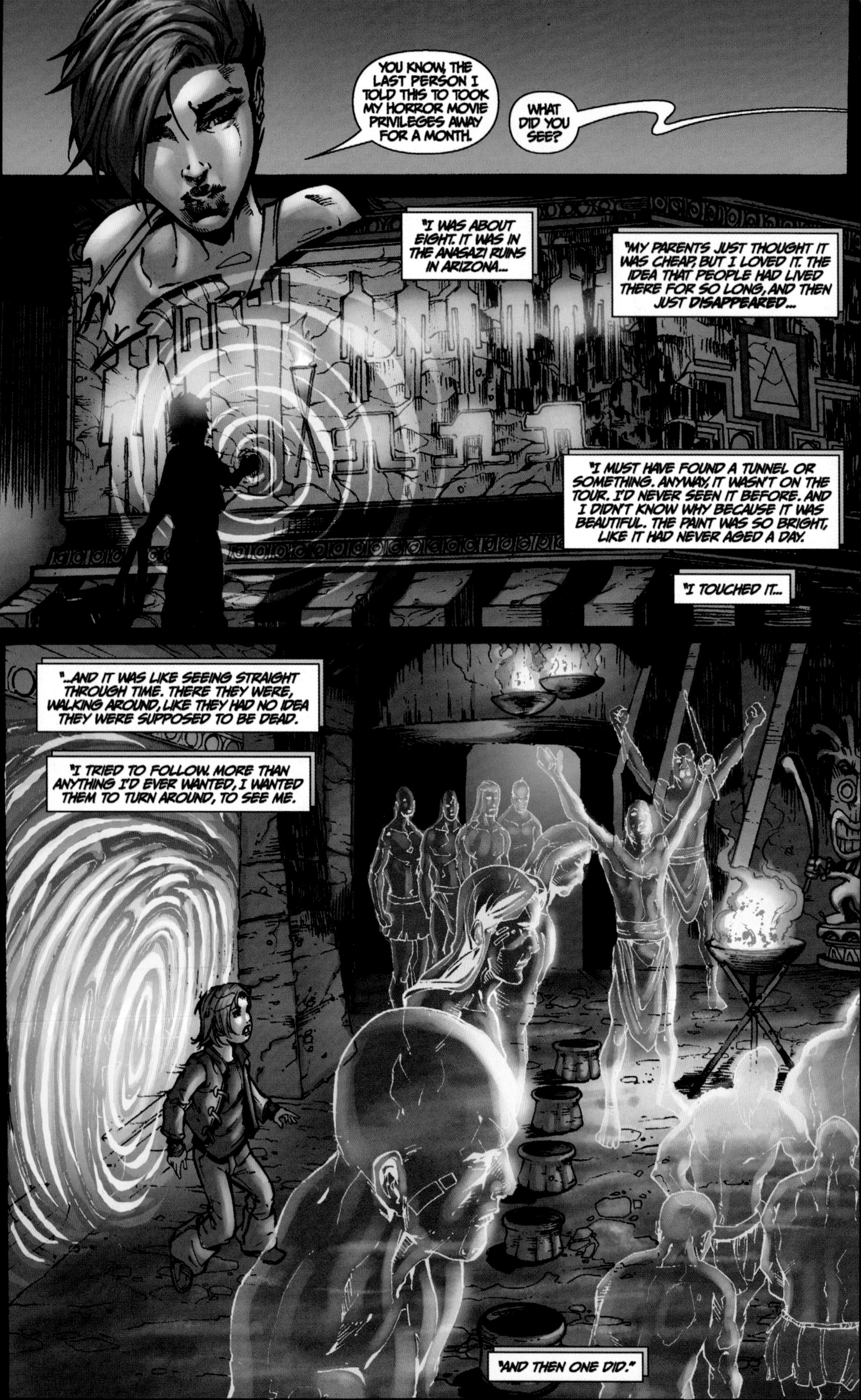
YOU KNOW, THE LAST PERSON I TOLD THIS TO TOOK MY HORROR MOVIE PRIVILEGES AWAY FOR A MONTH.
WHAT DID YOU SEE?
"I WAS ABOUT EIGHT. IT WAS IN THE ANASAZI RUINS IN ARIZONA...
"MY PARENTS JUST THOUGHT IT WAS CHEAP, BUT I LOVED IT. THE IDEA THAT PEOPLE HAD LIVED THERE FOR SO LONG, AND THEN JUST DISAPPEARED...
"I MUST HAVE FOUND A TUNNEL OR SOMETHING. ANYWAY, IT WASN'T ON THE TOUR. I'D NEVER SEEN IT BEFORE. AND I DIDN'T KNOW WHY BECAUSE IT WAS BEAUTIFUL. THE PAINT WAS SO BRIGHT, LIKE IT HAD NEVER AGED A DAY.
"I TOUCHED IT...
"...AND IT WAS LIKE SEEING STRAIGHT THROUGH TIME. THERE THEY WERE, WALKING AROUND, LIKE THEY HAD NO IDEA THEY WERE SUPPOSED TO BE DEAD.
"I TRIED TO FOLLOW. MORE THAN ANYTHING I'D EVER WANTED, I WANTED THEM TO TURN AROUND, TO SEE ME.
"AND THEN ONE DID."

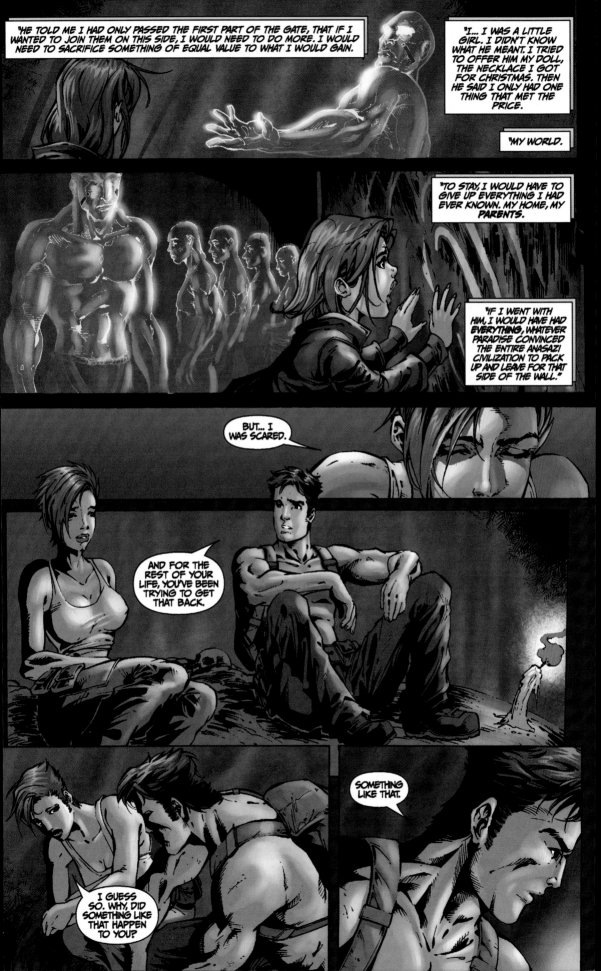

"HE TOLD ME I HAD ONLY PASSED THE FIRST PART OF THE GATE, THAT IF I WANTED TO JOIN THEM ON THIS SIDE, I WOULD NEED TO DO MORE. I WOULD NEED TO SACRIFICE SOMETHING OF EQUAL VALUE TO WHAT I WOULD GAIN.

"I... I WAS A LITTLE GIRL. I DIDN'T KNOW WHAT HE MEANT. I TRIED TO OFFER HIM MY DOLL, THE NECKLACE I GOT FOR CHRISTMAS. THEN HE SAID I ONLY HAD ONE THING THAT MET THE PRICE.

"MY WORLD.

"TO STAY, I WOULD HAVE TO GIVE UP EVERYTHING I HAD EVER KNOWN. MY HOME, MY PARENTS.

"IF I WENT WITH HIM, I WOULD HAVE HAD EVERYTHING, WHATEVER PARADISE CONVINCED THE ENTIRE ANASAZI CIVILIZATION TO PACK UP AND LEAVE FOR THAT SIDE OF THE WALL."

BUT... I WAS SCARED.

AND FOR THE REST OF YOUR LIFE, YOU'VE BEEN TRYING TO GET THAT BACK.

SOMETHING LIKE THAT.

I GUESS SO. WHY, DID SOMETHING LIKE THAT HAPPEN TO YOU?

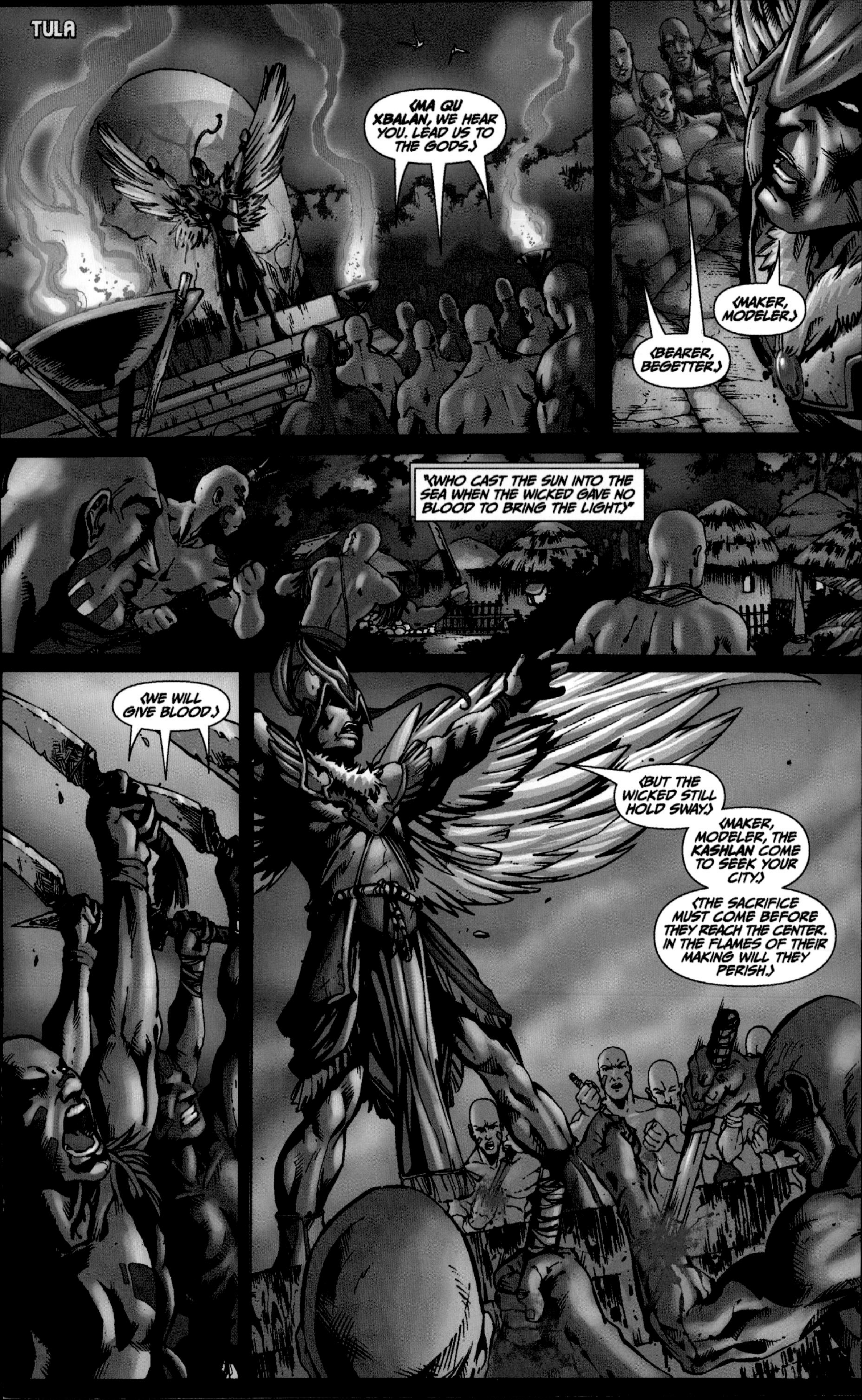
TULA
‹MA QU XBALAN, WE HEAR YOU. LEAD US TO THE GODS.›
‹MAKER, MODELER.›
‹BEARER, BEGETTER.›
"‹WHO CAST THE SUN INTO THE SEA WHEN THE WICKED GAVE NO BLOOD TO BRING THE LIGHT.›"
‹WE WILL GIVE BLOOD.›
‹BUT THE WICKED STILL HOLD SWAY.›
‹MAKER, MODELER, THE KASHLAN COME TO SEEK YOUR CITY.›
‹THE SACRIFICE MUST COME BEFORE THEY REACH THE CENTER. IN THE FLAMES OF THEIR MAKING WILL THEY PERISH.›

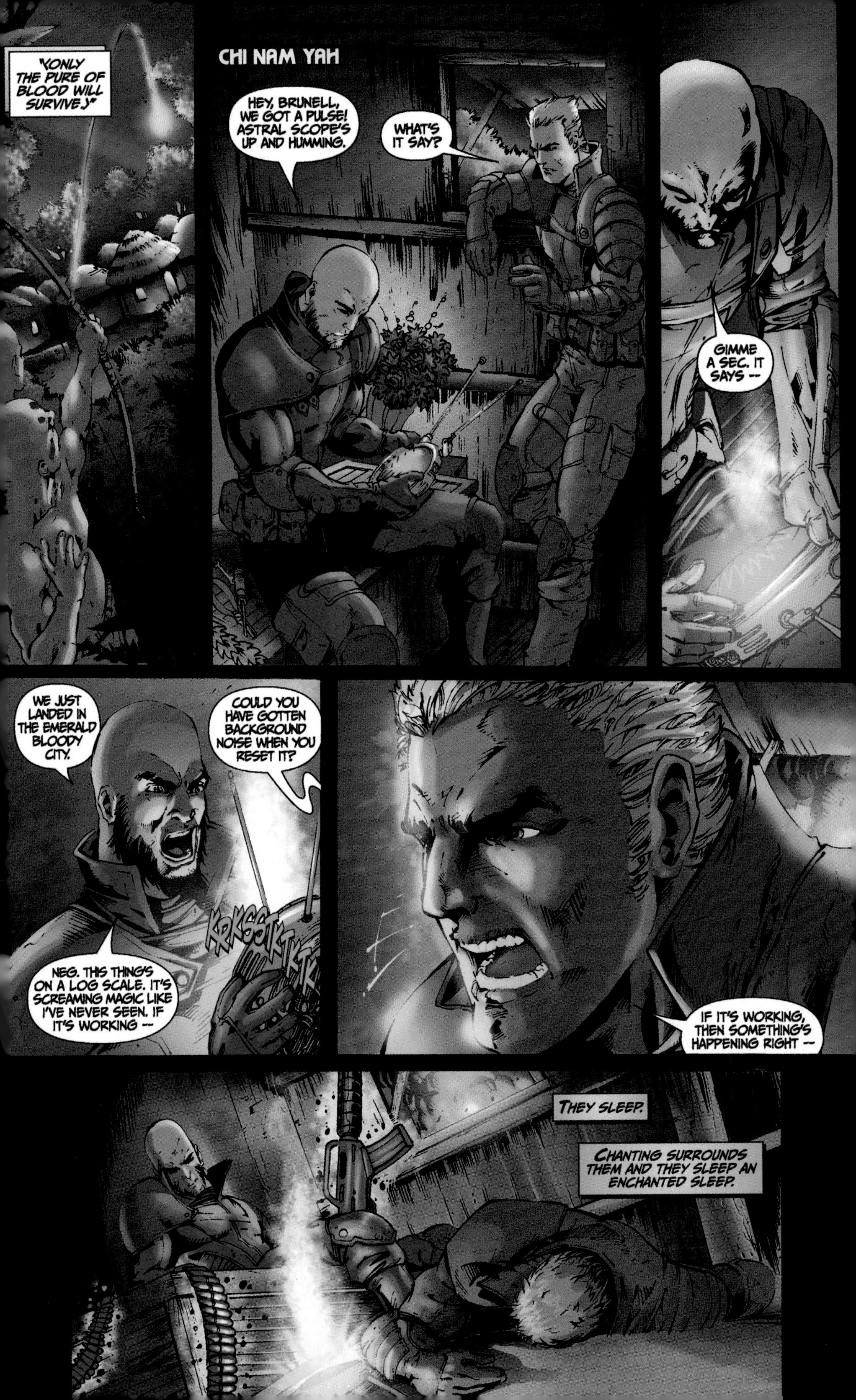
"‹ONLY THE PURE OF BLOOD WILL SURVIVE.›"
CHI NAM YAH
HEY, BRUNELL, WE GOT A PULSE! ASTRAL SCOPE'S UP AND HUMMING.
WHAT'S IT SAY?
GIMME A SEC. IT SAYS --
WE JUST LANDED IN THE EMERALD BLOODY CITY.
COULD YOU HAVE GOTTEN BACKGROUND NOISE WHEN YOU RESET IT?
KRKSSTKTKTK
NEG. THIS THING'S ON A LOG SCALE. IT'S SCREAMING MAGIC LIKE I'VE NEVER SEEN. IF IT'S WORKING --
IF IT'S WORKING, THEN SOMETHING'S HAPPENING RIGHT --
THEY SLEEP.
CHANTING SURROUNDS THEM AND THEY SLEEP AN ENCHANTED SLEEP.

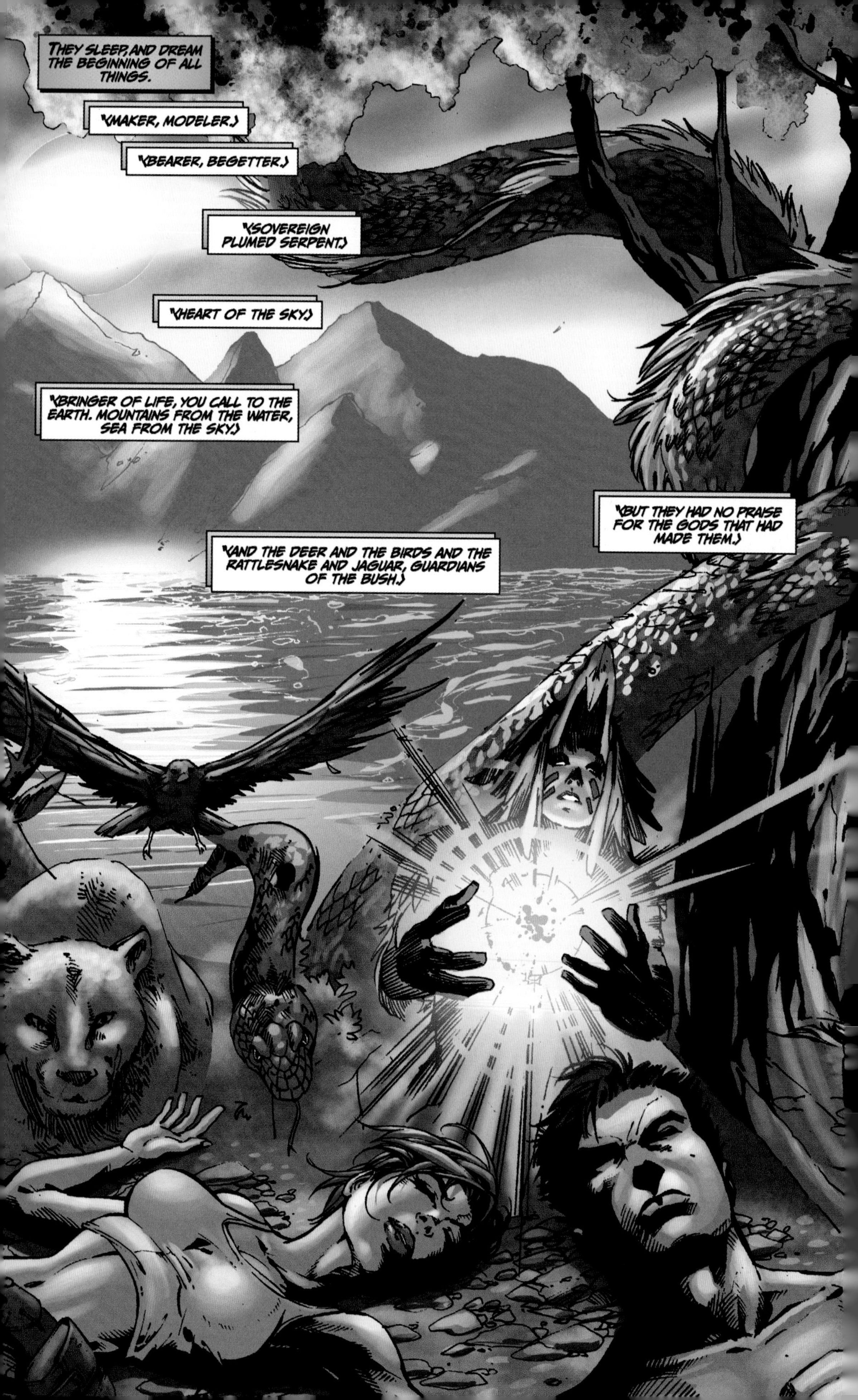
THEY SLEEP, AND DREAM THE BEGINNING OF ALL THINGS.
"<MAKER, MODELER.>
"<BEARER, BEGETTER.>
"<SOVEREIGN PLUMED SERPENT.>
"<HEART OF THE SKY.>
"<BRINGER OF LIFE, YOU CALL TO THE EARTH. MOUNTAINS FROM THE WATER, SEA FROM THE SKY.>
"<AND THE DEER AND THE BIRDS AND THE RATTLESNAKE AND JAGUAR, GUARDIANS OF THE BUSH.>
"<BUT THEY HAD NO PRAISE FOR THE GODS THAT HAD MADE THEM.>

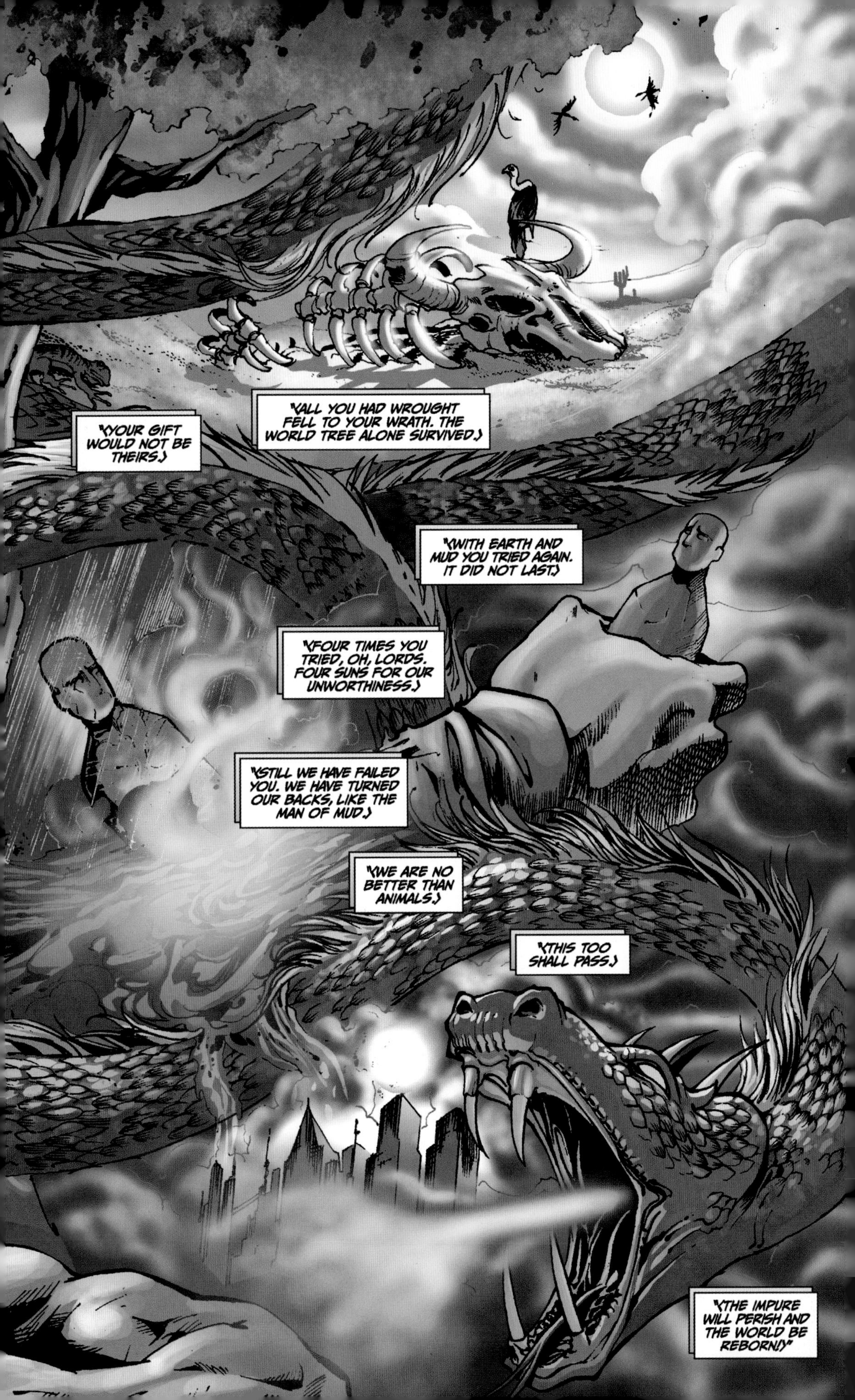
"<YOUR GIFT WOULD NOT BE THEIRS.>
"<ALL YOU HAD WROUGHT FELL TO YOUR WRATH. THE WORLD TREE ALONE SURVIVED.>
"<WITH EARTH AND MUD YOU TRIED AGAIN. IT DID NOT LAST.>
"<FOUR TIMES YOU TRIED, OH, LORDS. FOUR SUNS FOR OUR UNWORTHINESS.>
"<STILL WE HAVE FAILED YOU. WE HAVE TURNED OUR BACKS, LIKE THE MAN OF MUD.>
"<WE ARE NO BETTER THAN ANIMALS.>
"<THIS TOO SHALL PASS.>
"<THE IMPURE WILL PERISH AND THE WORLD BE REBORN!>"

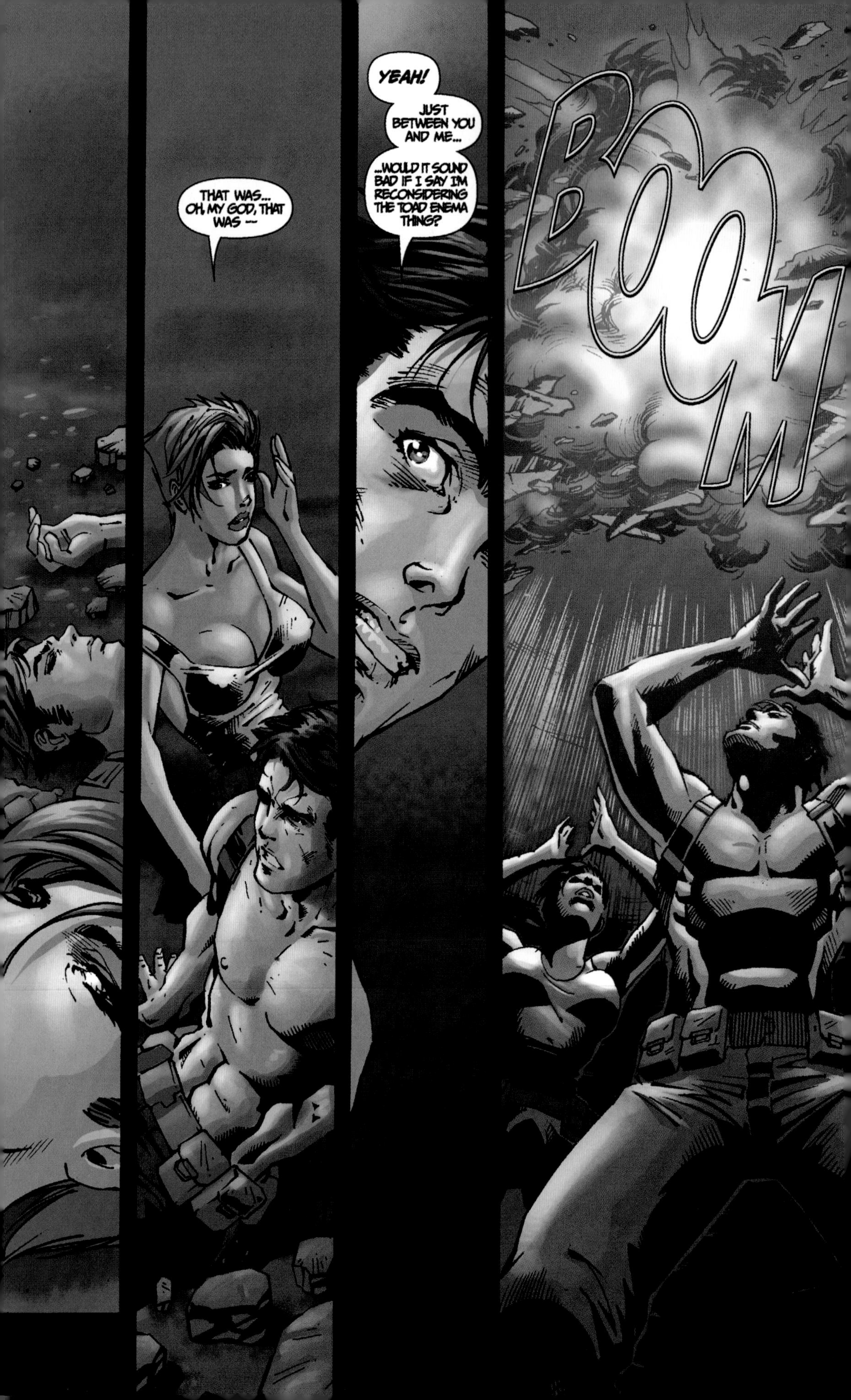
THAT WAS... OH, MY GOD, THAT WAS --
YEAH!
JUST BETWEEN YOU AND ME...
...WOULD IT SOUND BAD IF I SAY I'M RECONSIDERING THE TOAD ENEMA THING?
BOOM

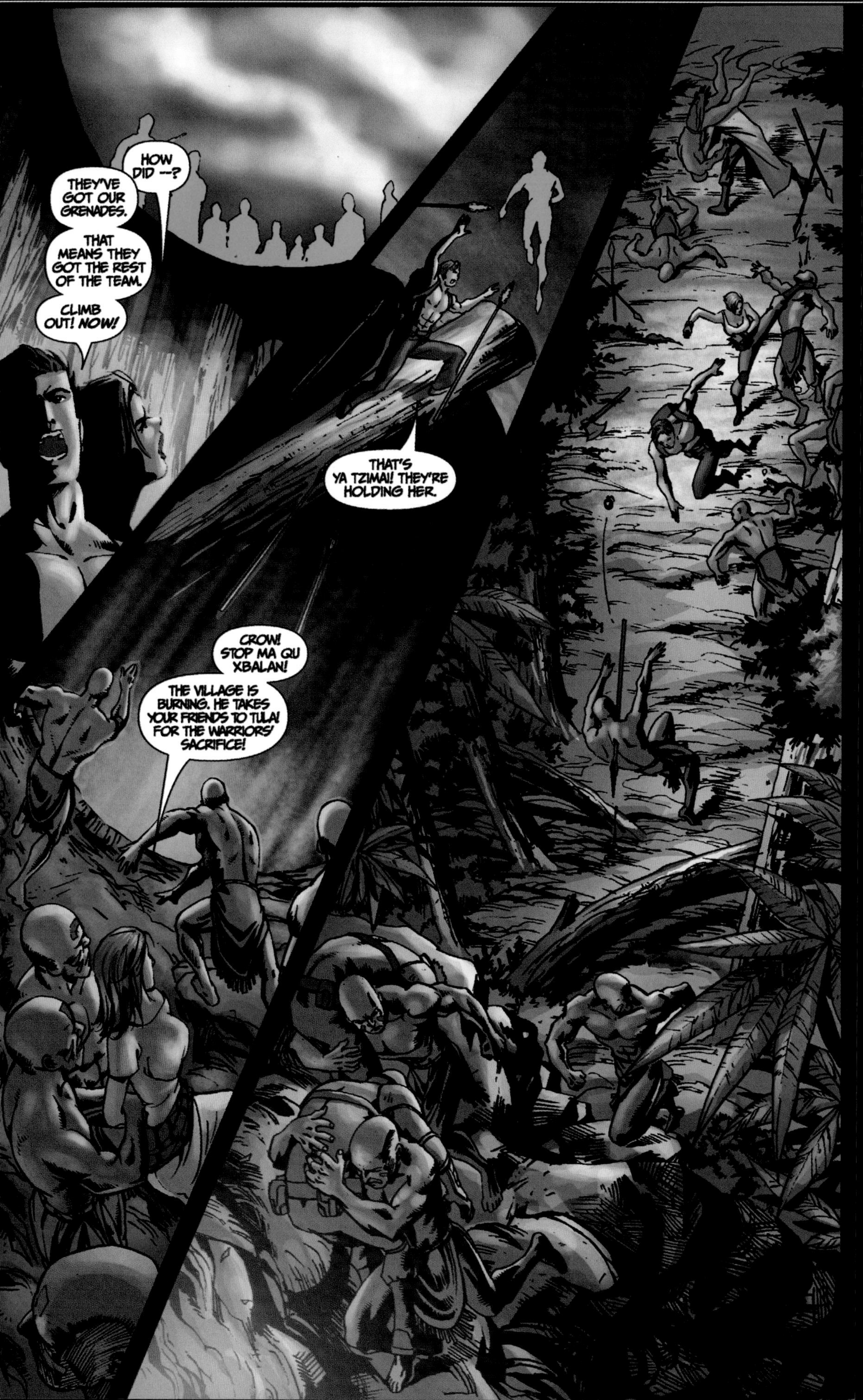
HOW DID --?
THEY'VE GOT OUR GRENADES.
THAT MEANS THEY GOT THE REST OF THE TEAM.
CLIMB OUT! NOW!
THAT'S YA TZIMA! THEY'RE HOLDING HER.
CROW! STOP MA QU XBALAN!
THE VILLAGE IS BURNING. HE TAKES YOUR FRIENDS TO TULA! FOR THE WARRIORS' SACRIFICE!

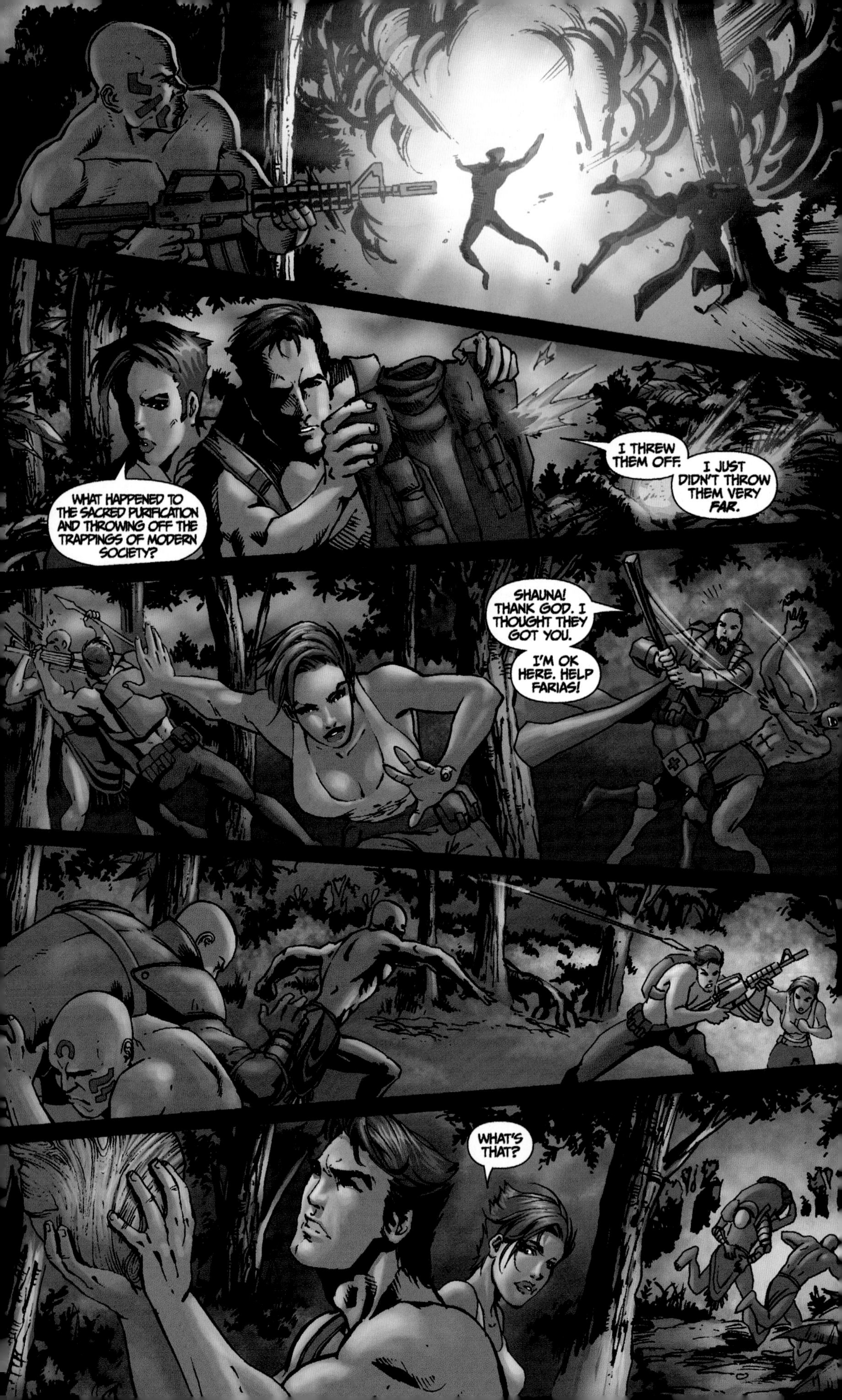

WHAT HAPPENED TO THE SACRED PURIFICATION AND THROWING OFF THE TRAPPINGS OF MODERN SOCIETY?
I THREW THEM OFF.
I JUST DIDN'T THROW THEM VERY FAR.
SHAUNA! THANK GOD. I THOUGHT THEY GOT YOU.
I'M OK HERE. HELP FARIAS!
WHAT'S THAT?

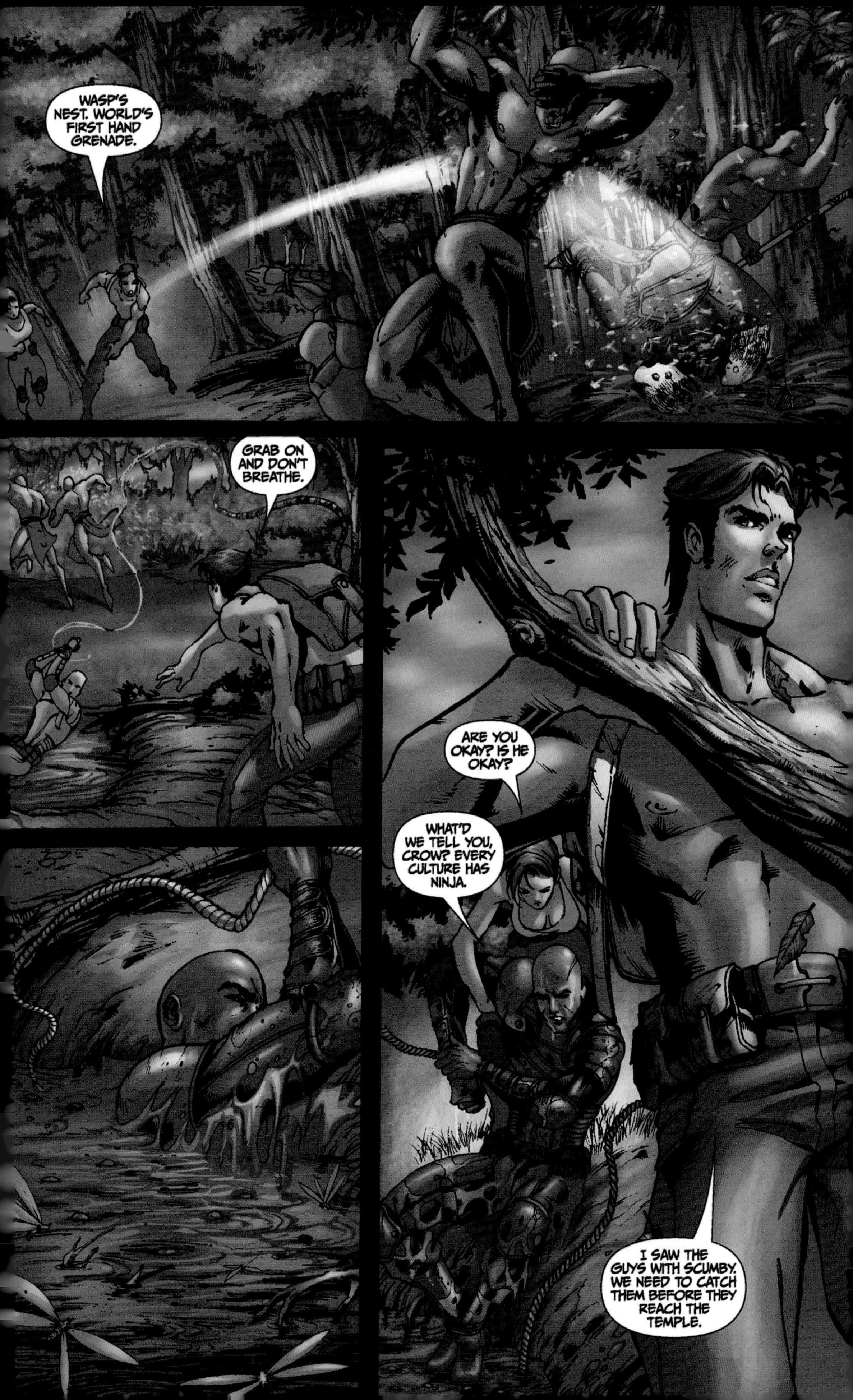
WASP'S NEST. WORLD'S FIRST HAND GRENADE.
GRAB ON AND DON'T BREATHE.
ARE YOU OKAY? IS HE OKAY?
WHAT'D WE TELL YOU, CROW? EVERY CULTURE HAS NINJA.
I SAW THE GUYS WITH SCUMBY. WE NEED TO CATCH THEM BEFORE THEY REACH THE TEMPLE.

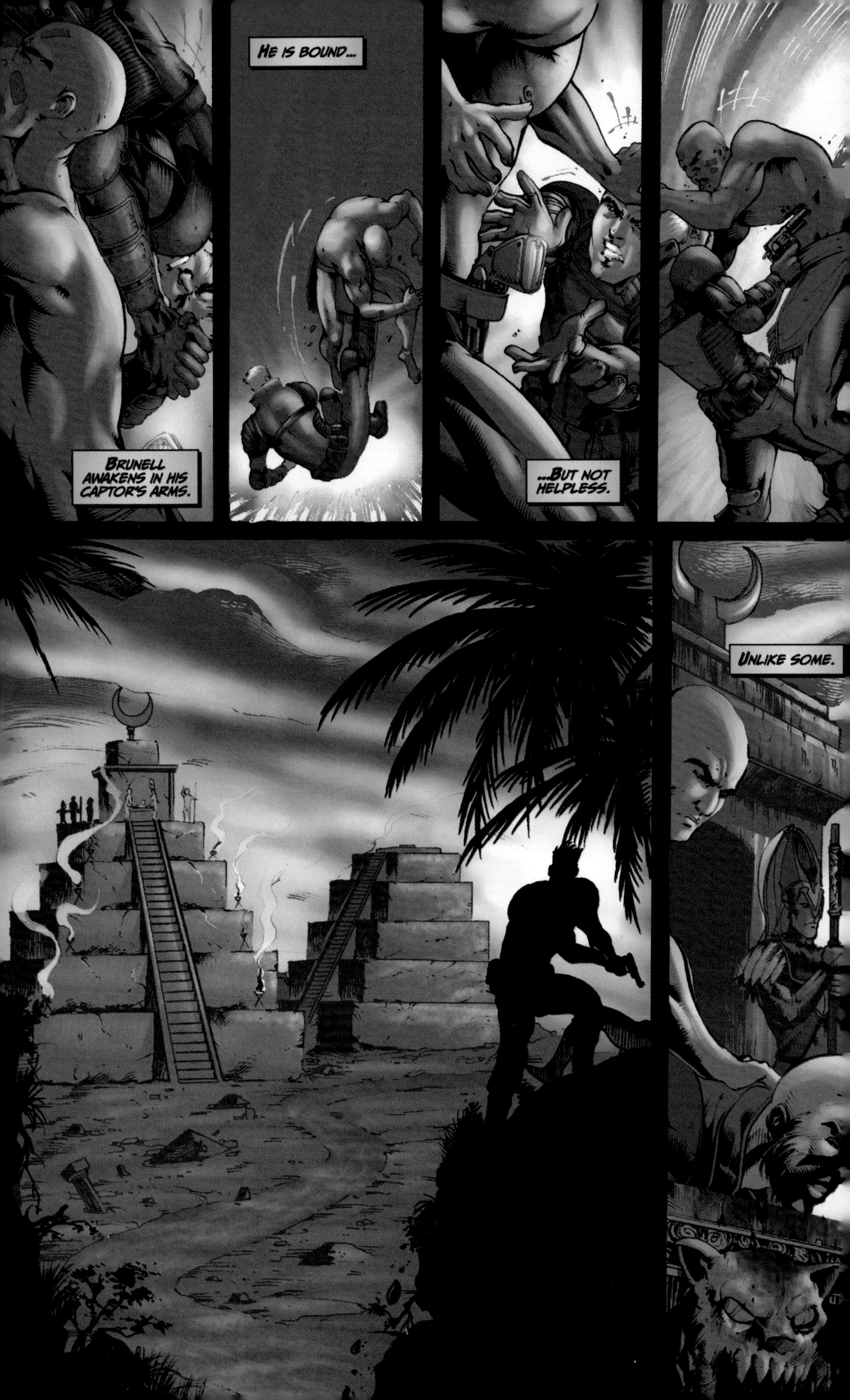
BRUNELL AWAKENS IN HIS CAPTOR'S ARMS.
HE IS BOUND...
...BUT NOT HELPLESS.
UNLIKE SOME.

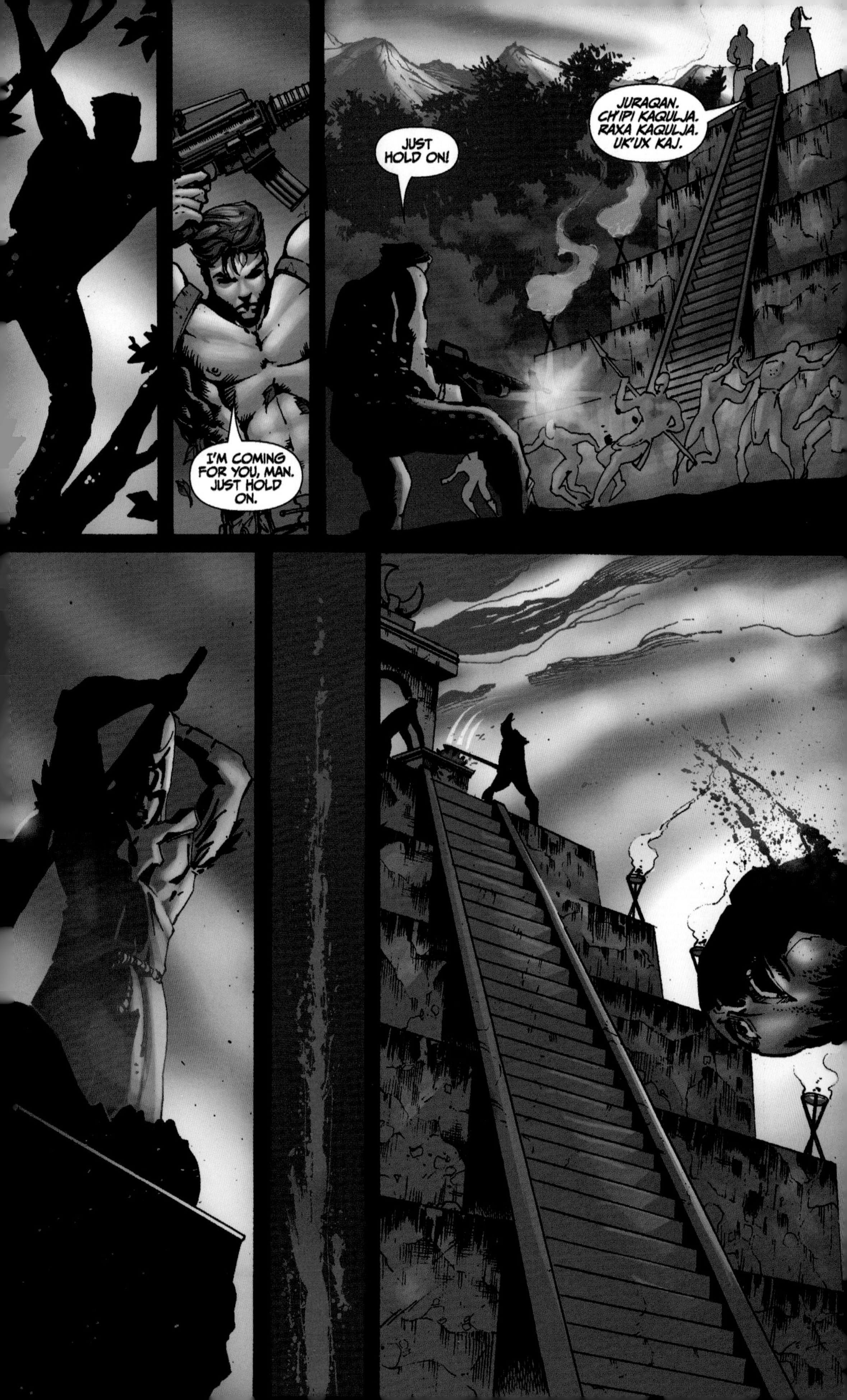
I'M COMING FOR YOU, MAN. JUST HOLD ON.
JUST HOLD ON!
JURAQAN. CH'IPI KAQULJA. RAXA KAQULJA. UK'UX KAJ.

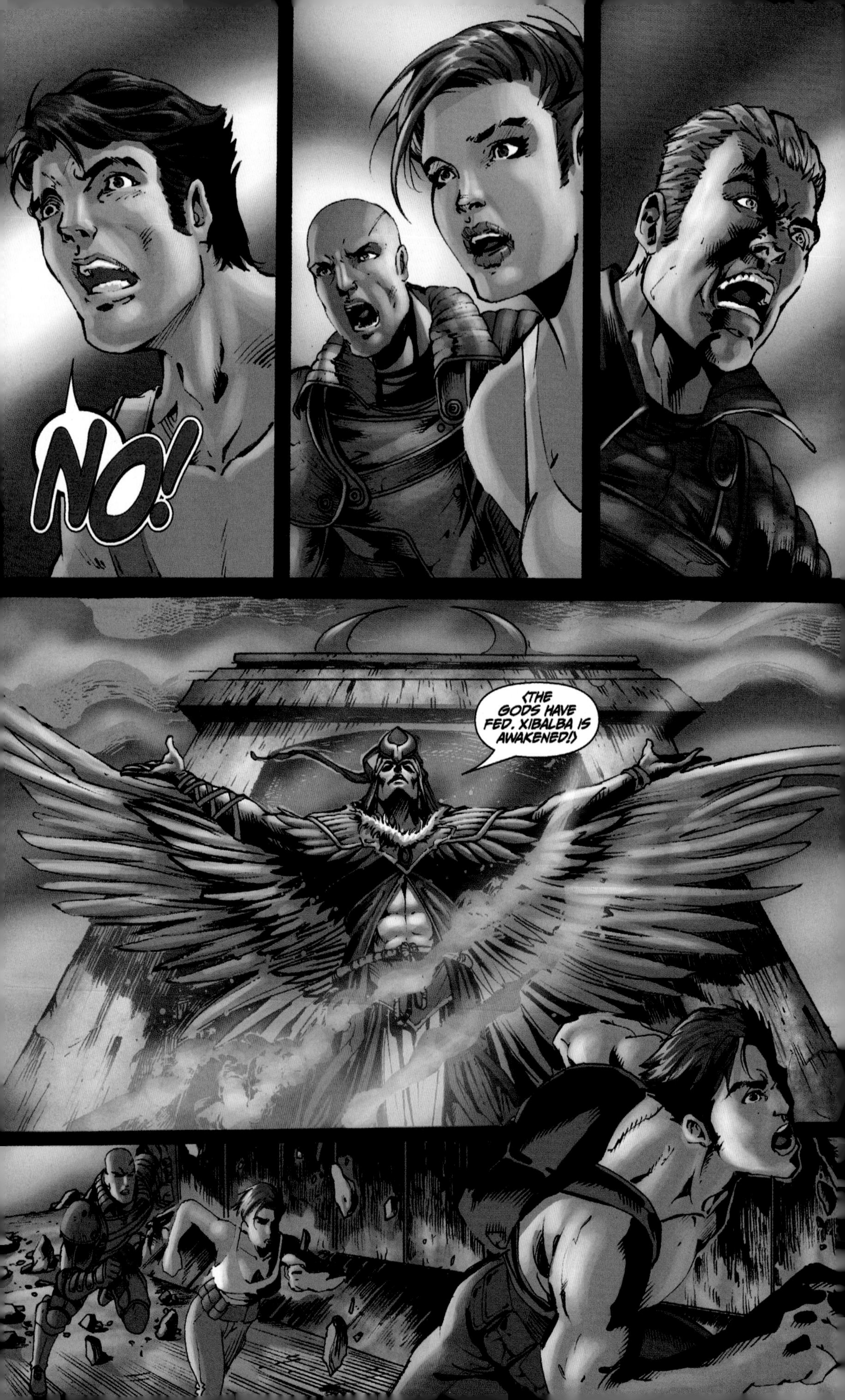
NO!
‹THE GODS HAVE FED. XIBALBA IS AWAKENED!›

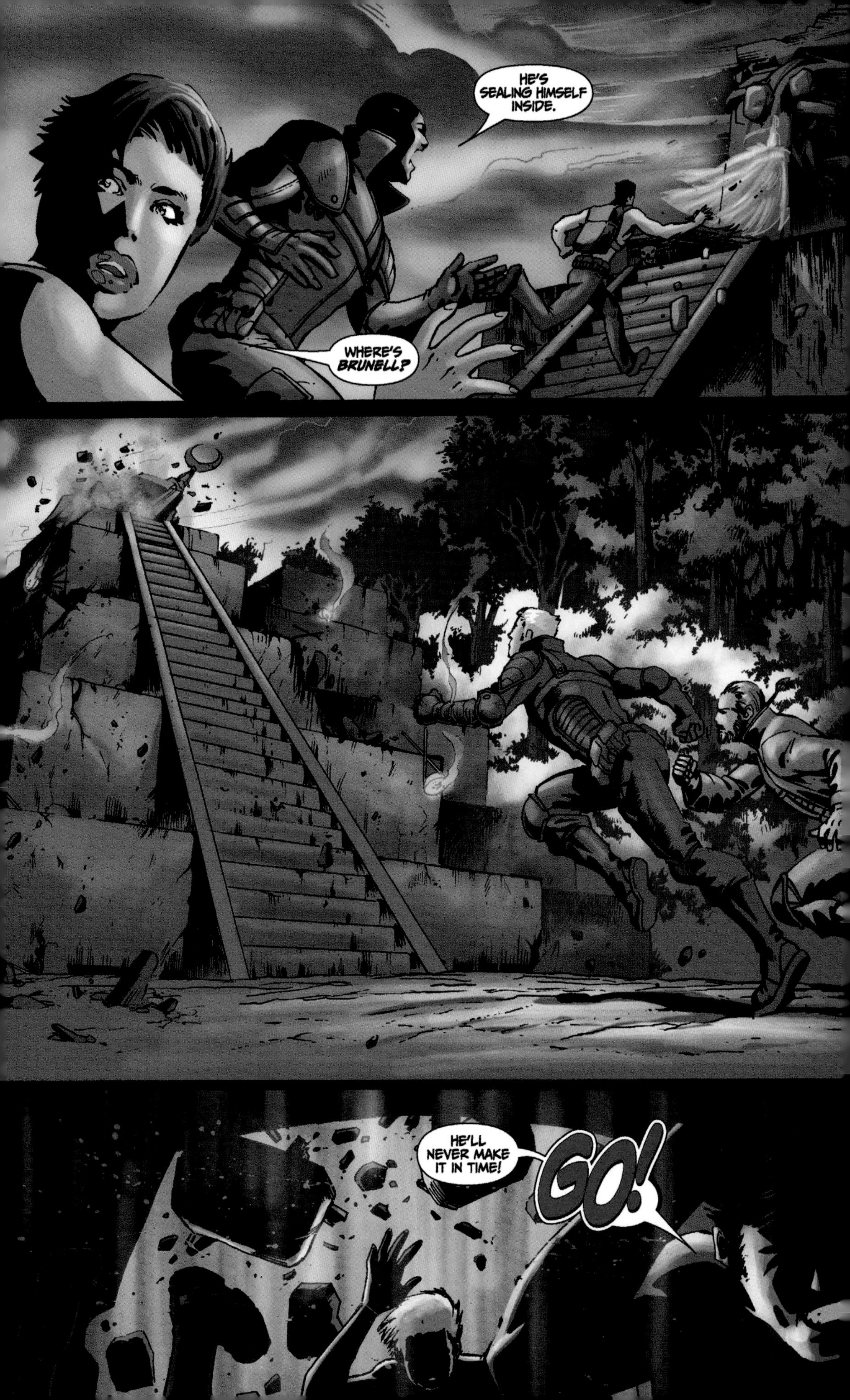
HE'S SEALING HIMSELF INSIDE.
WHERE'S BRUNELL?
HE'LL NEVER MAKE IT IN TIME!
GO!

CHAPTER 3

"There is no nonsense so errant that it cannot be made the creed of the vast majority by adequate governmental action."

-- Bertrand Russell

CONGRATULATIONS. WE UNDERSTAND SOME OF YOU HAVE REPORTED A POSSIBLE NUCLEAR THEFT FROM WHITE SANDS.

ANYONE WHO GOT THEIR STORY OUT BEFORE YESTERDAY GETS A FREE JAMBA JUICE. ON THE PRESIDENT.

EXCUSE ME?

IT WAS A TEST.

BUT, uh, SIR, WE HAVE A CREDIBLE REPORT OF A MINUTEMAN II NUCLEAR MISSILE WHICH HAS BEEN MISSING FOR --

RIGHT, TOM. AND WE'RE VERY IMPRESSED WITH YOUR RESPONSE TIME.

uh, I'M NOT TOM.

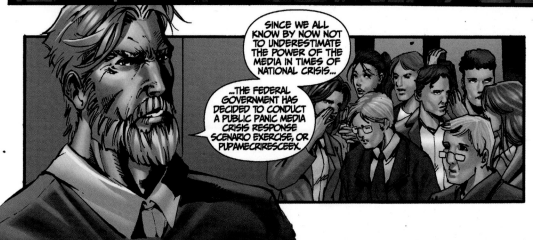

SINCE WE ALL KNOW BY NOW NOT TO UNDERESTIMATE THE POWER OF THE MEDIA IN TIMES OF NATIONAL CRISIS...

...THE FEDERAL GOVERNMENT HAS DECIDED TO CONDUCT A PUBLIC PANIC MEDIA CRISIS RESPONSE SCENARIO EXERCISE, OR PUPAMECRIRESCEEX.

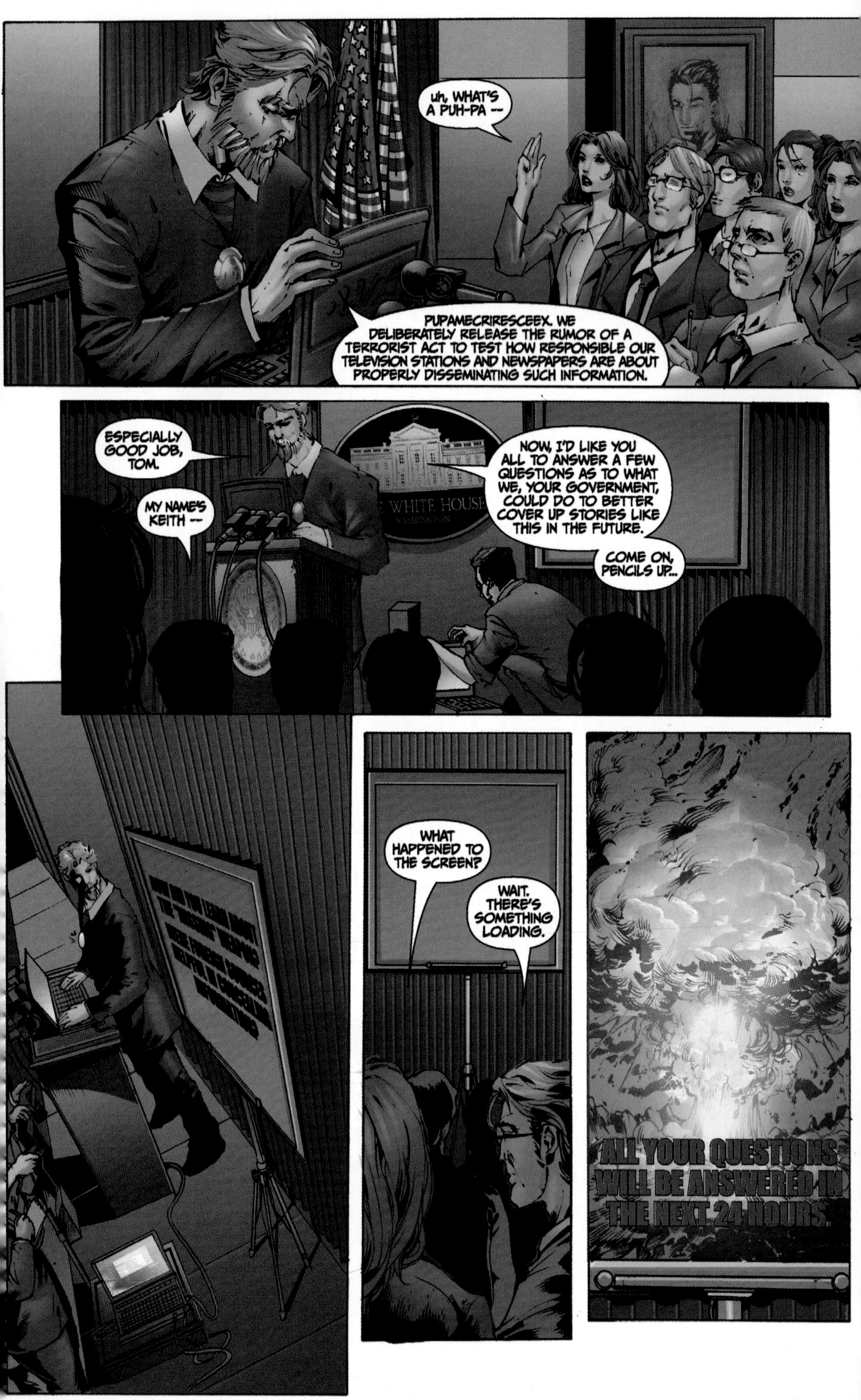
uh, WHAT'S A PUH-PA --
PUPAMECRIRESCEEX. WE DELIBERATELY RELEASE THE RUMOR OF A TERRORIST ACT TO TEST HOW RESPONSIBLE OUR TELEVISION STATIONS AND NEWSPAPERS ARE ABOUT PROPERLY DISSEMINATING SUCH INFORMATION.
ESPECIALLY GOOD JOB, TOM.
MY NAME'S KEITH --
NOW, I'D LIKE YOU ALL TO ANSWER A FEW QUESTIONS AS TO WHAT WE, YOUR GOVERNMENT, COULD DO TO BETTER COVER UP STORIES LIKE THIS IN THE FUTURE.
COME ON, PENCILS UP...
WHAT HAPPENED TO THE SCREEN?
WAIT. THERE'S SOMETHING LOADING.
ALL YOUR QUESTIONS WILL BE ANSWERED IN THE NEXT 24 HOURS.

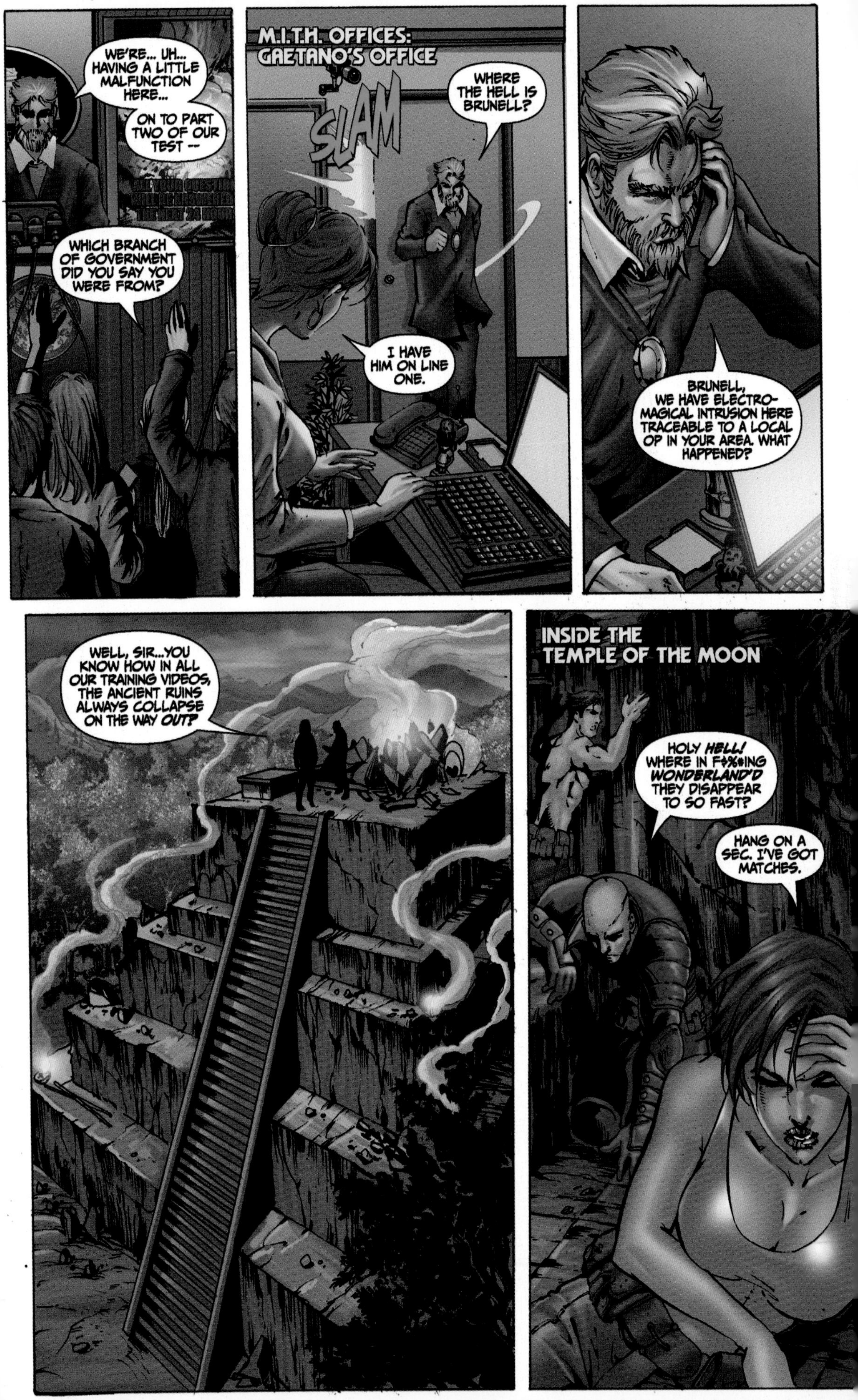
WE'RE... UH... HAVING A LITTLE MALFUNCTION HERE...
ON TO PART TWO OF OUR TEST --
WHICH BRANCH OF GOVERNMENT DID YOU SAY YOU WERE FROM?
M.I.T.H. OFFICES: GAETANO'S OFFICE
SLAM
WHERE THE HELL IS BRUNELL?
I HAVE HIM ON LINE ONE.
BRUNELL, WE HAVE ELECTRO-MAGICAL INTRUSION HERE TRACEABLE TO A LOCAL OP IN YOUR AREA. WHAT HAPPENED?
WELL, SIR...YOU KNOW HOW IN ALL OUR TRAINING VIDEOS, THE ANCIENT RUINS ALWAYS COLLAPSE ON THE WAY *OUT*?
INSIDE THE TEMPLE OF THE MOON
HOLY *HELL!* WHERE IN F‡%#ING *WONDERLAND'D* THEY DISAPPEAR TO SO FAST?
HANG ON A SEC. I'VE GOT MATCHES.

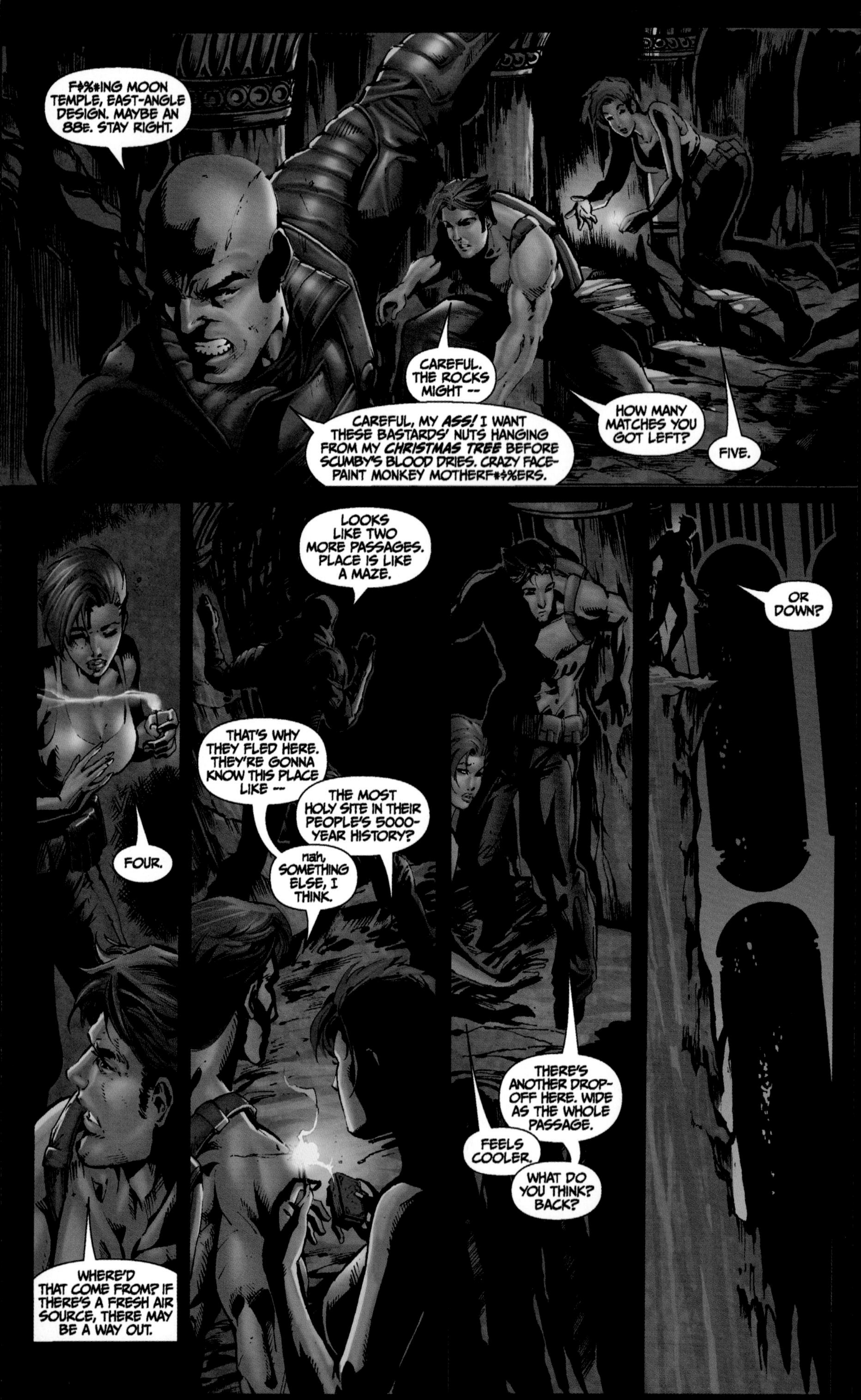
F#%#ING MOON TEMPLE, EAST-ANGLE DESIGN. MAYBE AN 88E. STAY RIGHT.
CAREFUL. THE ROCKS MIGHT --
CAREFUL, MY ASS! I WANT THESE BASTARDS' NUTS HANGING FROM MY CHRISTMAS TREE BEFORE SCUMBY'S BLOOD DRIES. CRAZY FACE-PAINT MONKEY MOTHERF#$%ERS.
HOW MANY MATCHES YOU GOT LEFT?
FIVE.
FOUR.
WHERE'D THAT COME FROM? IF THERE'S A FRESH AIR SOURCE, THERE MAY BE A WAY OUT.
LOOKS LIKE TWO MORE PASSAGES. PLACE IS LIKE A MAZE.
THAT'S WHY THEY FLED HERE. THEY'RE GONNA KNOW THIS PLACE LIKE --
THE MOST HOLY SITE IN THEIR PEOPLE'S 5000-YEAR HISTORY?
nah, SOMETHING ELSE, I THINK.
THERE'S ANOTHER DROP-OFF HERE. WIDE AS THE WHOLE PASSAGE.
FEELS COOLER.
WHAT DO YOU THINK? BACK?
OR DOWN?

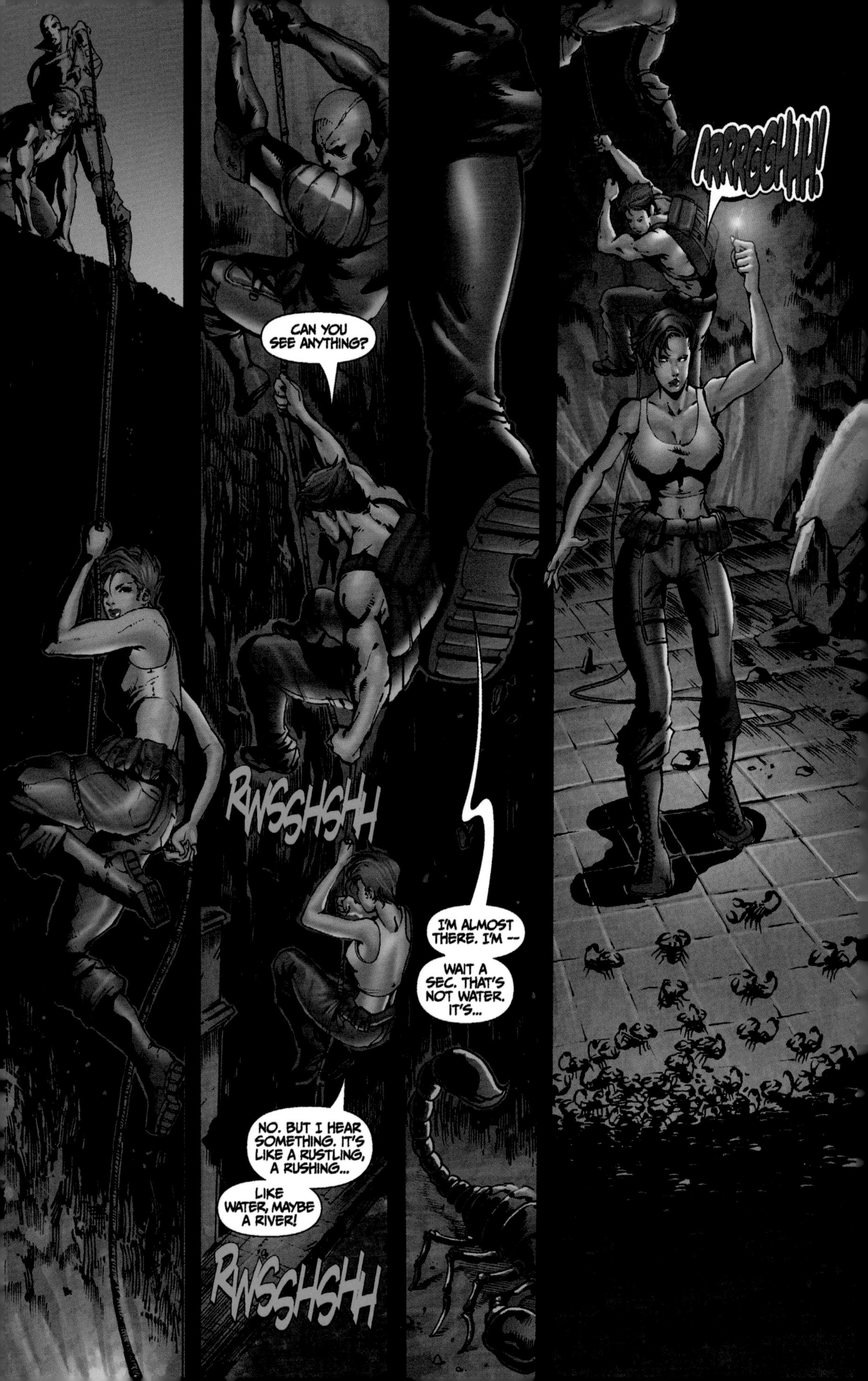
CAN YOU SEE ANYTHING?
RWSSHSHH
NO. BUT I HEAR SOMETHING. IT'S LIKE A RUSTLING, A RUSHING...
LIKE WATER, MAYBE A RIVER!
RWSSHSHH
I'M ALMOST THERE. I'M --
WAIT A SEC. THAT'S NOT WATER. IT'S...
ARRRGGHHH!

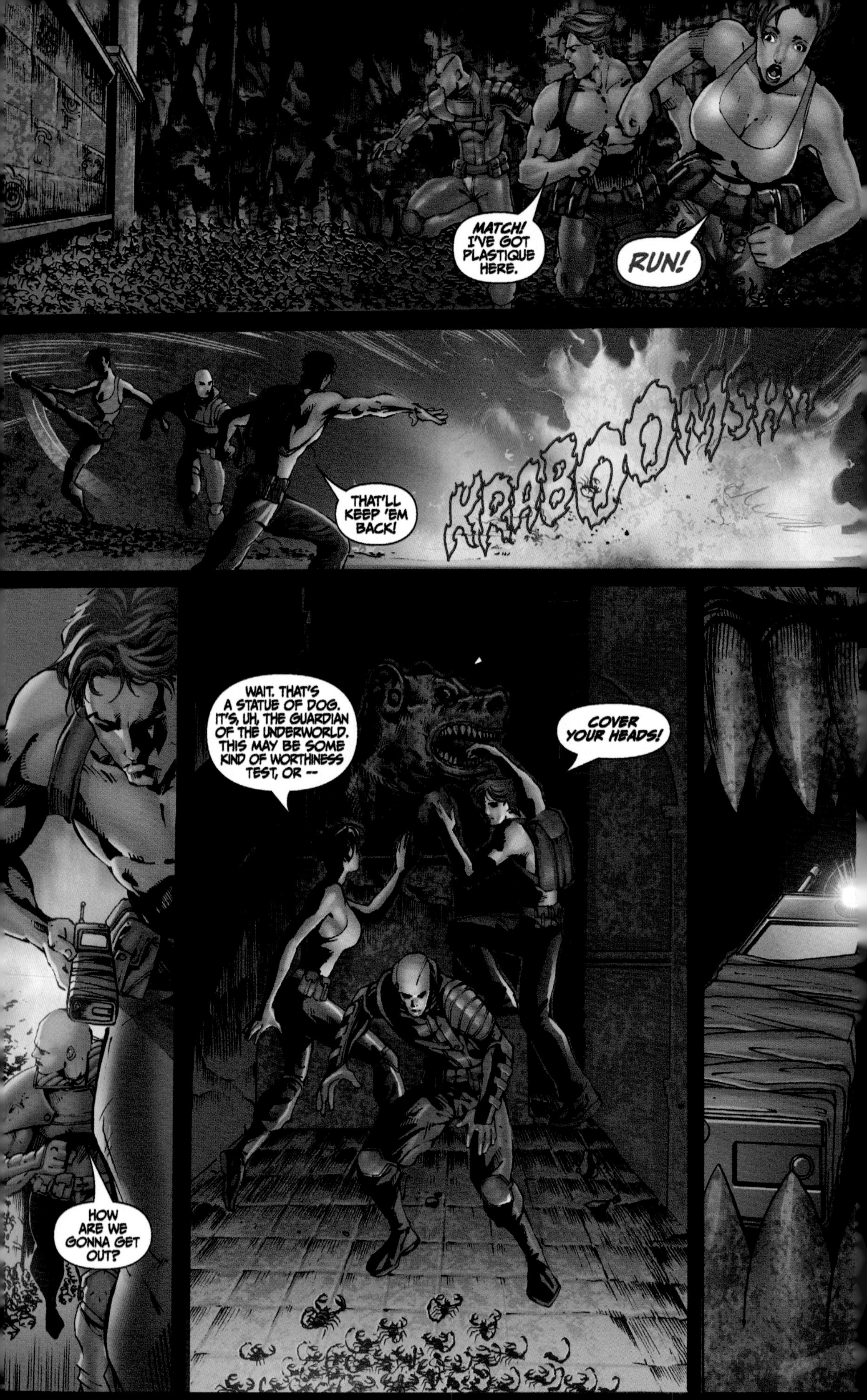
MATCH! I'VE GOT PLASTIQUE HERE.
RUN!
THAT'LL KEEP 'EM BACK!
KRABOOMSHH
HOW ARE WE GONNA GET OUT?
WAIT. THAT'S A STATUE OF DOG. IT'S, UH, THE GUARDIAN OF THE UNDERWORLD. THIS MAY BE SOME KIND OF WORTHINESS TEST, OR --
COVER YOUR HEADS!

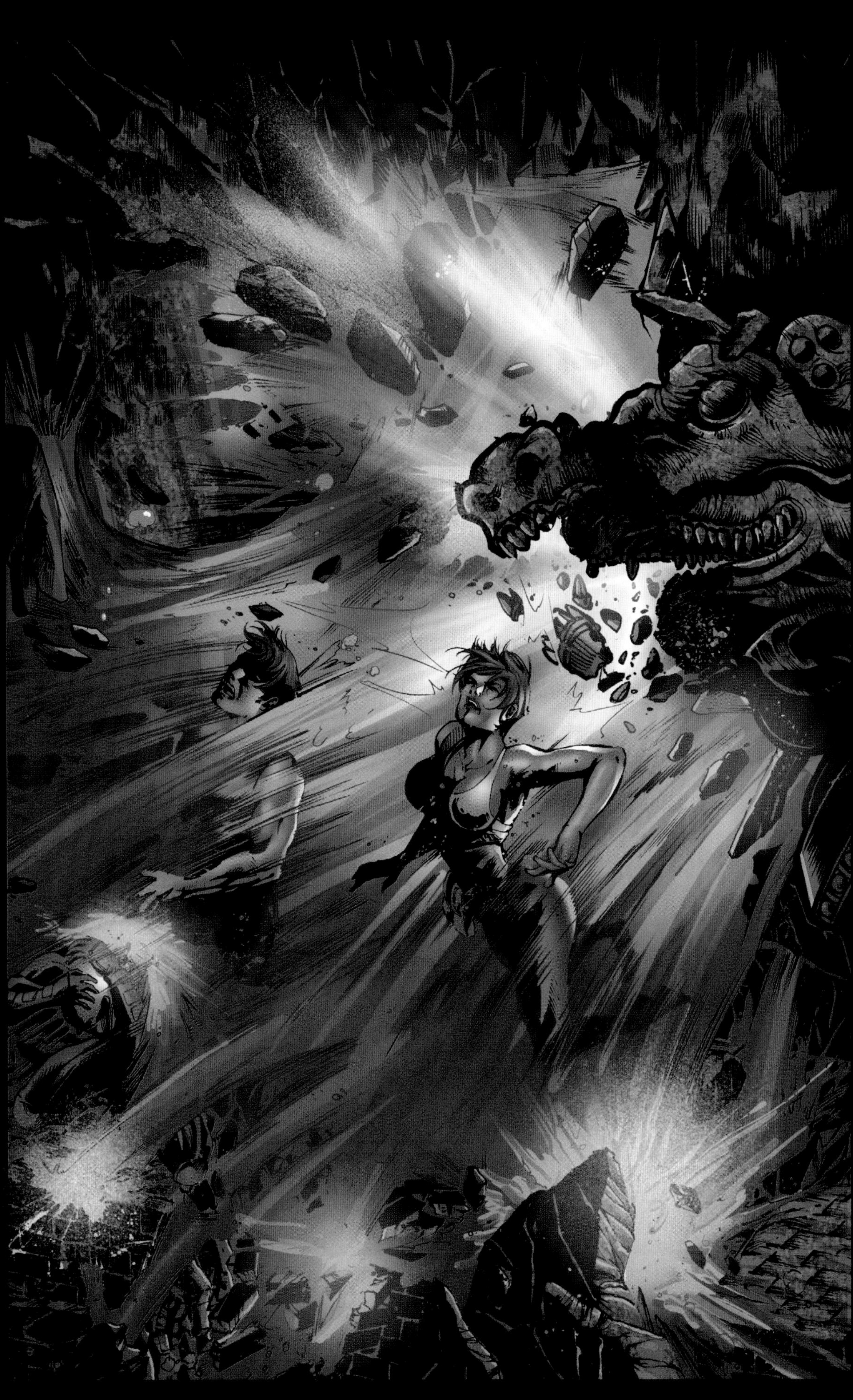

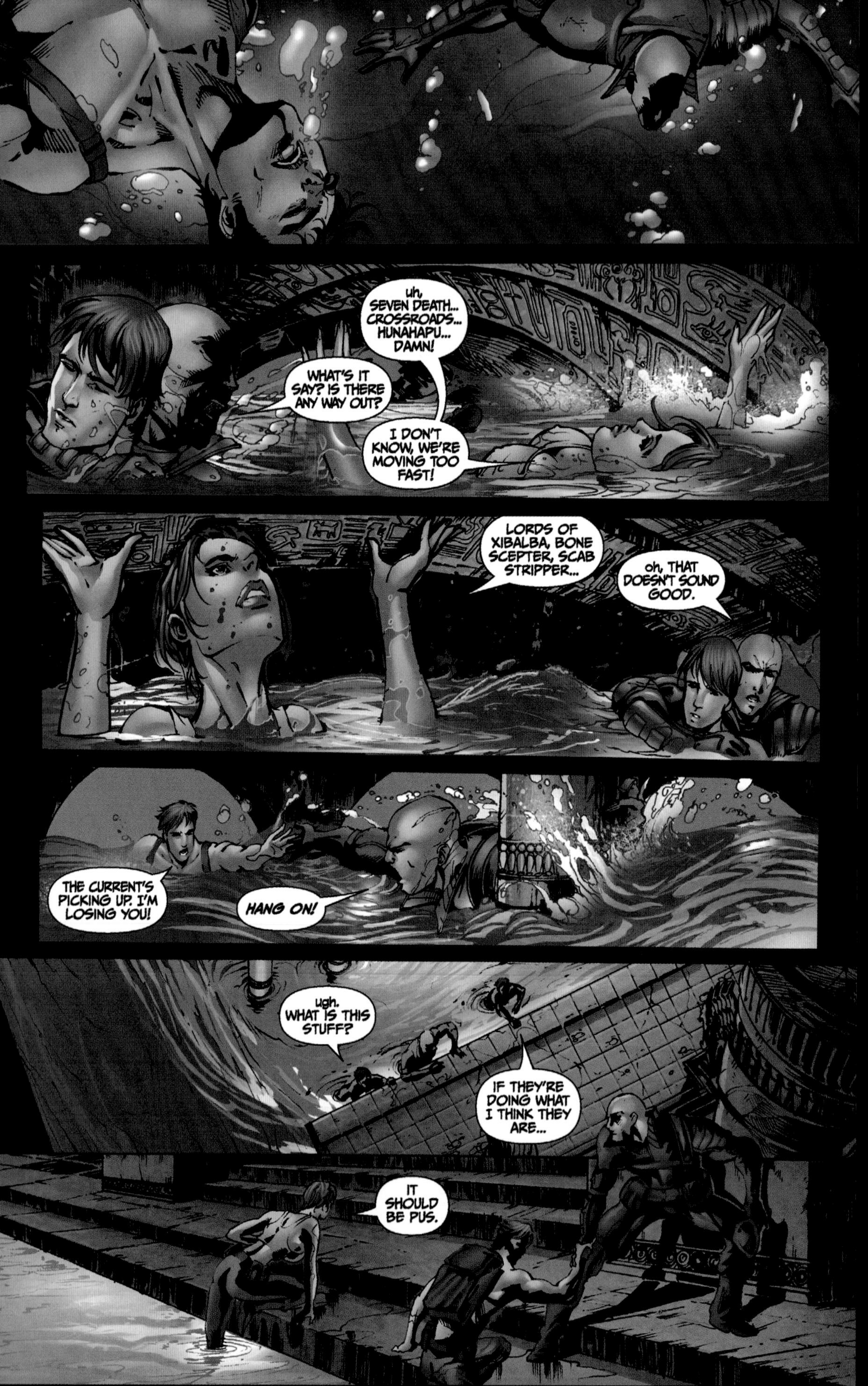
uh, SEVEN DEATH... CROSSROADS... HUNAHAPU... DAMN!
WHAT'S IT SAY? IS THERE ANY WAY OUT?
I DON'T KNOW, WE'RE MOVING TOO FAST!
LORDS OF XIBALBA, BONE SCEPTER, SCAB STRIPPER...
oh, THAT DOESN'T SOUND GOOD.
THE CURRENT'S PICKING UP. I'M LOSING YOU!
HANG ON!
ugh. WHAT IS THIS STUFF?
IF THEY'RE DOING WHAT I THINK THEY ARE...
IT SHOULD BE PUS.

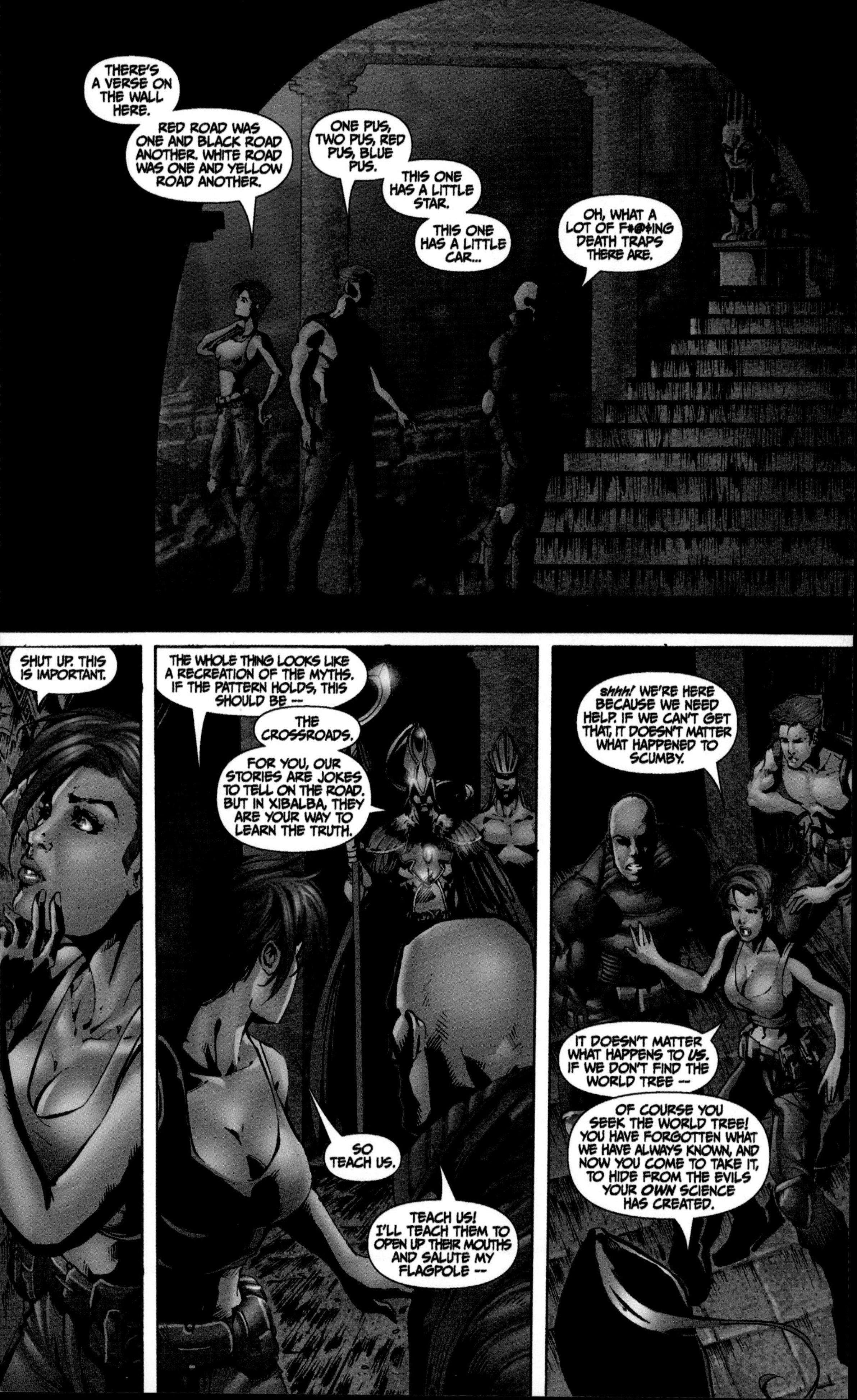

THERE'S A VERSE ON THE WALL HERE.
RED ROAD WAS ONE AND BLACK ROAD ANOTHER. WHITE ROAD WAS ONE AND YELLOW ROAD ANOTHER.
ONE PUS, TWO PUS, RED PUS, BLUE PUS.
THIS ONE HAS A LITTLE STAR.
THIS ONE HAS A LITTLE CAR...
OH, WHAT A LOT OF F#@$ING DEATH TRAPS THERE ARE.
SHUT UP. THIS IS IMPORTANT.
THE WHOLE THING LOOKS LIKE A RECREATION OF THE MYTHS. IF THE PATTERN HOLDS, THIS SHOULD BE --
THE CROSSROADS.
FOR YOU, OUR STORIES ARE JOKES TO TELL ON THE ROAD. BUT IN XIBALBA, THEY ARE YOUR WAY TO LEARN THE TRUTH.
SO TEACH US.
TEACH US! I'LL TEACH THEM TO OPEN UP THEIR MOUTHS AND SALUTE MY FLAGPOLE --
shhh! WE'RE HERE BECAUSE WE NEED HELP. IF WE CAN'T GET THAT, IT DOESN'T MATTER WHAT HAPPENED TO SCUMBY.
IT DOESN'T MATTER WHAT HAPPENS TO US. IF WE DON'T FIND THE WORLD TREE --
OF COURSE YOU SEEK THE WORLD TREE! YOU HAVE FORGOTTEN WHAT WE HAVE ALWAYS KNOWN, AND NOW YOU COME TO TAKE IT, TO HIDE FROM THE EVILS YOUR OWN SCIENCE HAS CREATED.

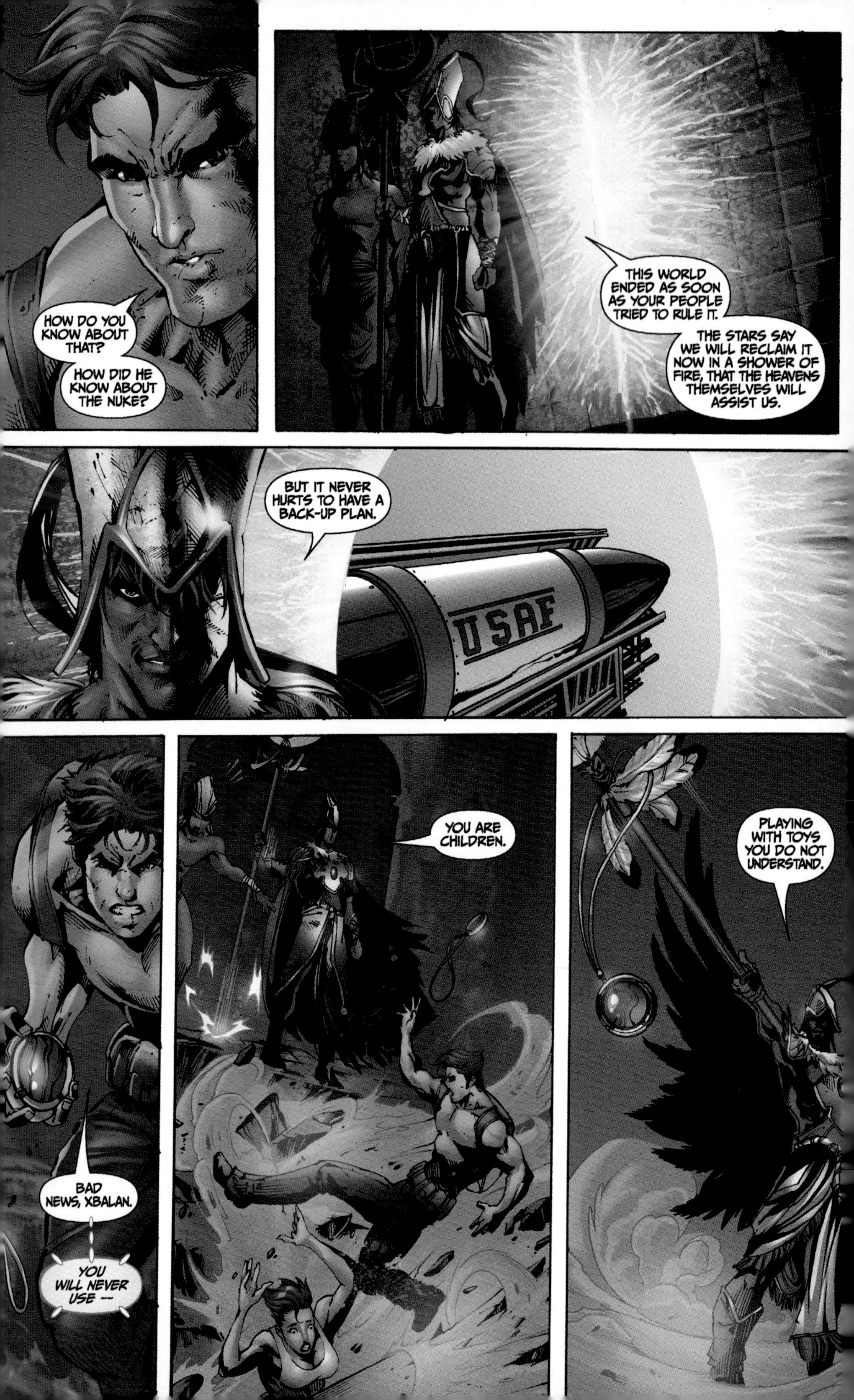
HOW DO YOU KNOW ABOUT THAT?
HOW DID HE KNOW ABOUT THE NUKE?
THIS WORLD ENDED AS SOON AS YOUR PEOPLE TRIED TO RULE IT.
THE STARS SAY WE WILL RECLAIM IT NOW IN A SHOWER OF FIRE, THAT THE HEAVENS THEMSELVES WILL ASSIST US.
BUT IT NEVER HURTS TO HAVE A BACK-UP PLAN.
USAF
BAD NEWS, XBALAN.
YOU WILL NEVER USE --
YOU ARE CHILDREN.
PLAYING WITH TOYS YOU DO NOT UNDERSTAND.

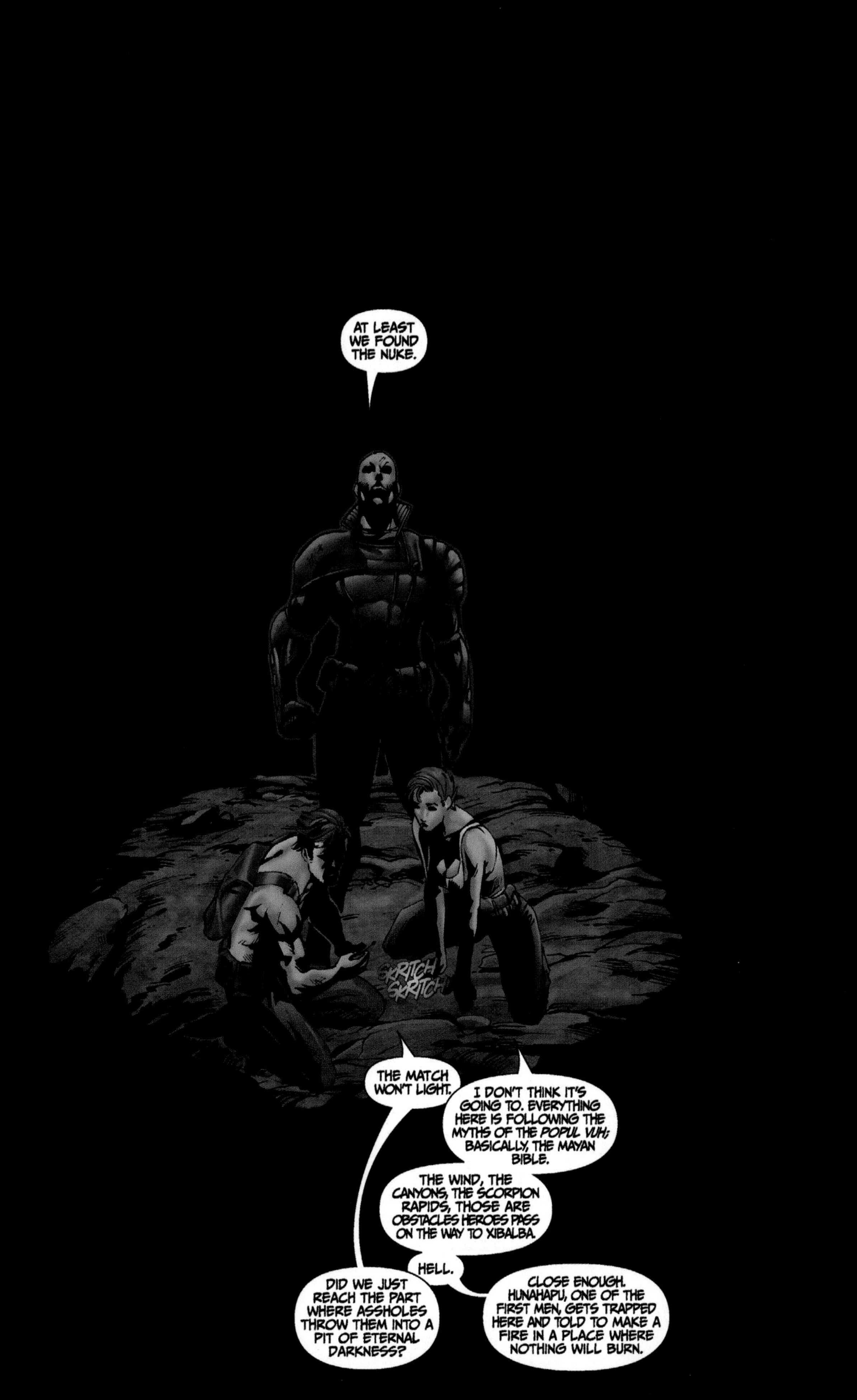
AT LEAST WE FOUND THE NUKE.
SKRITCH SKRITCH
THE MATCH WON'T LIGHT.
I DON'T THINK IT'S GOING TO. EVERYTHING HERE IS FOLLOWING THE MYTHS OF THE *POPUL VUH*; BASICALLY, THE MAYAN BIBLE.
THE WIND, THE CANYONS, THE SCORPION RAPIDS, THOSE ARE OBSTACLES HEROES PASS ON THE WAY TO XIBALBA.
HELL.
CLOSE ENOUGH. HUNAHAPU, ONE OF THE FIRST MEN, GETS TRAPPED HERE AND TOLD TO MAKE A FIRE IN A PLACE WHERE NOTHING WILL BURN.
DID WE JUST REACH THE PART WHERE ASSHOLES THROW THEM INTO A PIT OF ETERNAL DARKNESS?

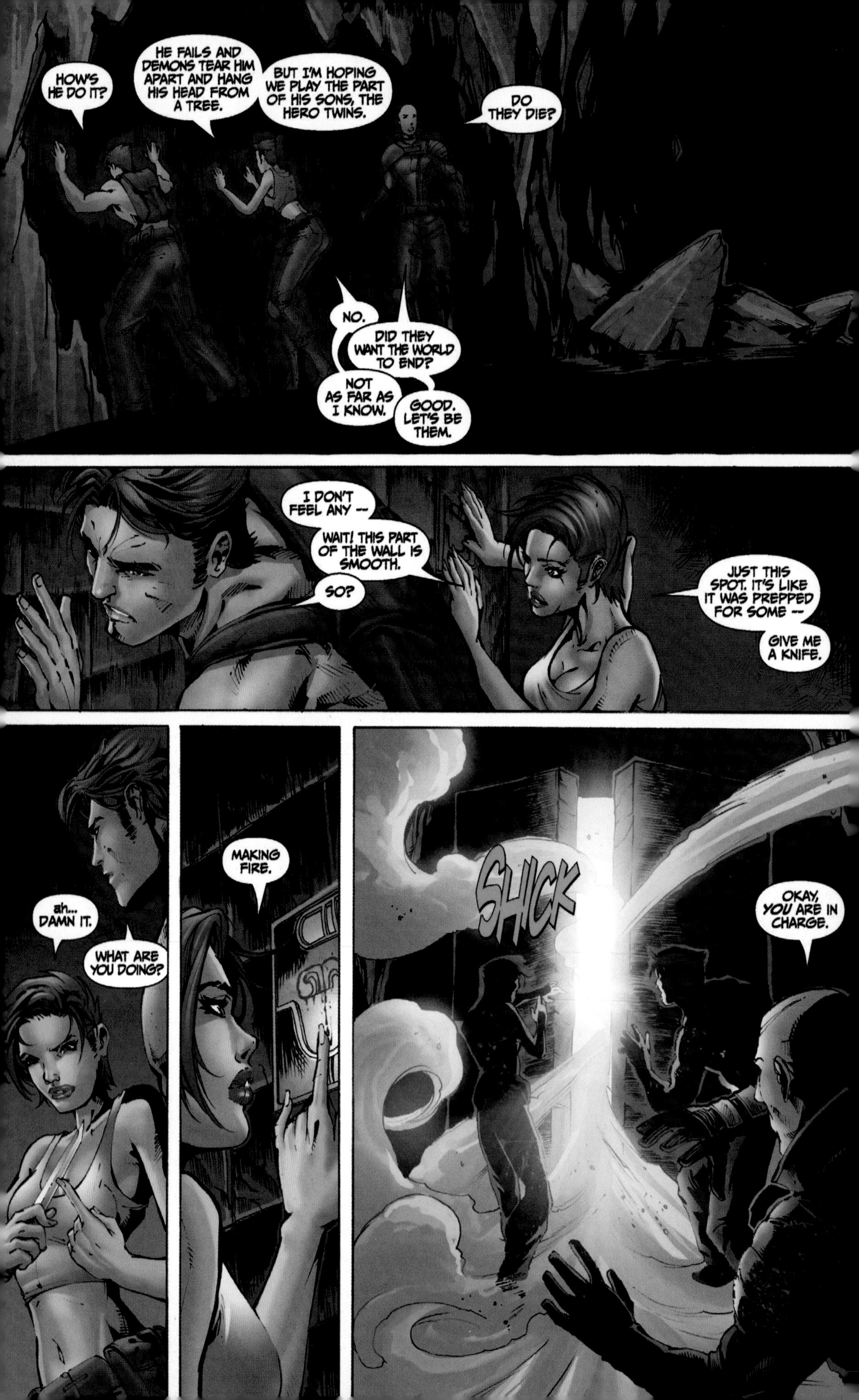
HOW'S HE DO IT?
HE FAILS AND DEMONS TEAR HIM APART AND HANG HIS HEAD FROM A TREE.
BUT I'M HOPING WE PLAY THE PART OF HIS SONS, THE HERO TWINS.
DO THEY DIE?
NO.
DID THEY WANT THE WORLD TO END?
NOT AS FAR AS I KNOW.
GOOD. LET'S BE THEM.
I DON'T FEEL ANY --
WAIT! THIS PART OF THE WALL IS SMOOTH.
SO?
JUST THIS SPOT. IT'S LIKE IT WAS PREPPED FOR SOME --
GIVE ME A KNIFE.
ah... DAMN IT.
WHAT ARE YOU DOING?
MAKING FIRE.
SHICK
OKAY, YOU ARE IN CHARGE.

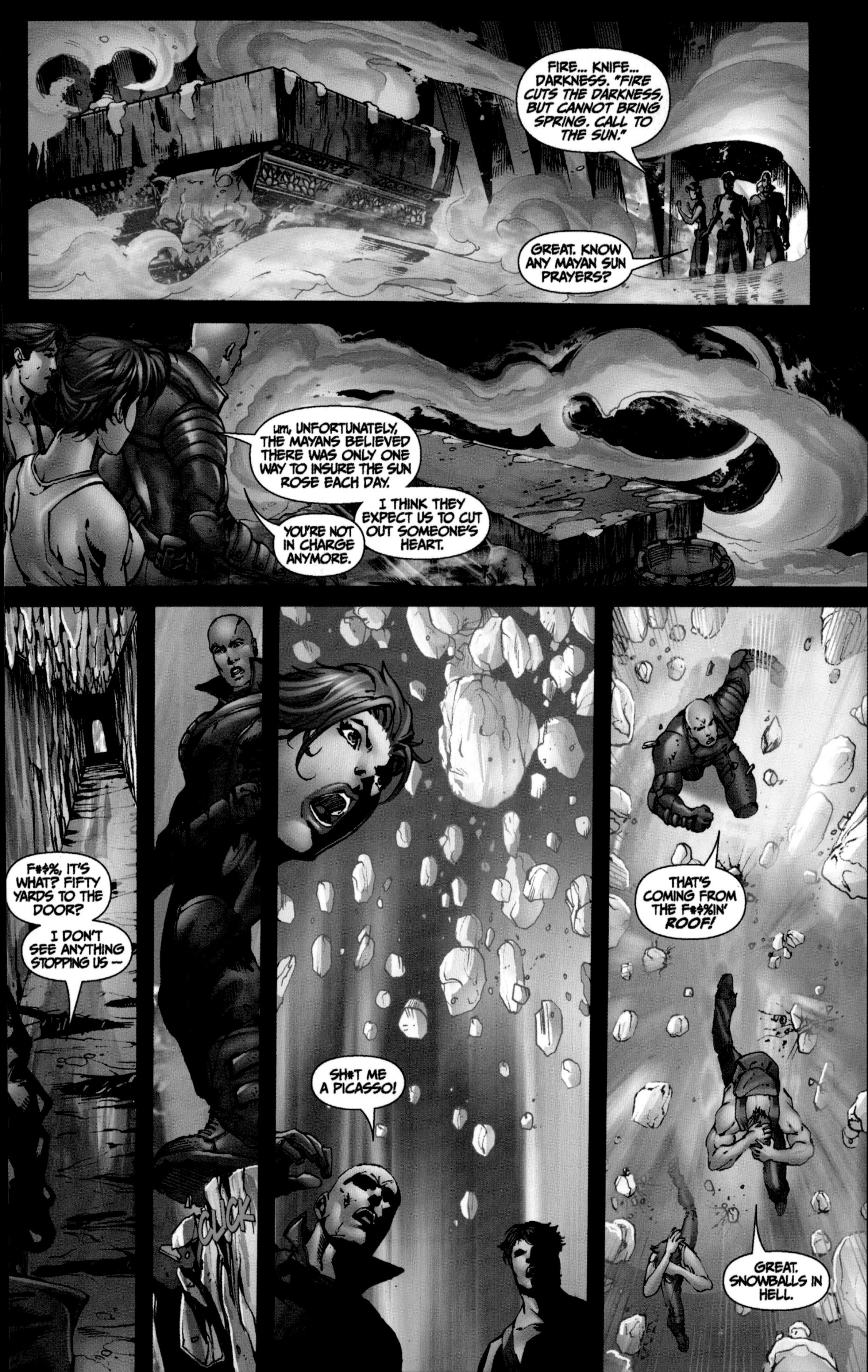
FIRE... KNIFE... DARKNESS. "FIRE CUTS THE DARKNESS, BUT CANNOT BRING SPRING. CALL TO THE SUN."
GREAT. KNOW ANY MAYAN SUN PRAYERS?
um, UNFORTUNATELY, THE MAYANS BELIEVED THERE WAS ONLY ONE WAY TO INSURE THE SUN ROSE EACH DAY.
I THINK THEY EXPECT US TO CUT OUT SOMEONE'S HEART.
YOU'RE NOT IN CHARGE ANYMORE.
F#$%, IT'S WHAT? FIFTY YARDS TO THE DOOR?
I DON'T SEE ANYTHING STOPPING US --
CLICK
SH#T ME A PICASSO!
THAT'S COMING FROM THE F#$%IN' ROOF!
GREAT. SNOWBALLS IN HELL.

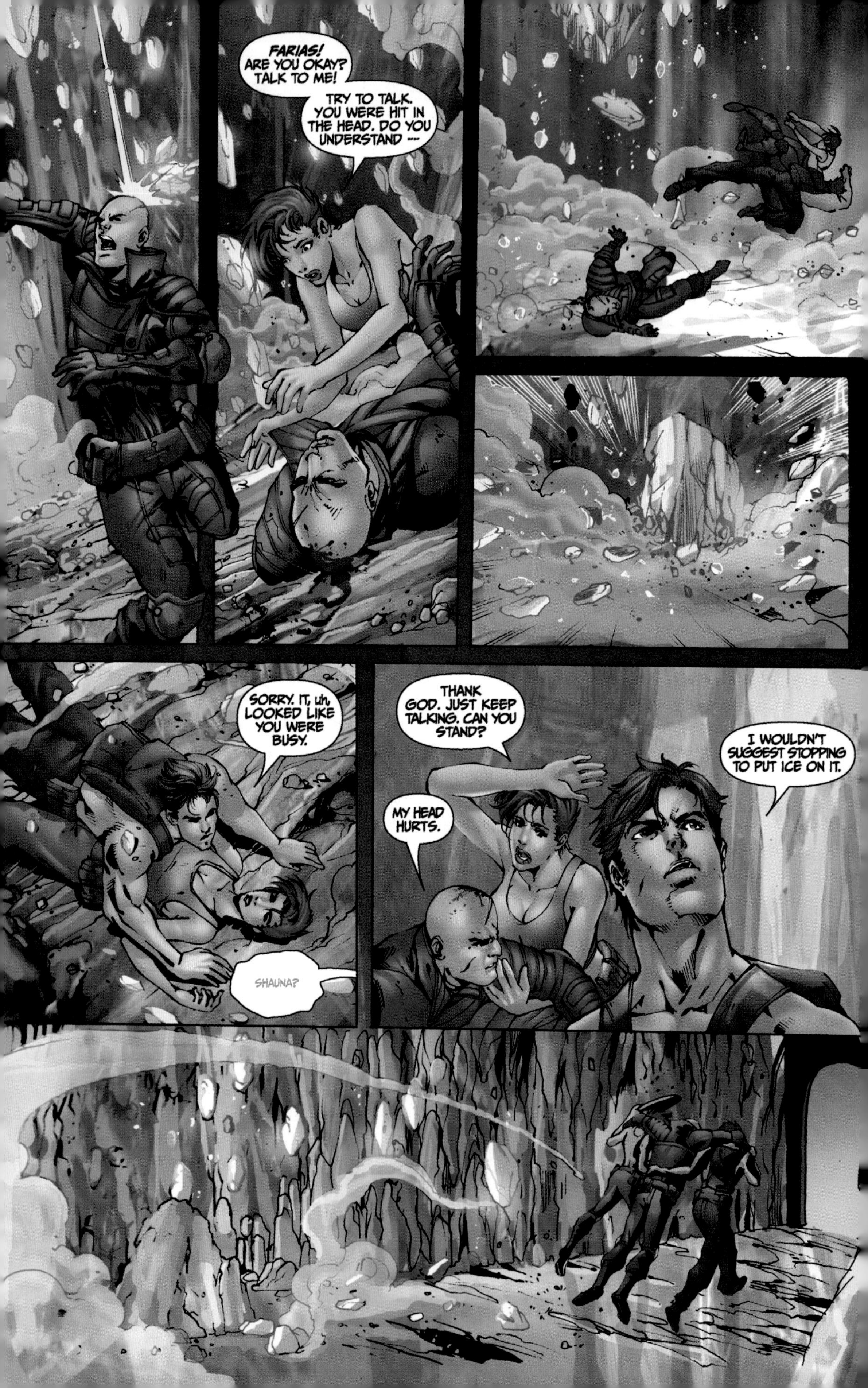
FARIAS! ARE YOU OKAY? TALK TO ME!
TRY TO TALK. YOU WERE HIT IN THE HEAD. DO YOU UNDERSTAND ---
SORRY. IT, uh, LOOKED LIKE YOU WERE BUSY.
SHAUNA?
THANK GOD. JUST KEEP TALKING. CAN YOU STAND?
MY HEAD HURTS.
I WOULDN'T SUGGEST STOPPING TO PUT ICE ON IT.

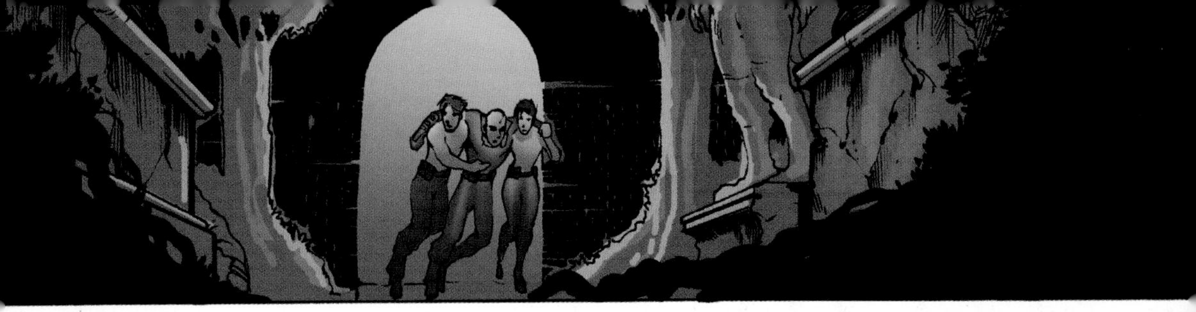

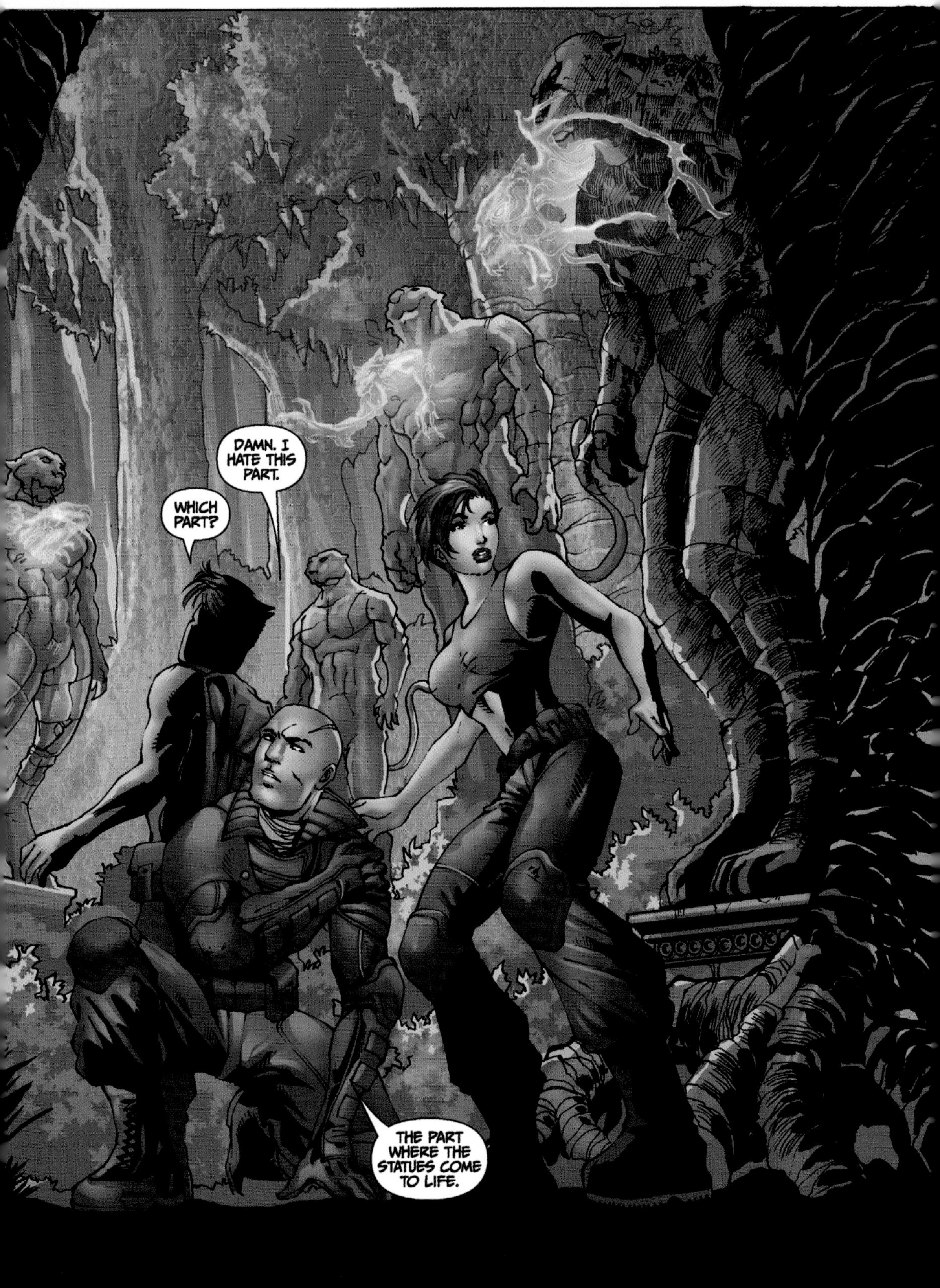
WHICH PART?
DAMN. I HATE THIS PART.
THE PART WHERE THE STATUES COME TO LIFE.

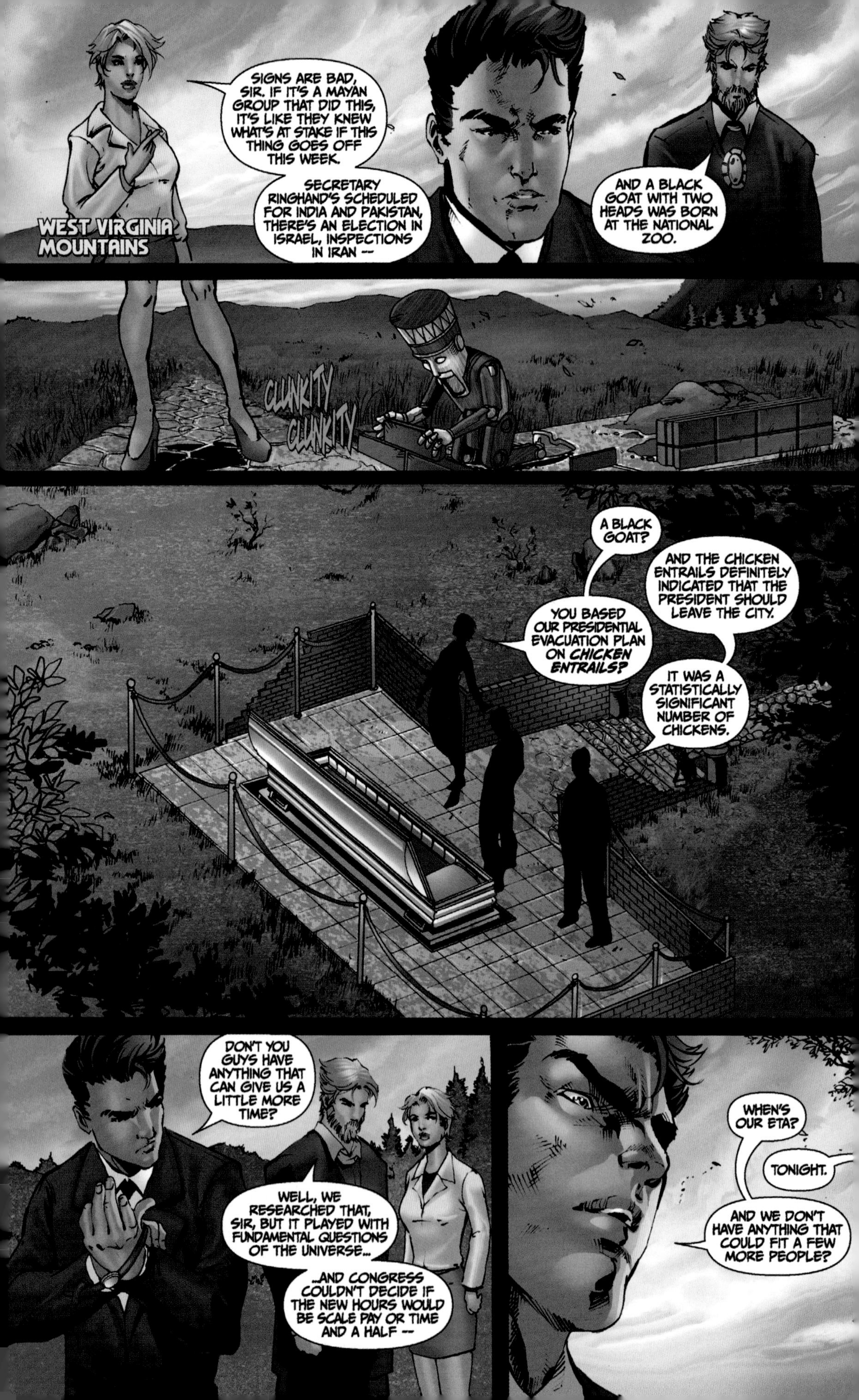
WEST VIRGINIA MOUNTAINS
SIGNS ARE BAD, SIR. IF IT'S A MAYAN GROUP THAT DID THIS, IT'S LIKE THEY KNEW WHAT'S AT STAKE IF THIS THING GOES OFF THIS WEEK.
SECRETARY RINGHAND'S SCHEDULED FOR INDIA AND PAKISTAN, THERE'S AN ELECTION IN ISRAEL, INSPECTIONS IN IRAN --
AND A BLACK GOAT WITH TWO HEADS WAS BORN AT THE NATIONAL ZOO.
CLUNKITY CLUNKITY
A BLACK GOAT?
YOU BASED OUR PRESIDENTIAL EVACUATION PLAN ON CHICKEN ENTRAILS?
AND THE CHICKEN ENTRAILS DEFINITELY INDICATED THAT THE PRESIDENT SHOULD LEAVE THE CITY.
IT WAS A STATISTICALLY SIGNIFICANT NUMBER OF CHICKENS.
DON'T YOU GUYS HAVE ANYTHING THAT CAN GIVE US A LITTLE MORE TIME?
WELL, WE RESEARCHED THAT, SIR, BUT IT PLAYED WITH FUNDAMENTAL QUESTIONS OF THE UNIVERSE...
...AND CONGRESS COULDN'T DECIDE IF THE NEW HOURS WOULD BE SCALE PAY OR TIME AND A HALF --
WHEN'S OUR ETA?
TONIGHT.
AND WE DON'T HAVE ANYTHING THAT COULD FIT A FEW MORE PEOPLE?

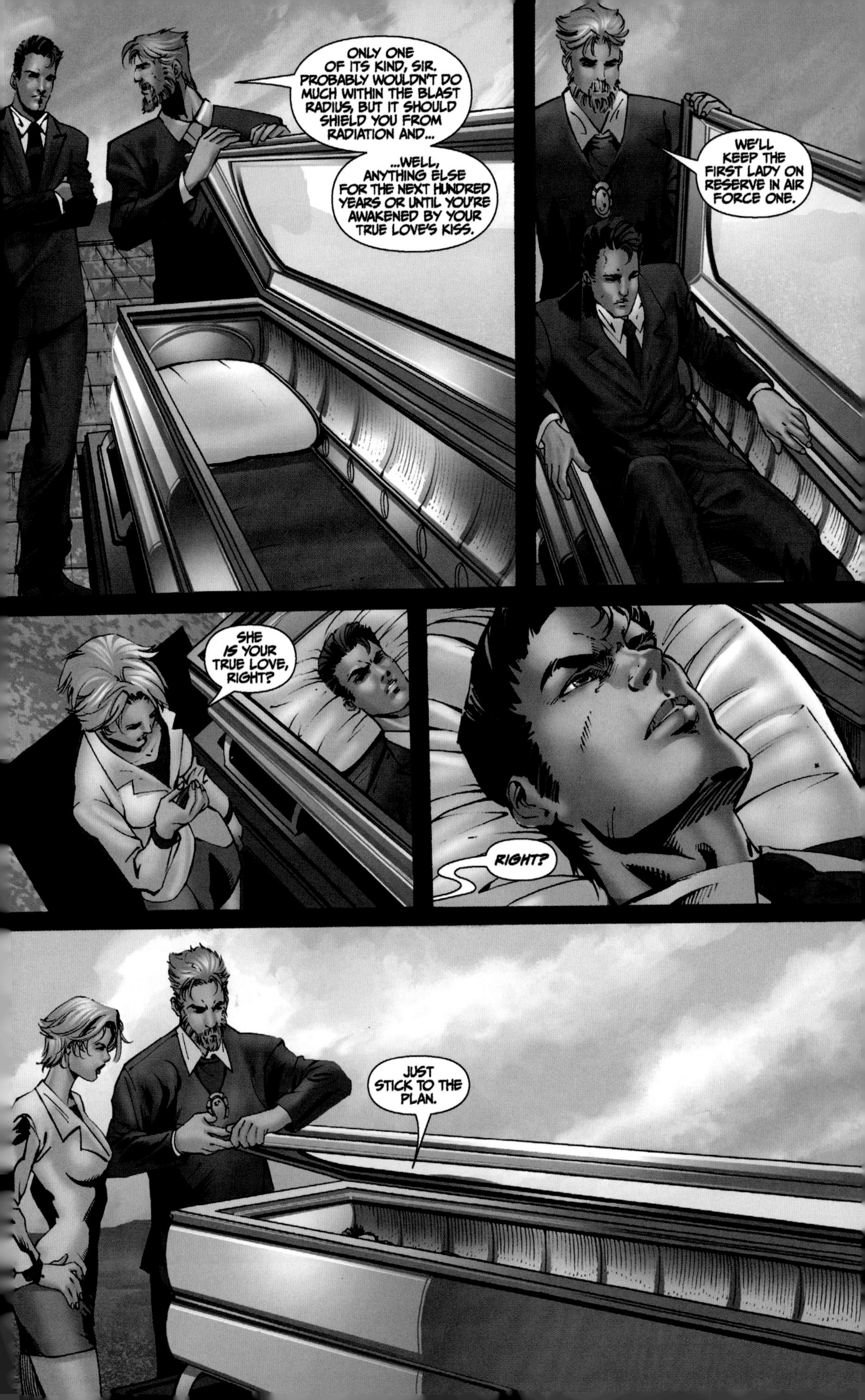
ONLY ONE OF ITS KIND, SIR. PROBABLY WOULDN'T DO MUCH WITHIN THE BLAST RADIUS, BUT IT SHOULD SHIELD YOU FROM RADIATION AND...
...WELL, ANYTHING ELSE FOR THE NEXT HUNDRED YEARS OR UNTIL YOU'RE AWAKENED BY YOUR TRUE LOVE'S KISS.
WE'LL KEEP THE FIRST LADY ON RESERVE IN AIR FORCE ONE.
SHE *IS* YOUR TRUE LOVE, RIGHT?
RIGHT?
JUST STICK TO THE PLAN.

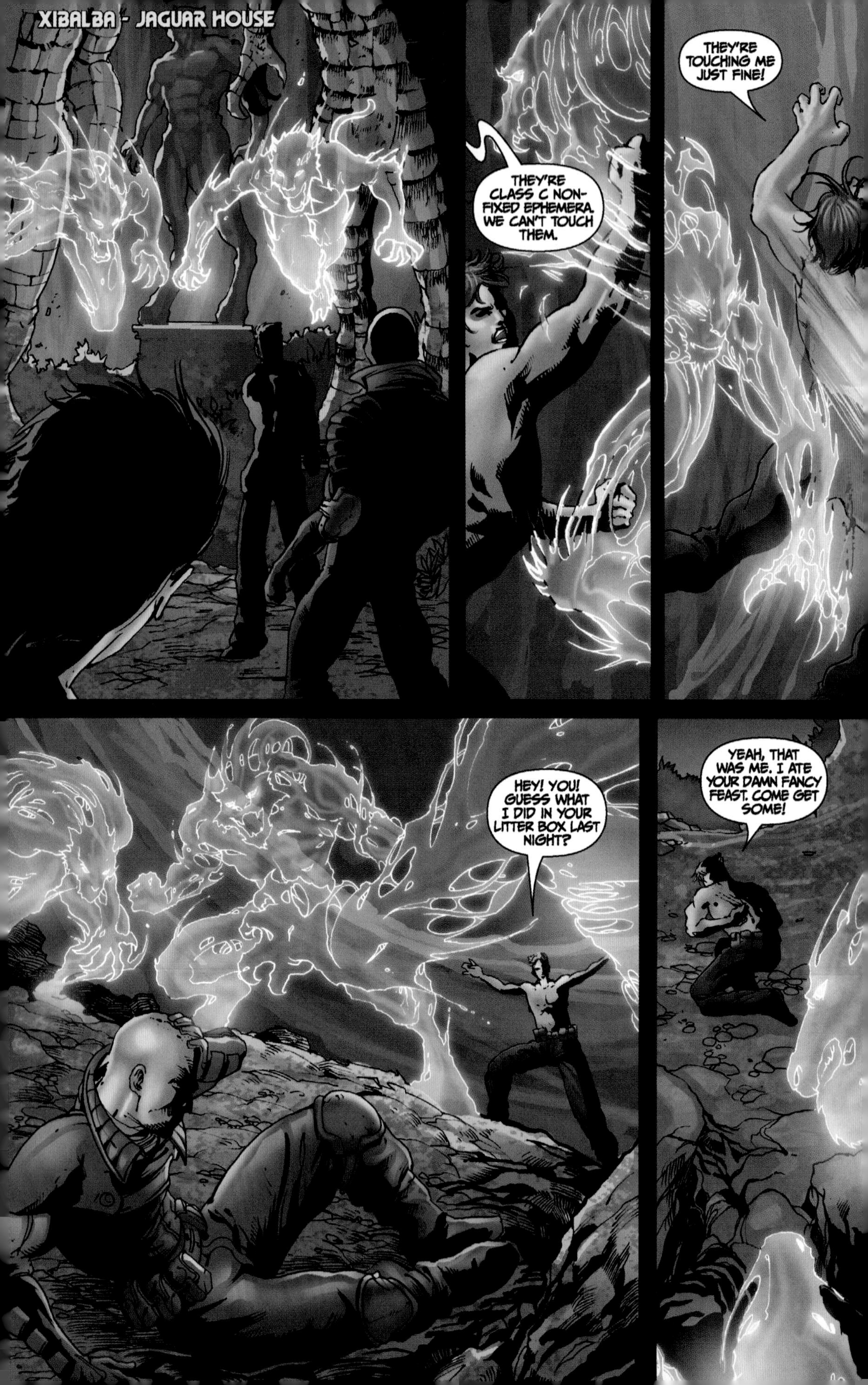
XIBALBA - JAGUAR HOUSE
THEY'RE CLASS C NON-FIXED EPHEMERA. WE CAN'T TOUCH THEM.
THEY'RE TOUCHING ME JUST FINE!
HEY! YOU! GUESS WHAT I DID IN YOUR LITTER BOX LAST NIGHT?
YEAH, THAT WAS ME. I ATE YOUR DAMN FANCY FEAST. COME GET SOME!

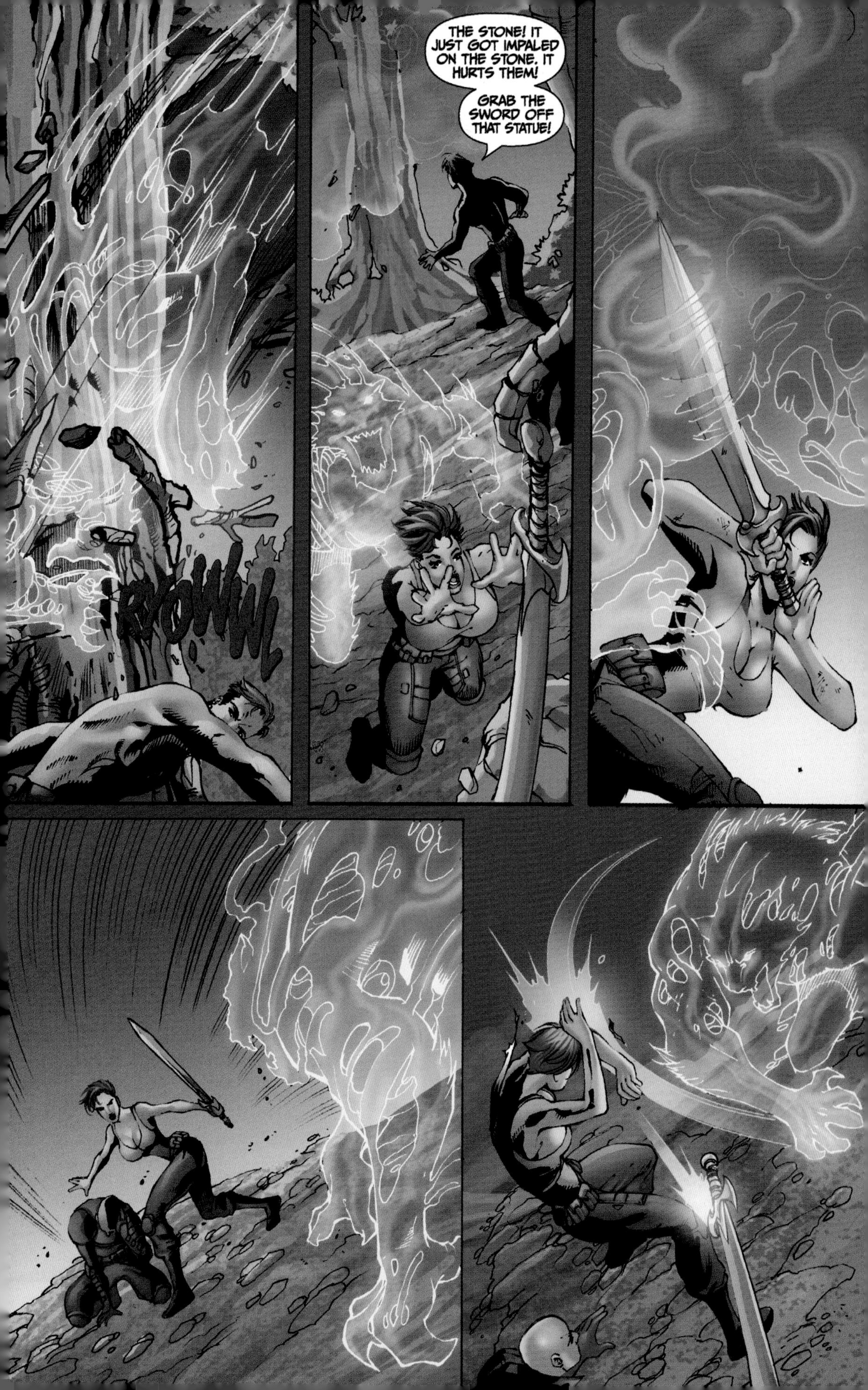
RYOWWL
THE STONE! IT JUST GOT IMPALED ON THE STONE. IT HURTS THEM!
GRAB THE SWORD OFF THAT STATUE!

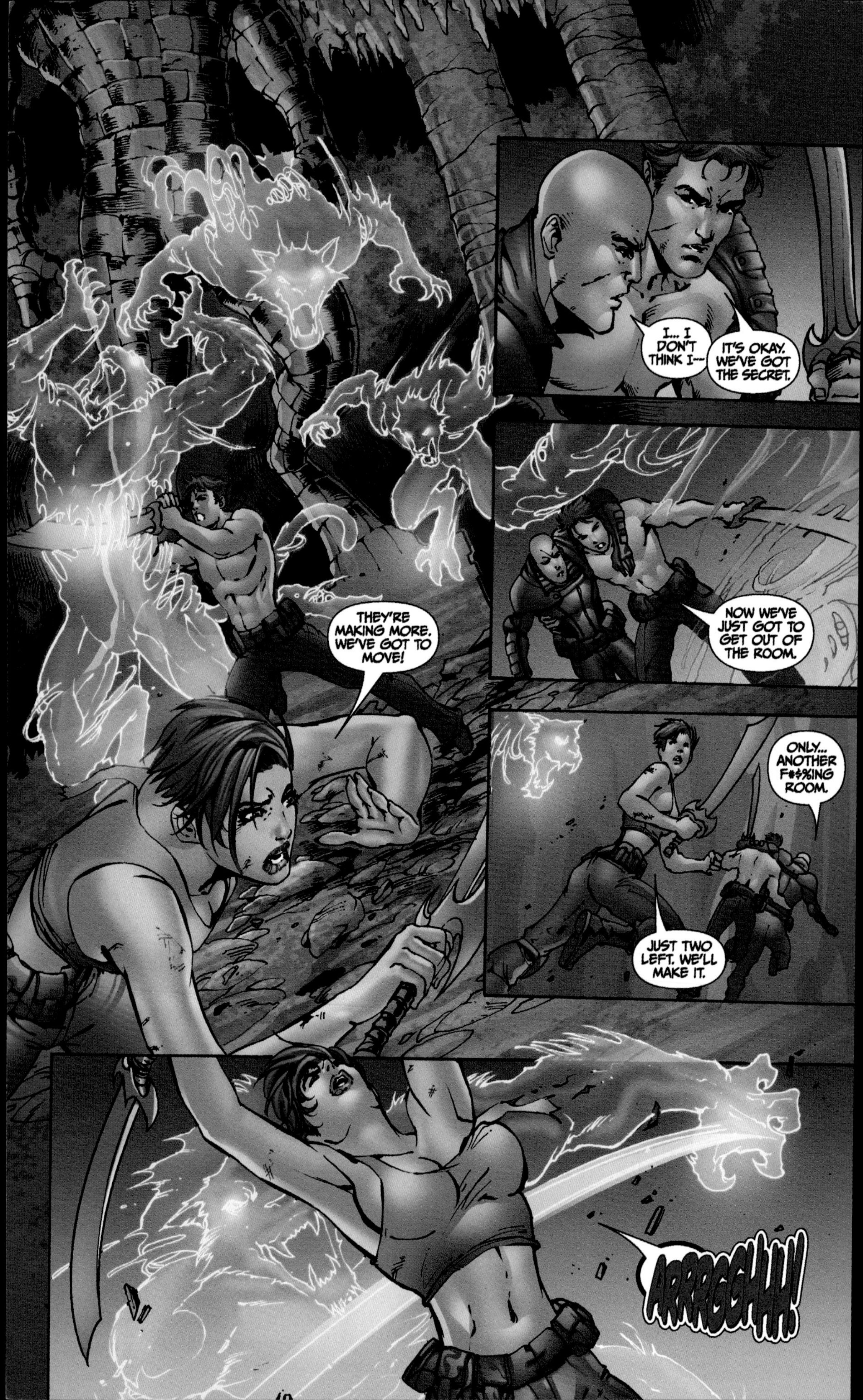
I... I DON'T THINK I--
IT'S OKAY. WE'VE GOT THE SECRET.
THEY'RE MAKING MORE. WE'VE GOT TO MOVE!
NOW WE'VE JUST GOT TO GET OUT OF THE ROOM.
ONLY... ANOTHER F#$%ING ROOM.
JUST TWO LEFT. WE'LL MAKE IT.
ARRRGGHHH!

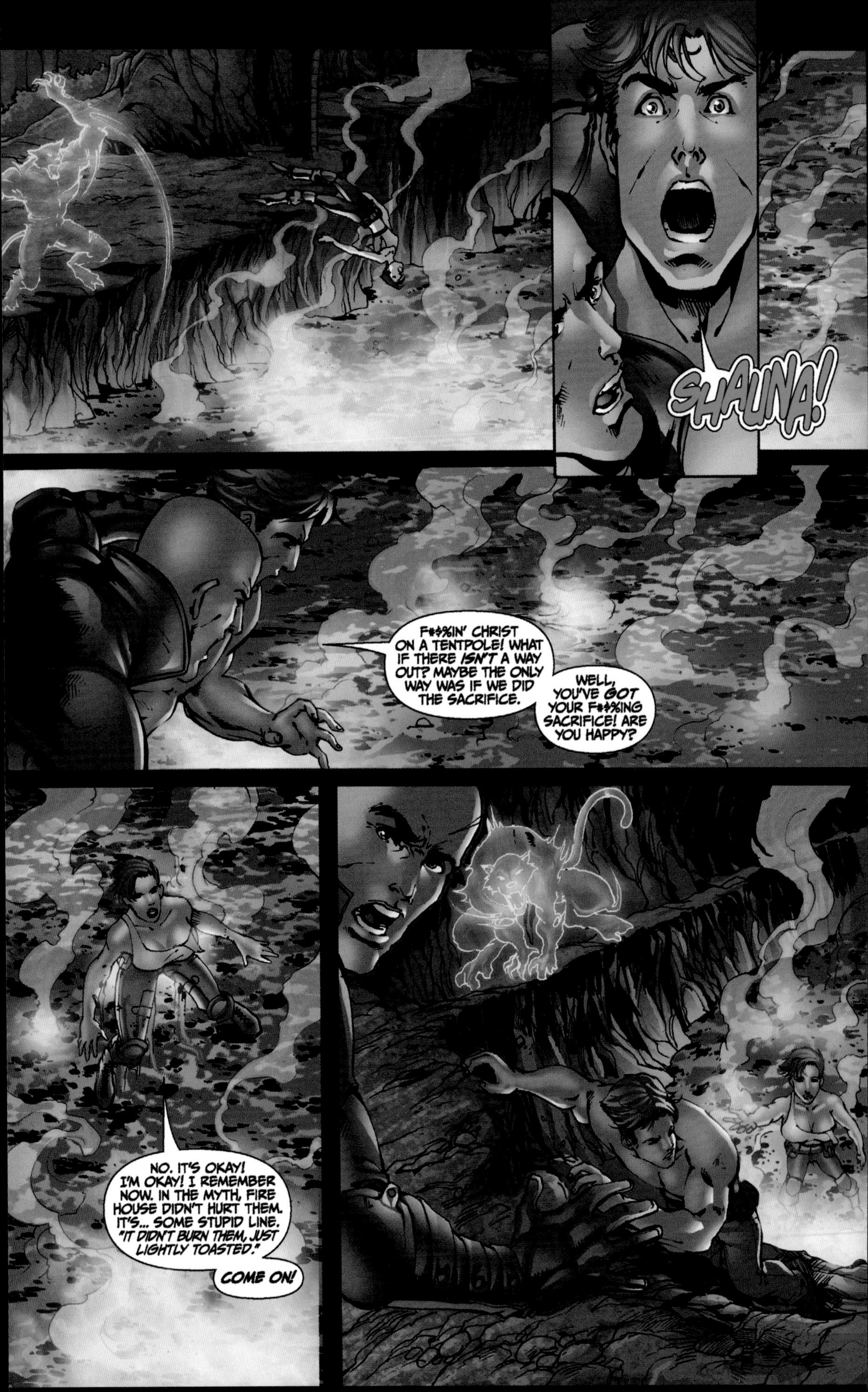
SHAUNA!
F#$%IN' CHRIST ON A TENTPOLE! WHAT IF THERE *ISN'T* A WAY OUT? MAYBE THE ONLY WAY WAS IF WE DID THE SACRIFICE.
WELL, YOU'VE *GOT* YOUR F#$%ING SACRIFICE! ARE YOU HAPPY?
NO. IT'S OKAY! I'M OKAY! I REMEMBER NOW. IN THE MYTH, FIRE HOUSE DIDN'T HURT THEM. IT'S... SOME STUPID LINE. *"IT DIDN'T BURN THEM, JUST LIGHTLY TOASTED."*
COME ON!

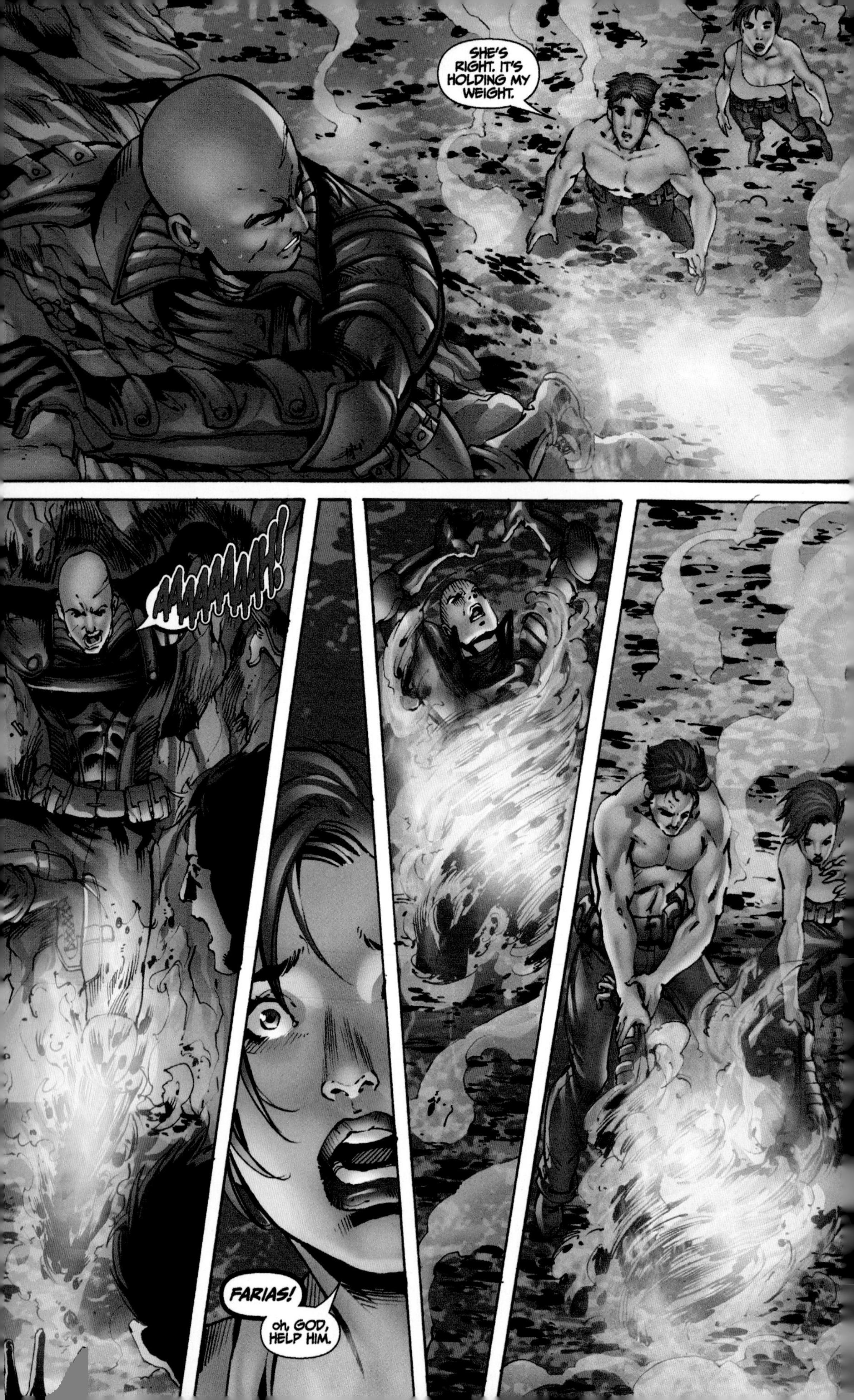
SHE'S RIGHT. IT'S HOLDING MY WEIGHT.
AAAAAAAH!
FARIAS!
oh, GOD, HELP HIM.

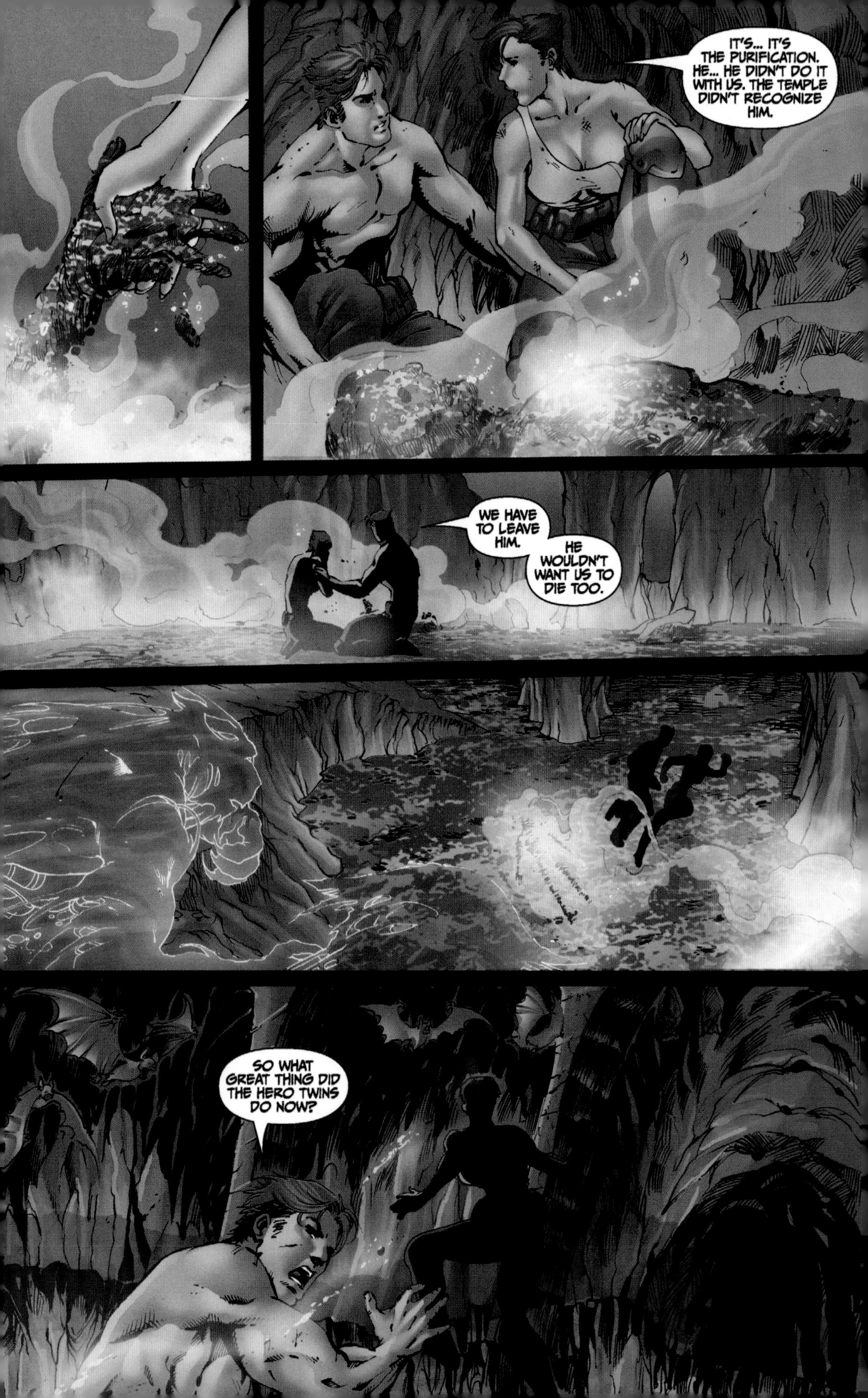
IT'S... IT'S THE PURIFICATION. HE... HE DIDN'T DO IT WITH US. THE TEMPLE DIDN'T RECOGNIZE HIM.
WE HAVE TO LEAVE HIM.
HE WOULDN'T WANT US TO DIE TOO.
SO WHAT GREAT THING DID THE HERO TWINS DO NOW?

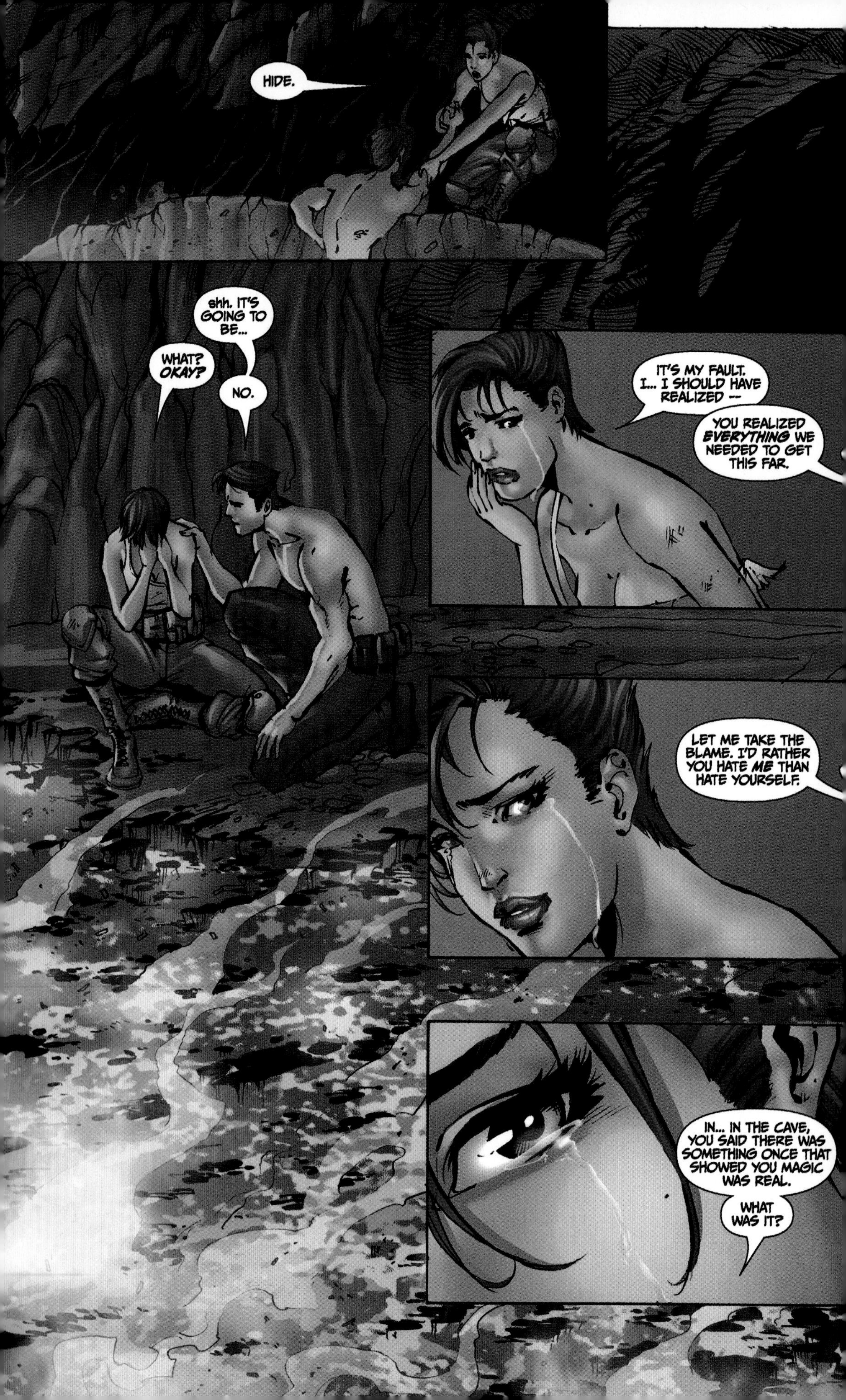
HIDE.
shh. IT'S GOING TO BE...
WHAT? OKAY?
NO.
IT'S MY FAULT. I... I SHOULD HAVE REALIZED --
YOU REALIZED EVERYTHING WE NEEDED TO GET THIS FAR.
LET ME TAKE THE BLAME. I'D RATHER YOU HATE ME THAN HATE YOURSELF.
IN... IN THE CAVE, YOU SAID THERE WAS SOMETHING ONCE THAT SHOWED YOU MAGIC WAS REAL.
WHAT WAS IT?

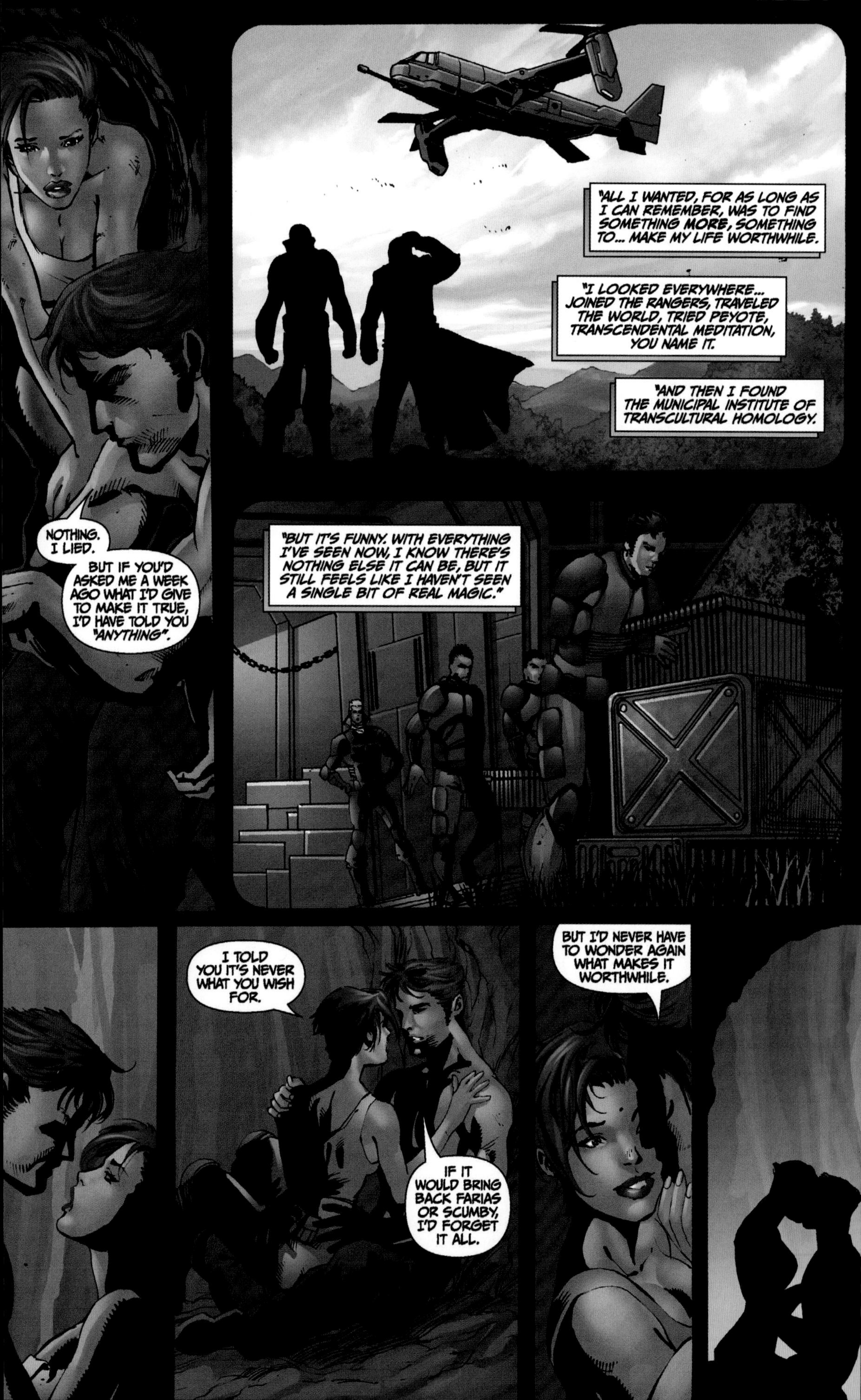
"ALL I WANTED, FOR AS LONG AS I CAN REMEMBER, WAS TO FIND SOMETHING MORE, SOMETHING TO... MAKE MY LIFE WORTHWHILE.
"I LOOKED EVERYWHERE... JOINED THE RANGERS, TRAVELED THE WORLD, TRIED PEYOTE, TRANSCENDENTAL MEDITATION, YOU NAME IT.
"AND THEN I FOUND THE MUNICIPAL INSTITUTE OF TRANSCULTURAL HOMOLOGY.
NOTHING. I LIED.
BUT IF YOU'D ASKED ME A WEEK AGO WHAT I'D GIVE TO MAKE IT TRUE, I'D HAVE TOLD YOU "ANYTHING".
"BUT IT'S FUNNY. WITH EVERYTHING I'VE SEEN NOW, I KNOW THERE'S NOTHING ELSE IT CAN BE, BUT IT STILL FEELS LIKE I HAVEN'T SEEN A SINGLE BIT OF REAL MAGIC."
I TOLD YOU IT'S NEVER WHAT YOU WISH FOR.
IF IT WOULD BRING BACK FARIAS OR SCUMBY, I'D FORGET IT ALL.
BUT I'D NEVER HAVE TO WONDER AGAIN WHAT MAKES IT WORTHWHILE.

M.I.T.H.™

CHAPTER 4

"Reality is that which, when you stop believing in it, doesn't go away."

-- Philip K. Dick

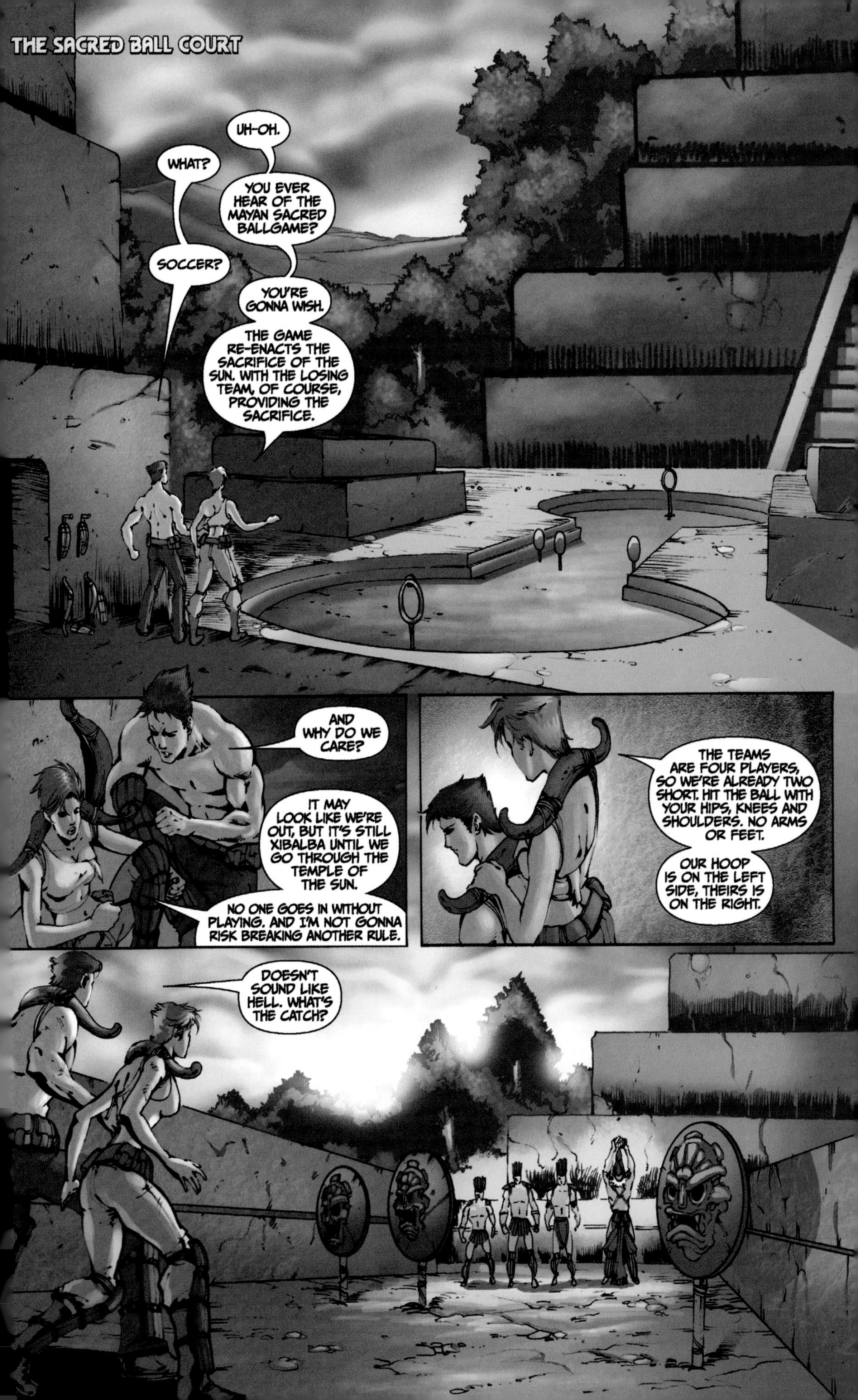
THE SACRED BALL COURT
UH-OH.
WHAT?
YOU EVER HEAR OF THE MAYAN SACRED BALLGAME?
SOCCER?
YOU'RE GONNA WISH.
THE GAME RE-ENACTS THE SACRIFICE OF THE SUN. WITH THE LOSING TEAM, OF COURSE, PROVIDING THE SACRIFICE.
AND WHY DO WE CARE?
IT MAY LOOK LIKE WE'RE OUT, BUT IT'S STILL XIBALBA UNTIL WE GO THROUGH THE TEMPLE OF THE SUN.
NO ONE GOES IN WITHOUT PLAYING. AND I'M NOT GONNA RISK BREAKING ANOTHER RULE.
THE TEAMS ARE FOUR PLAYERS, SO WE'RE ALREADY TWO SHORT. HIT THE BALL WITH YOUR HIPS, KNEES AND SHOULDERS. NO ARMS OR FEET.
OUR HOOP IS ON THE LEFT SIDE, THEIRS IS ON THE RIGHT.
DOESN'T SOUND LIKE HELL. WHAT'S THE CATCH?

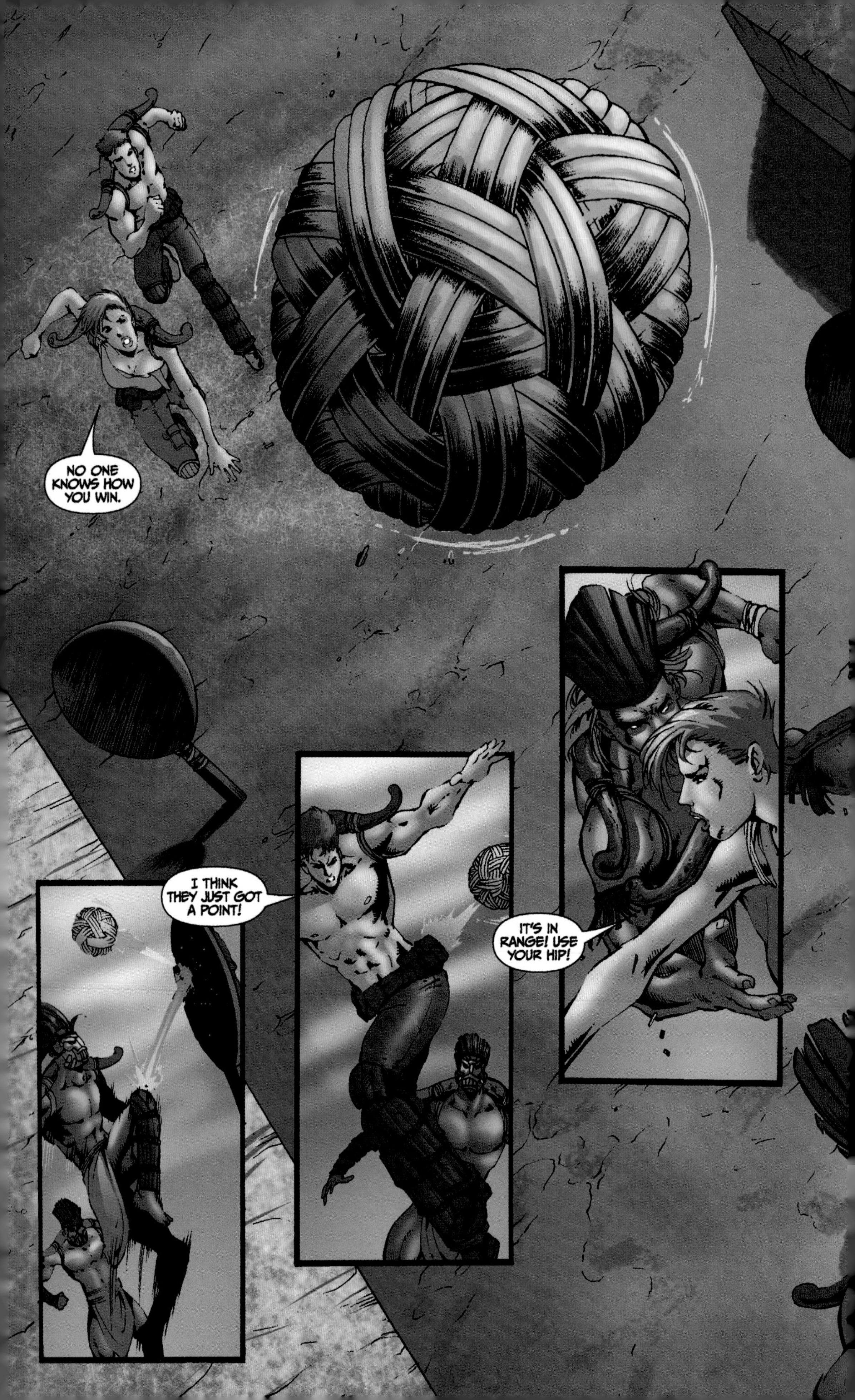
NO ONE KNOWS HOW YOU WIN.
I THINK THEY JUST GOT A POINT!
IT'S IN RANGE! USE YOUR HIP!

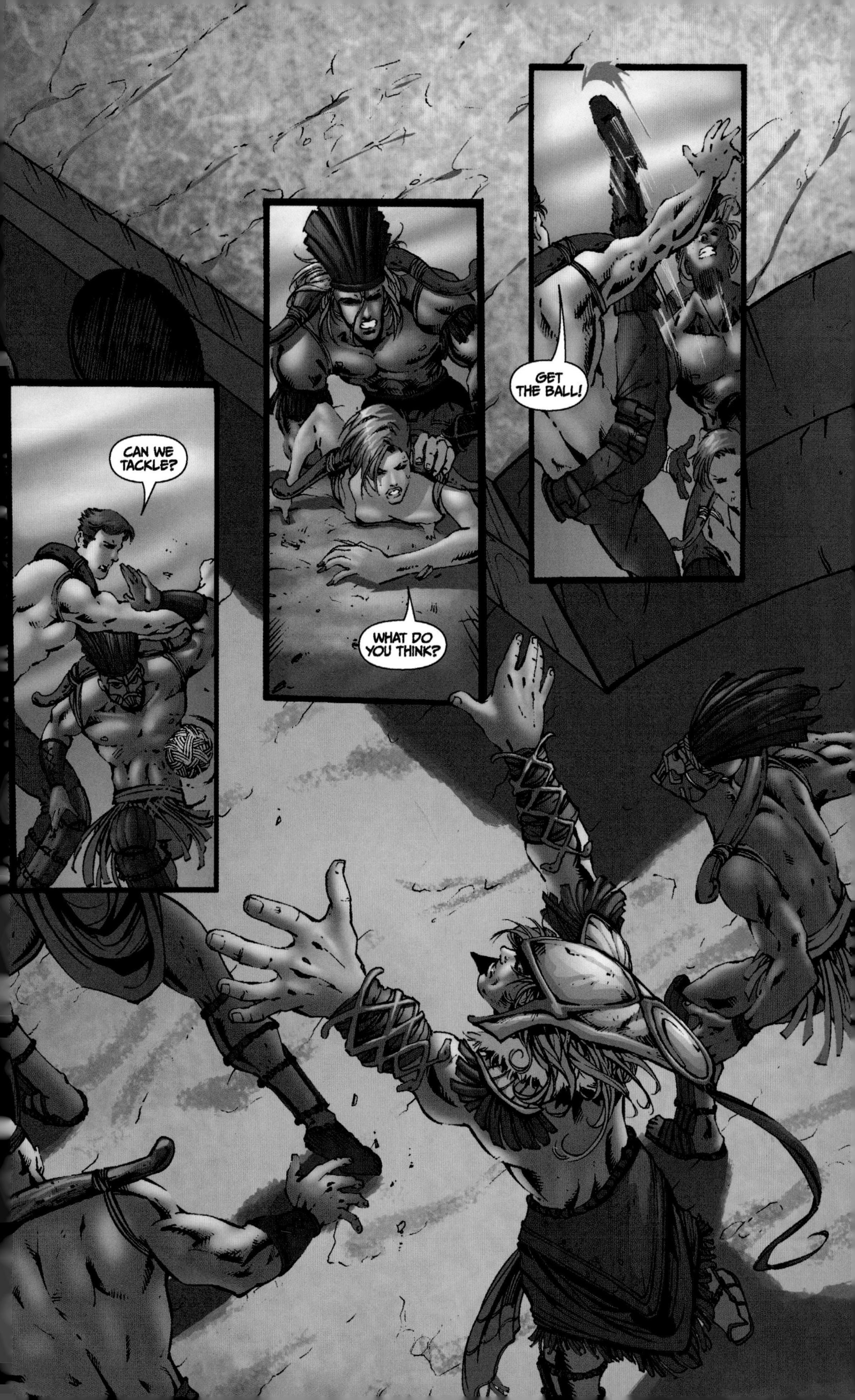
CAN WE TACKLE?
WHAT DO YOU THINK?
GET THE BALL!

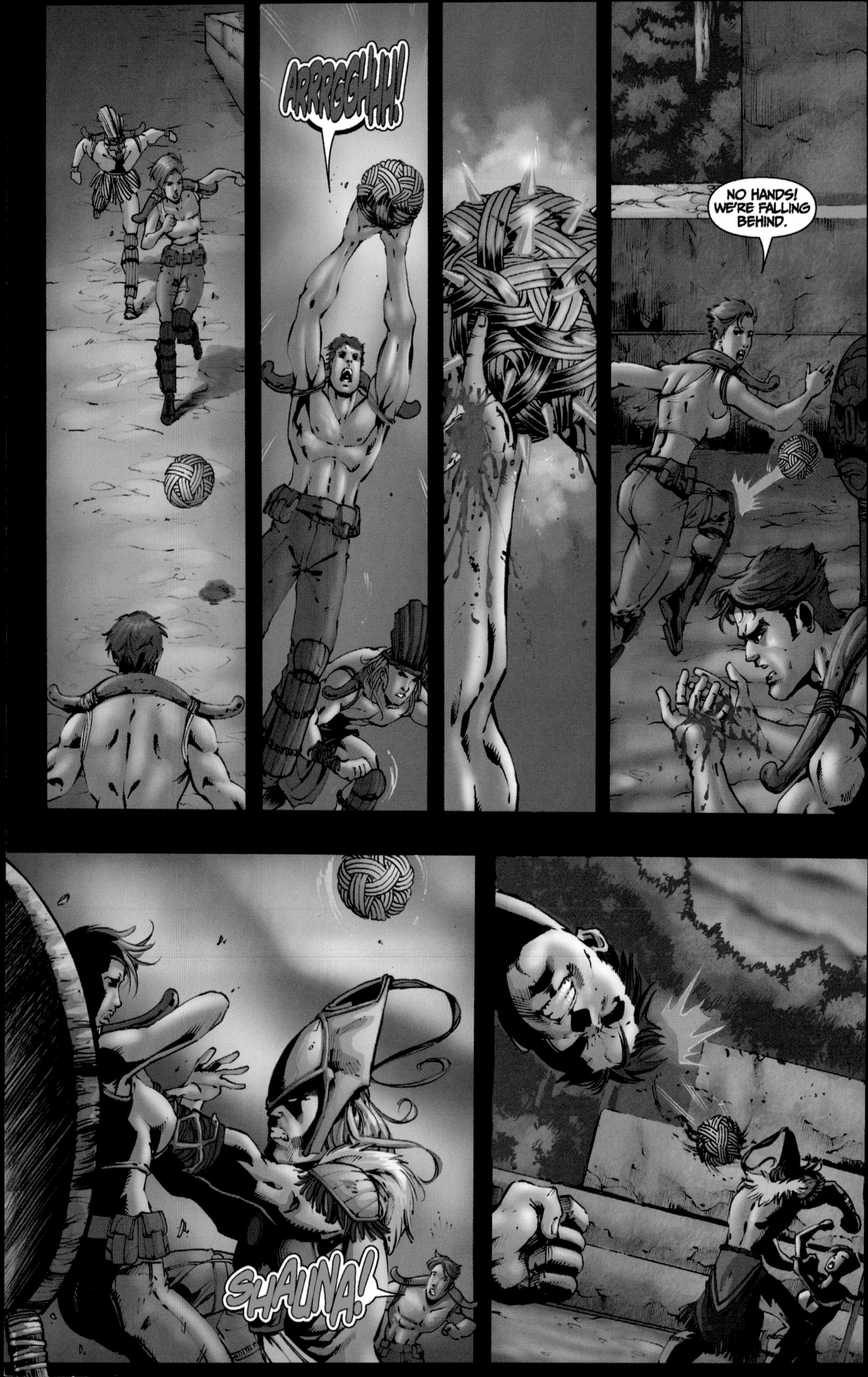
ARRRGGHHH!
NO HANDS! WE'RE FALLING BEHIND.
SHAUNA!

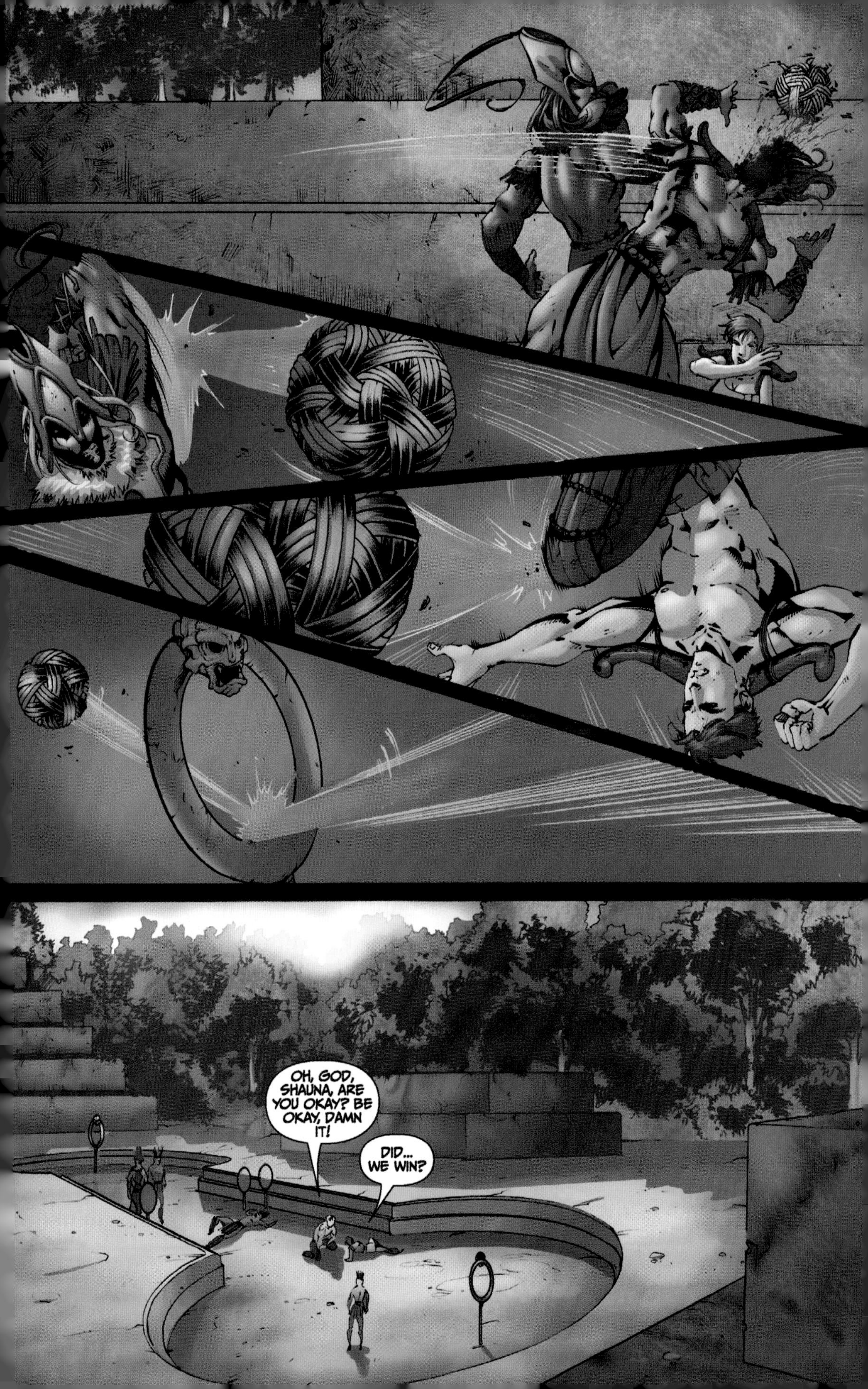
OH, GOD, SHAUNA, ARE YOU OKAY? BE OKAY, DAMN IT!
DID... WE WIN?

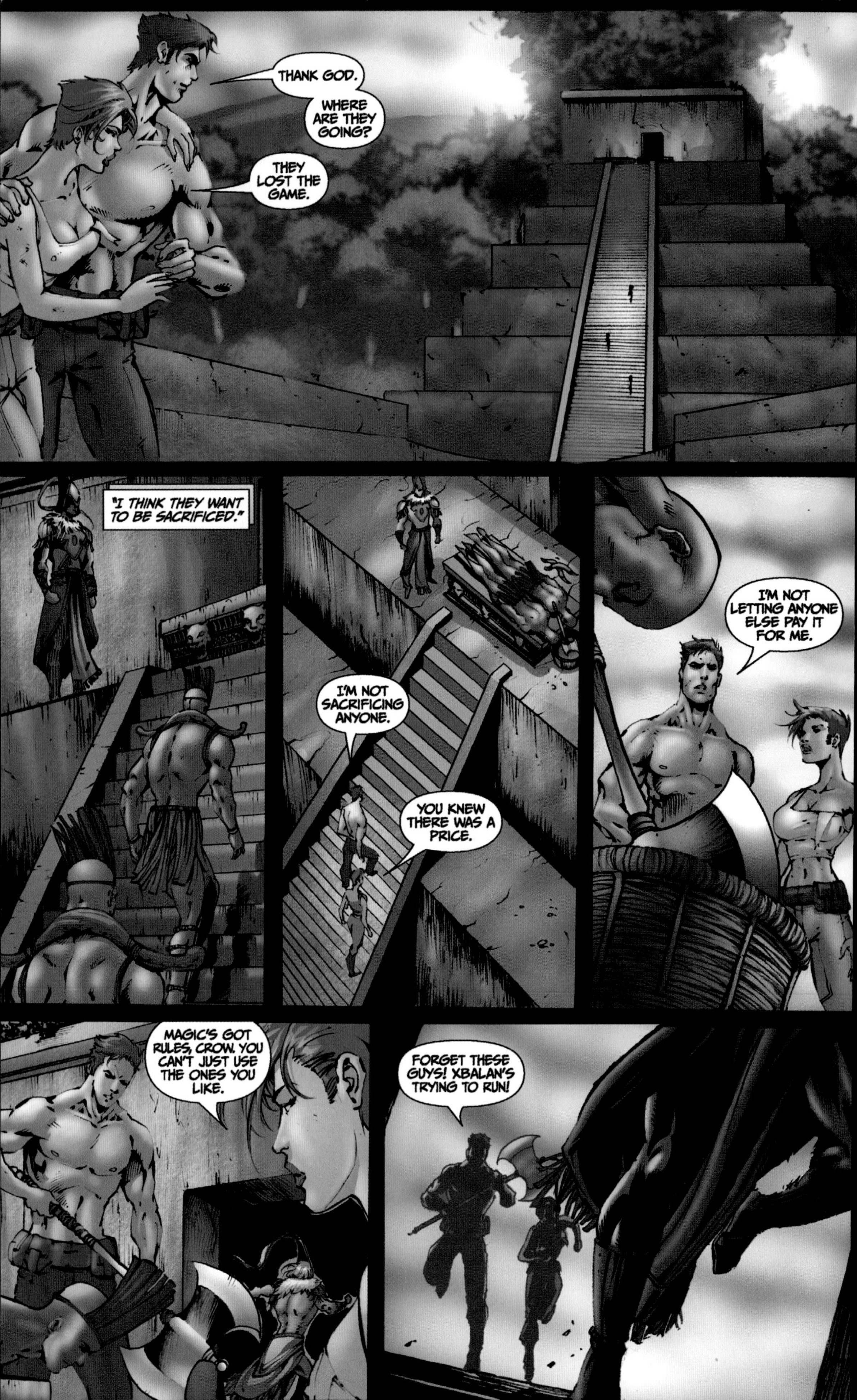
THANK GOD.
WHERE ARE THEY GOING?
THEY LOST THE GAME.
"I THINK THEY WANT TO BE SACRIFICED."
I'M NOT SACRIFICING ANYONE.
YOU KNEW THERE WAS A PRICE.
I'M NOT LETTING ANYONE ELSE PAY IT FOR ME.
MAGIC'S GOT RULES, CROW. YOU CAN'T JUST USE THE ONES YOU LIKE.
FORGET THESE GUYS! XBALAN'S TRYING TO RUN!

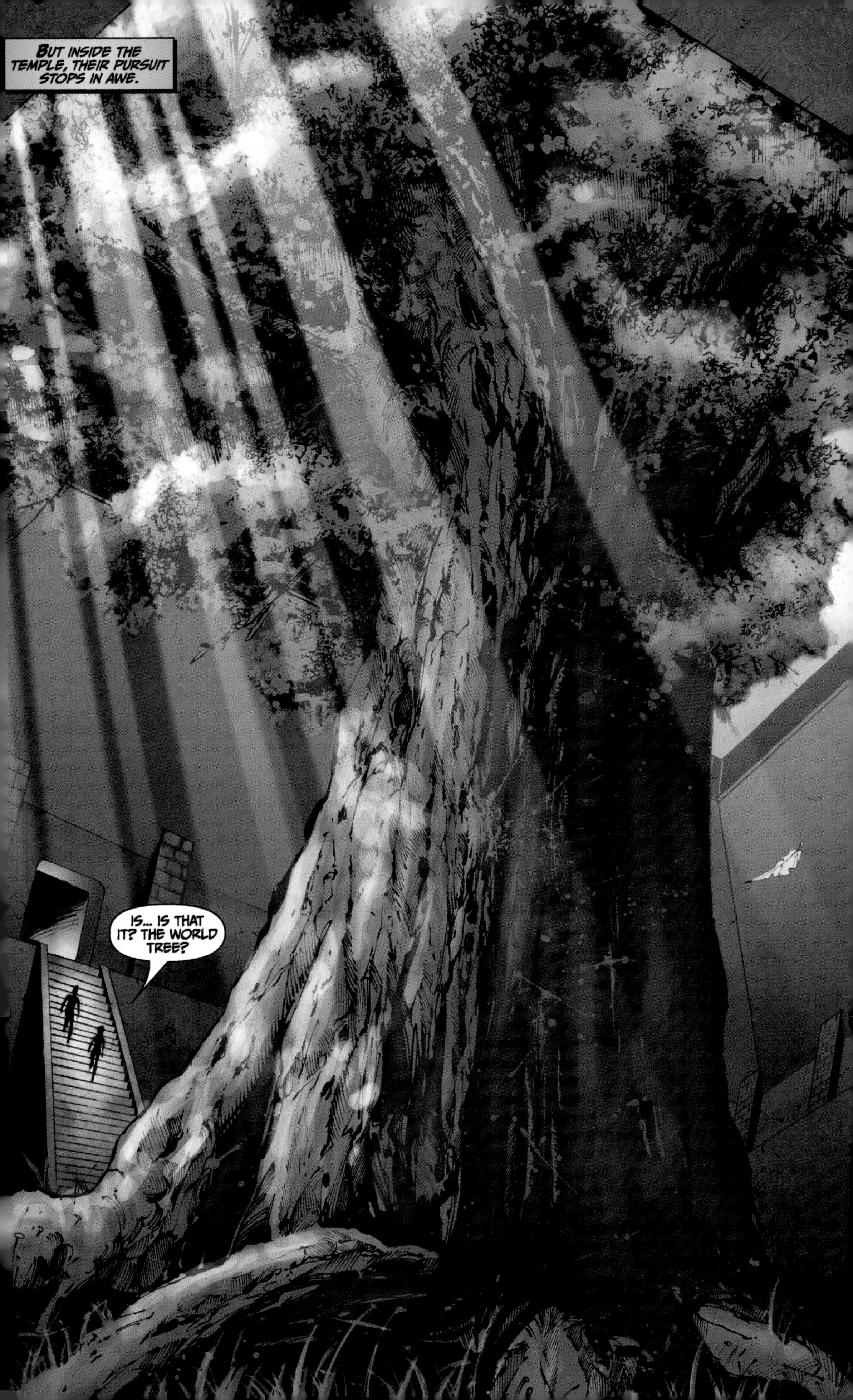
BUT INSIDE THE TEMPLE, THEIR PURSUIT STOPS IN AWE.
IS... IS THAT IT? THE WORLD TREE?

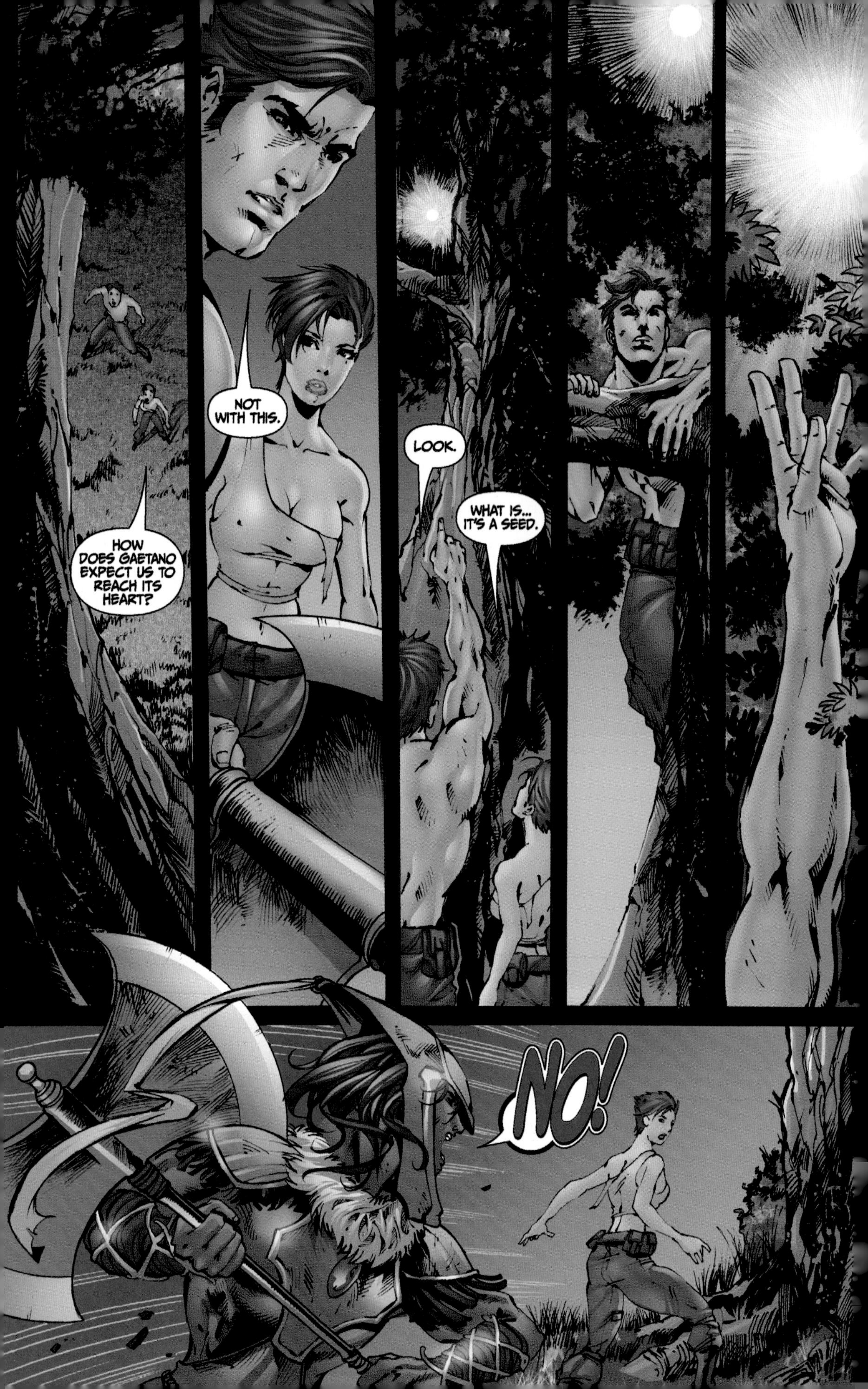
HOW DOES GAETANO EXPECT US TO REACH ITS HEART?
NOT WITH THIS.
LOOK.
WHAT IS... IT'S A SEED.
NO!

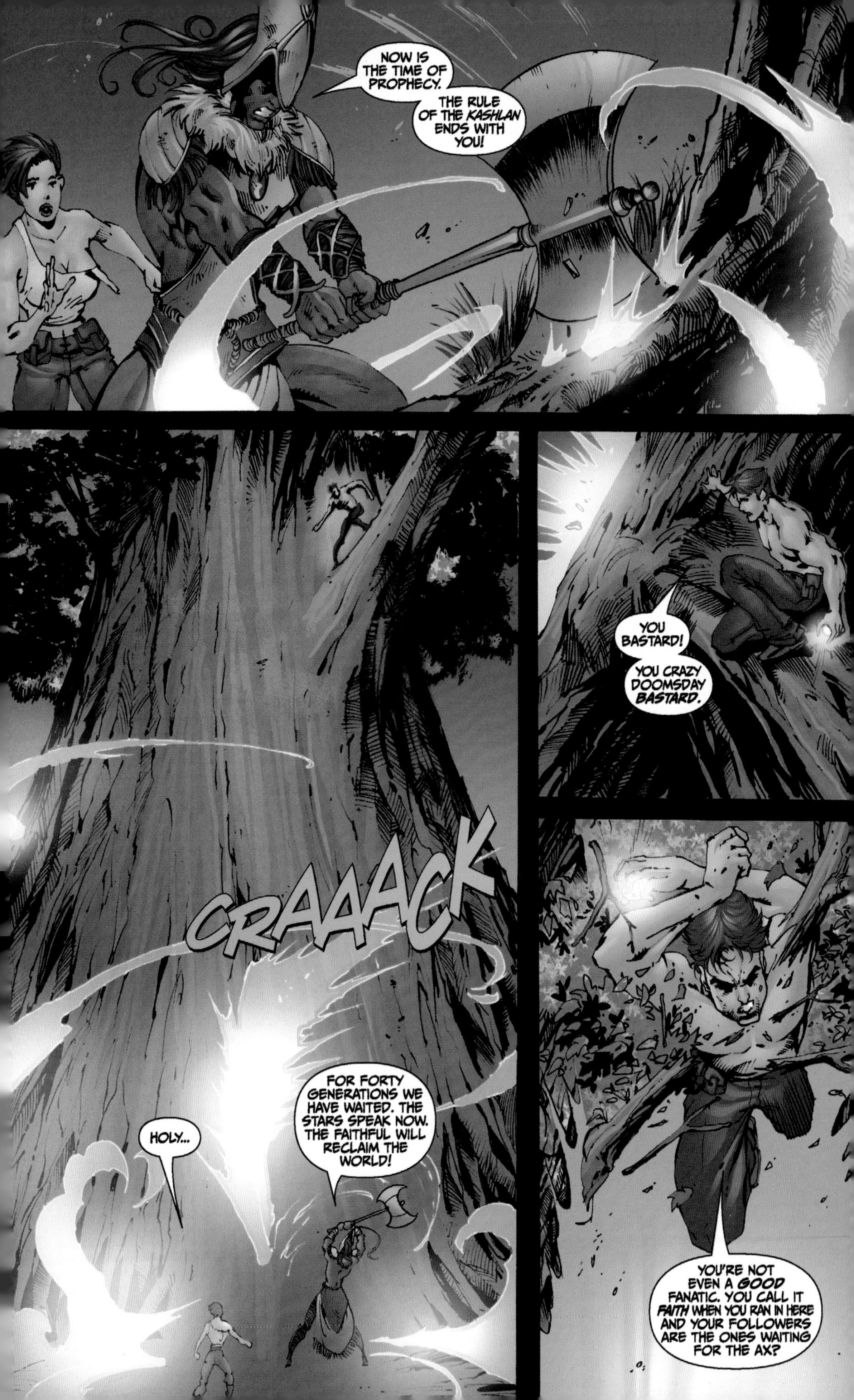
NOW IS THE TIME OF PROPHECY.
THE RULE OF THE KASHLAN ENDS WITH YOU!
YOU BASTARD!
YOU CRAZY DOOMSDAY BASTARD.
CRAAACK
HOLY...
FOR FORTY GENERATIONS WE HAVE WAITED. THE STARS SPEAK NOW. THE FAITHFUL WILL RECLAIM THE WORLD!
YOU'RE NOT EVEN A GOOD FANATIC. YOU CALL IT FAITH WHEN YOU RAN IN HERE AND YOUR FOLLOWERS ARE THE ONES WAITING FOR THE AX?

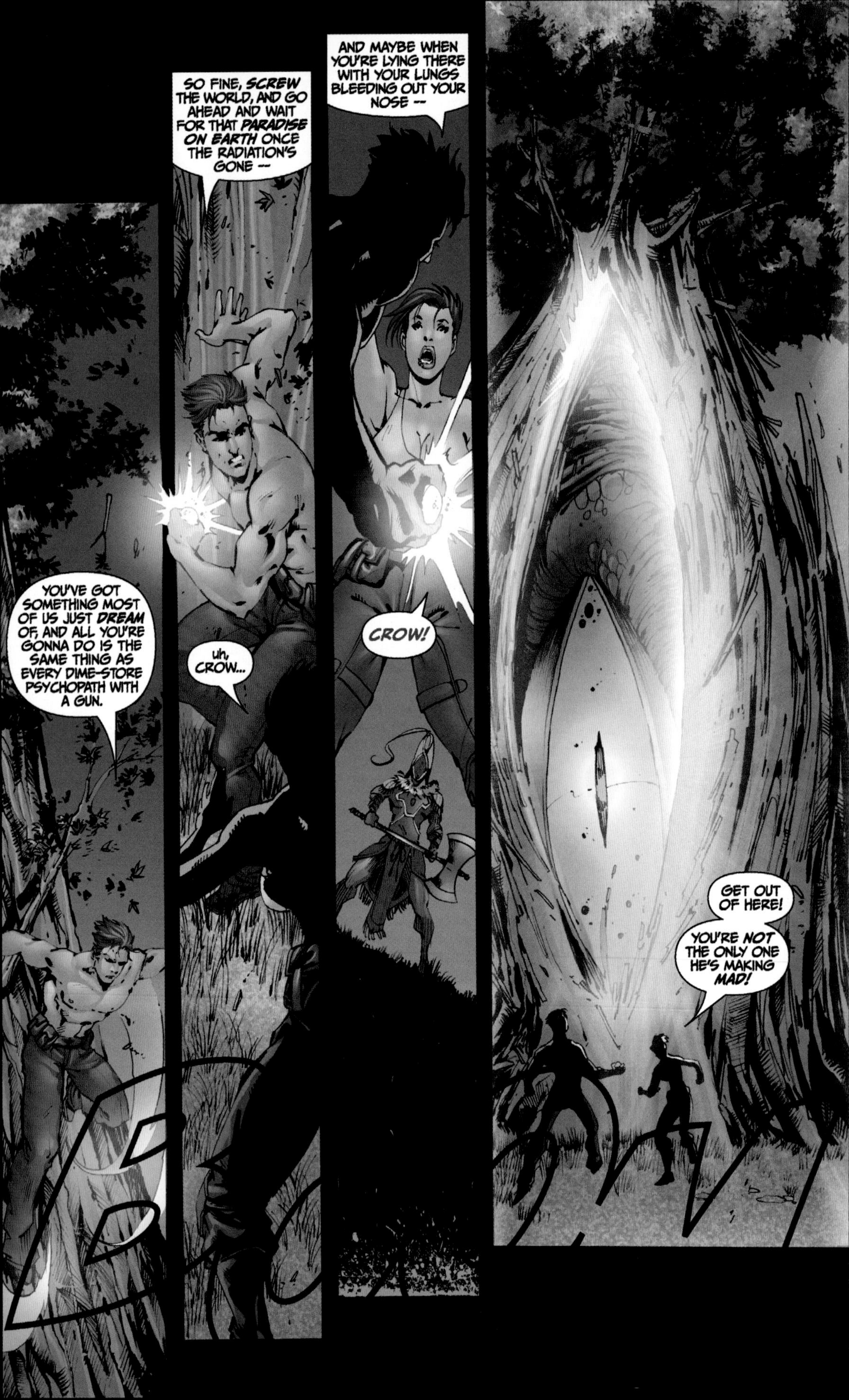
SO FINE, SCREW THE WORLD, AND GO AHEAD AND WAIT FOR THAT PARADISE ON EARTH ONCE THE RADIATION'S GONE --
AND MAYBE WHEN YOU'RE LYING THERE WITH YOUR LUNGS BLEEDING OUT YOUR NOSE --
YOU'VE GOT SOMETHING MOST OF US JUST DREAM OF, AND ALL YOU'RE GONNA DO IS THE SAME THING AS EVERY DIME-STORE PSYCHOPATH WITH A GUN.
uh, CROW...
CROW!
GET OUT OF HERE!
YOU'RE NOT THE ONLY ONE HE'S MAKING MAD!

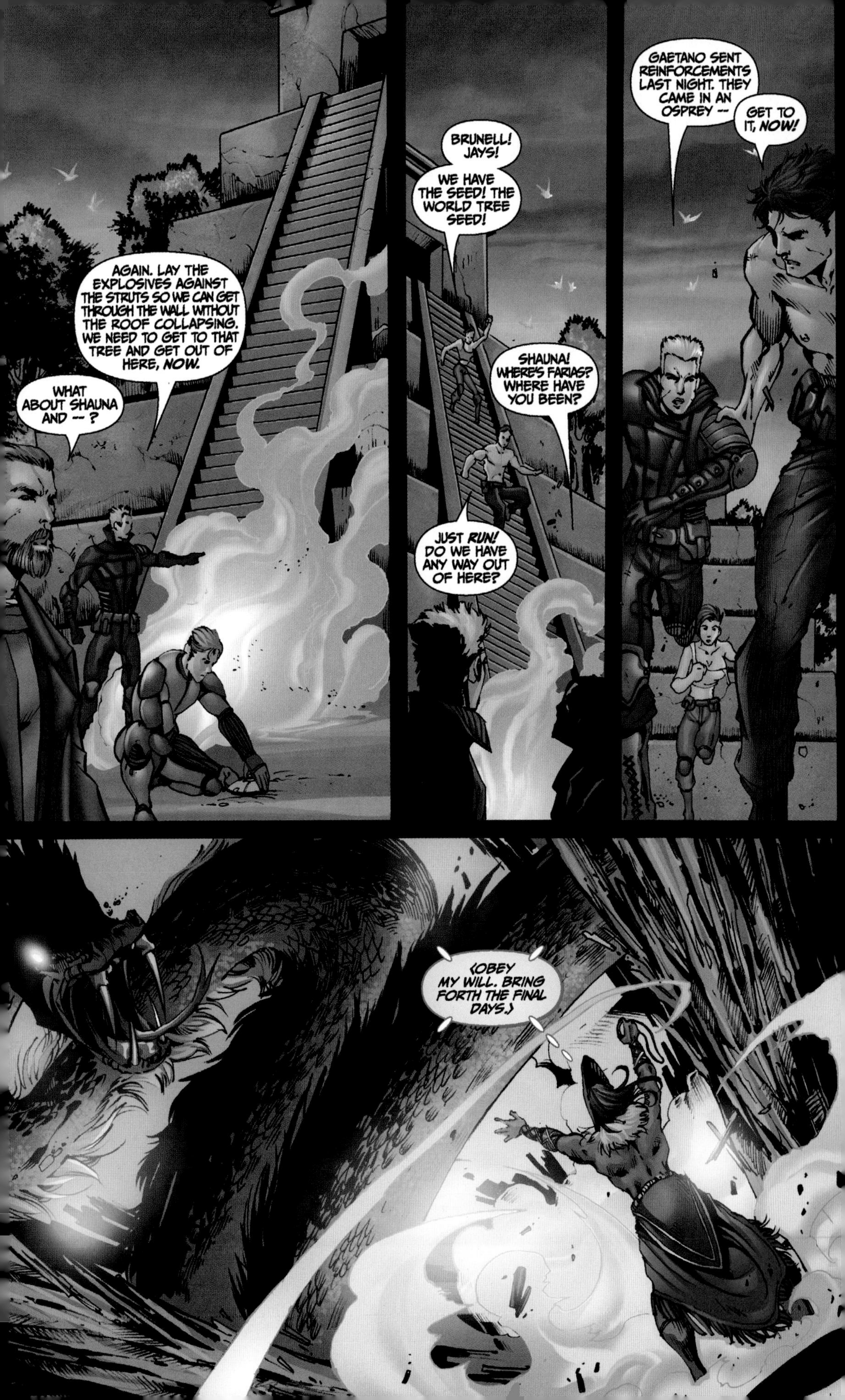
AGAIN. LAY THE EXPLOSIVES AGAINST THE STRUTS SO WE CAN GET THROUGH THE WALL WITHOUT THE ROOF COLLAPSING. WE NEED TO GET TO THAT TREE AND GET OUT OF HERE, NOW.
WHAT ABOUT SHAUNA AND -- ?
BRUNELL! JAYS!
WE HAVE THE SEED! THE WORLD TREE SEED!
SHAUNA! WHERE'S FARIAS? WHERE HAVE YOU BEEN?
JUST RUN! DO WE HAVE ANY WAY OUT OF HERE?
GAETANO SENT REINFORCEMENTS LAST NIGHT. THEY CAME IN AN OSPREY --
GET TO IT, NOW!
‹OBEY MY WILL. BRING FORTH THE FINAL DAYS.›

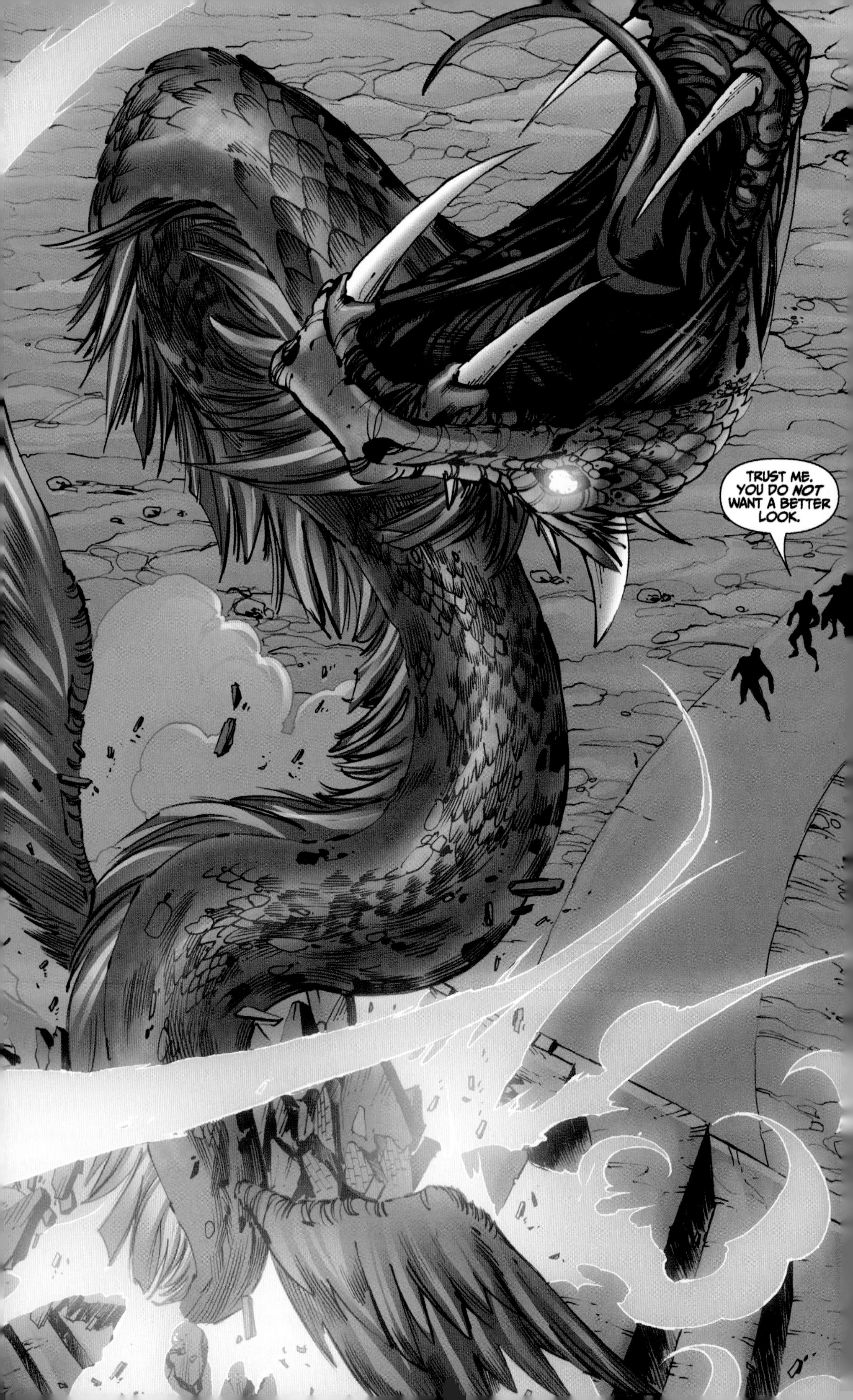
TRUST ME. YOU DO NOT WANT A BETTER LOOK.

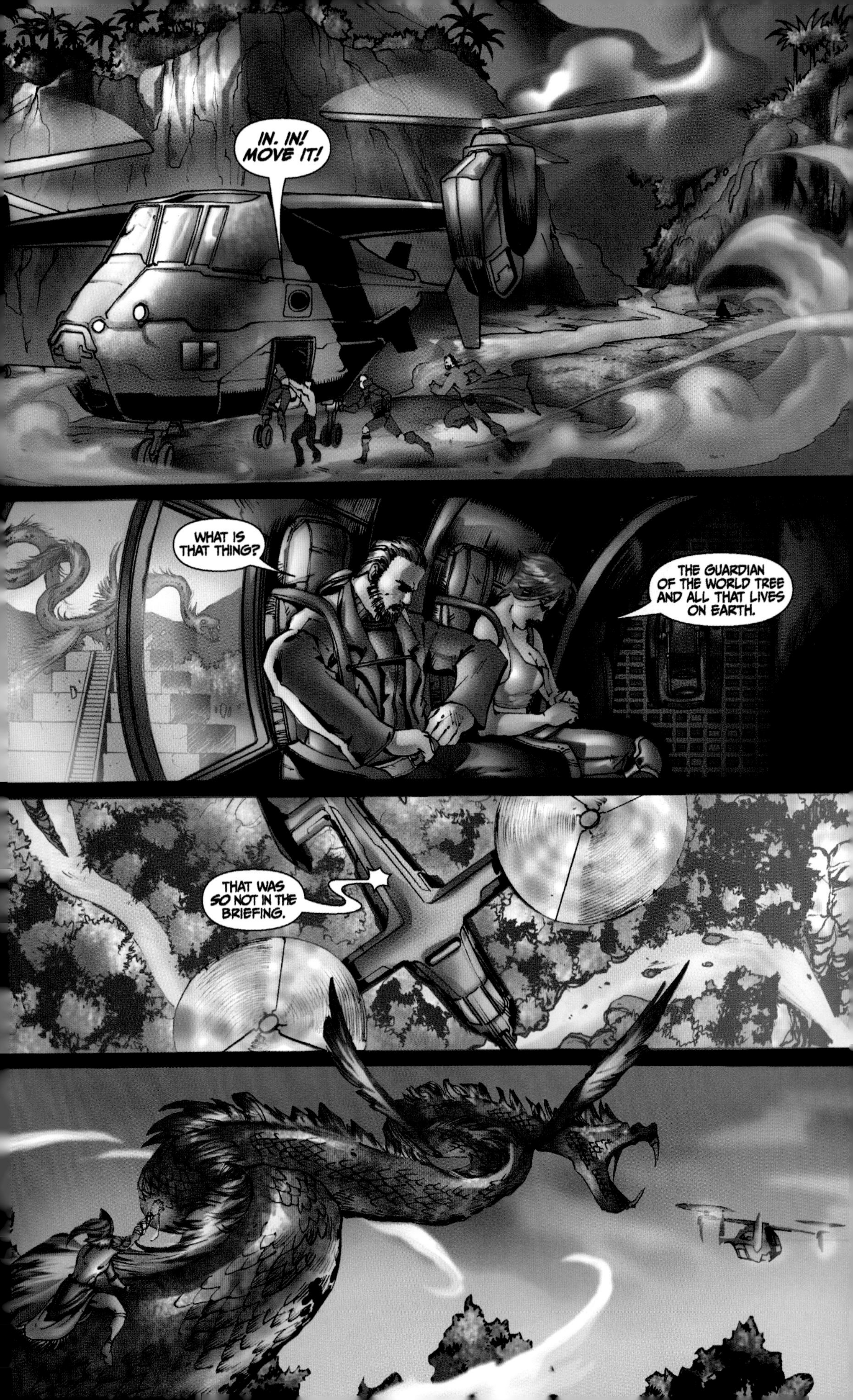
IN. IN! MOVE IT!
WHAT IS THAT THING?
THE GUARDIAN OF THE WORLD TREE AND ALL THAT LIVES ON EARTH.
THAT WAS SO NOT IN THE BRIEFING.

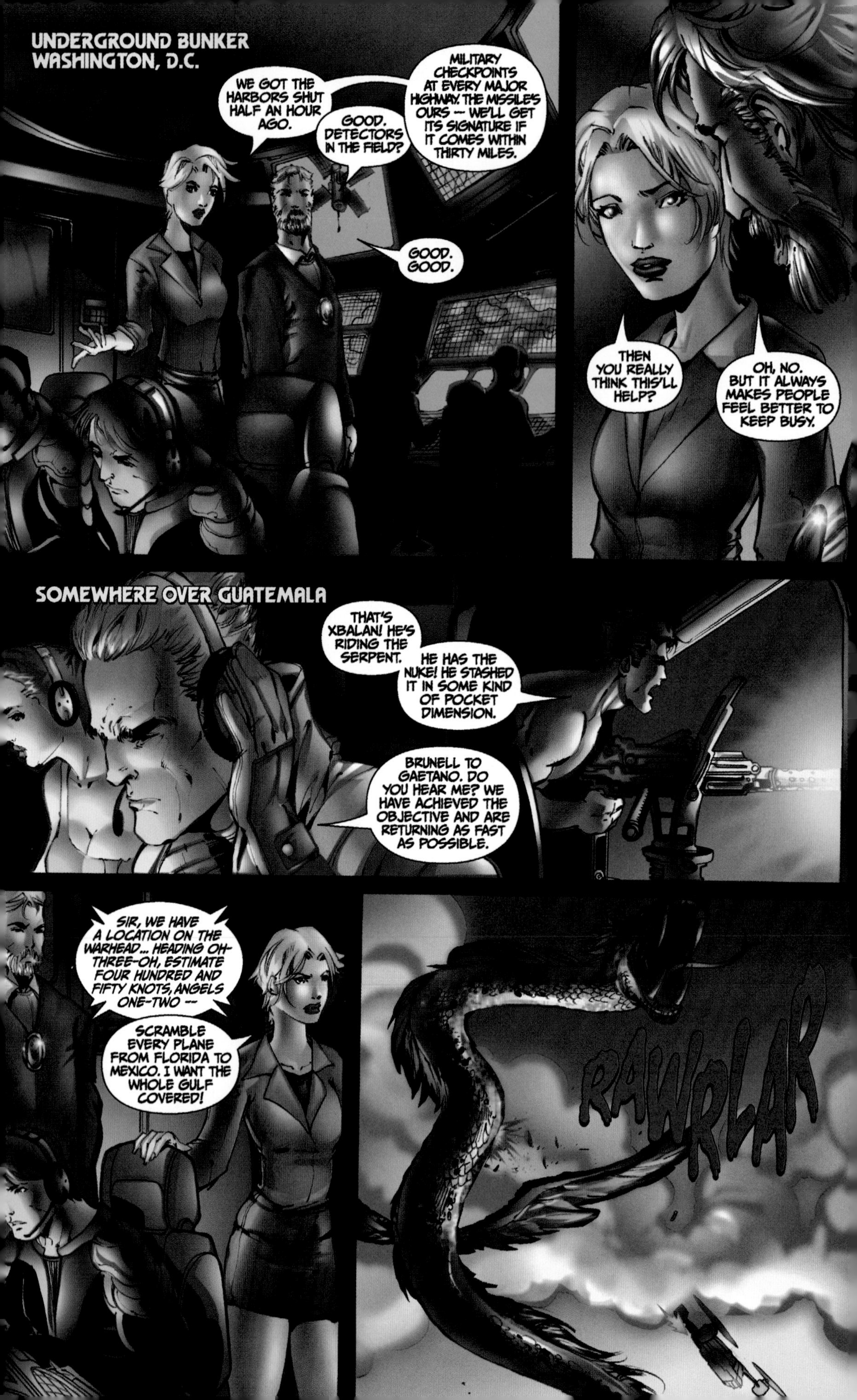
UNDERGROUND BUNKER
WASHINGTON, D.C.
WE GOT THE HARBORS SHUT HALF AN HOUR AGO.
GOOD. DETECTORS IN THE FIELD?
MILITARY CHECKPOINTS AT EVERY MAJOR HIGHWAY. THE MISSILE'S OURS -- WE'LL GET ITS SIGNATURE IF IT COMES WITHIN THIRTY MILES.
GOOD. GOOD.
THEN YOU REALLY THINK THIS'LL HELP?
OH, NO. BUT IT ALWAYS MAKES PEOPLE FEEL BETTER TO KEEP BUSY.
SOMEWHERE OVER GUATEMALA
THAT'S XBALAN! HE'S RIDING THE SERPENT.
HE HAS THE NUKE! HE STASHED IT IN SOME KIND OF POCKET DIMENSION.
BRUNELL TO GAETANO. DO YOU HEAR ME? WE HAVE ACHIEVED THE OBJECTIVE AND ARE RETURNING AS FAST AS POSSIBLE.
SIR, WE HAVE A LOCATION ON THE WARHEAD... HEADING OH-THREE-OH, ESTIMATE FOUR HUNDRED AND FIFTY KNOTS, ANGELS ONE-TWO --
SCRAMBLE EVERY PLANE FROM FLORIDA TO MEXICO. I WANT THE WHOLE GULF COVERED!
RAWRLAR

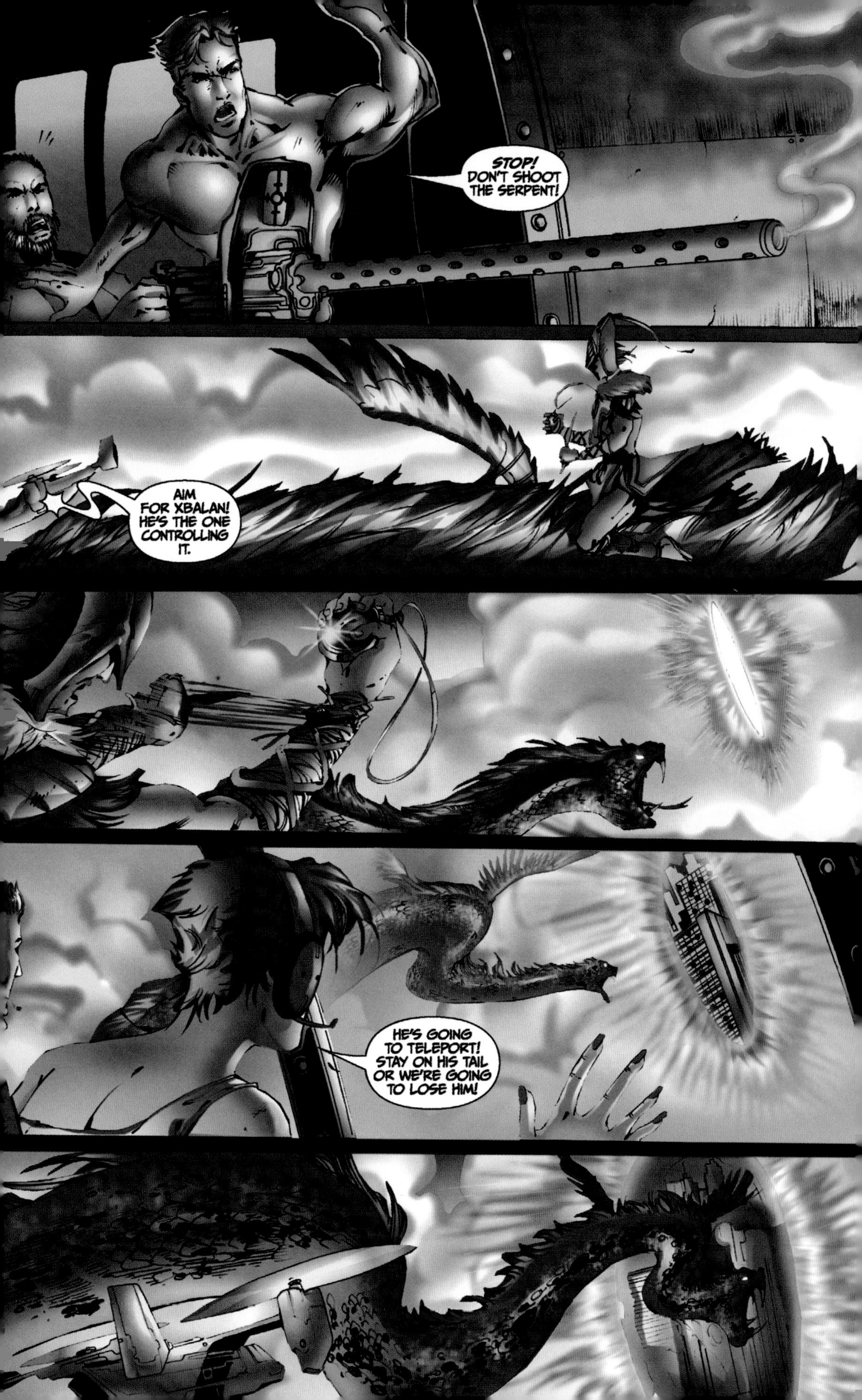
STOP! DON'T SHOOT THE SERPENT!
AIM FOR XBALAN! HE'S THE ONE CONTROLLING IT.
HE'S GOING TO TELEPORT! STAY ON HIS TAIL OR WE'RE GOING TO LOSE HIM!

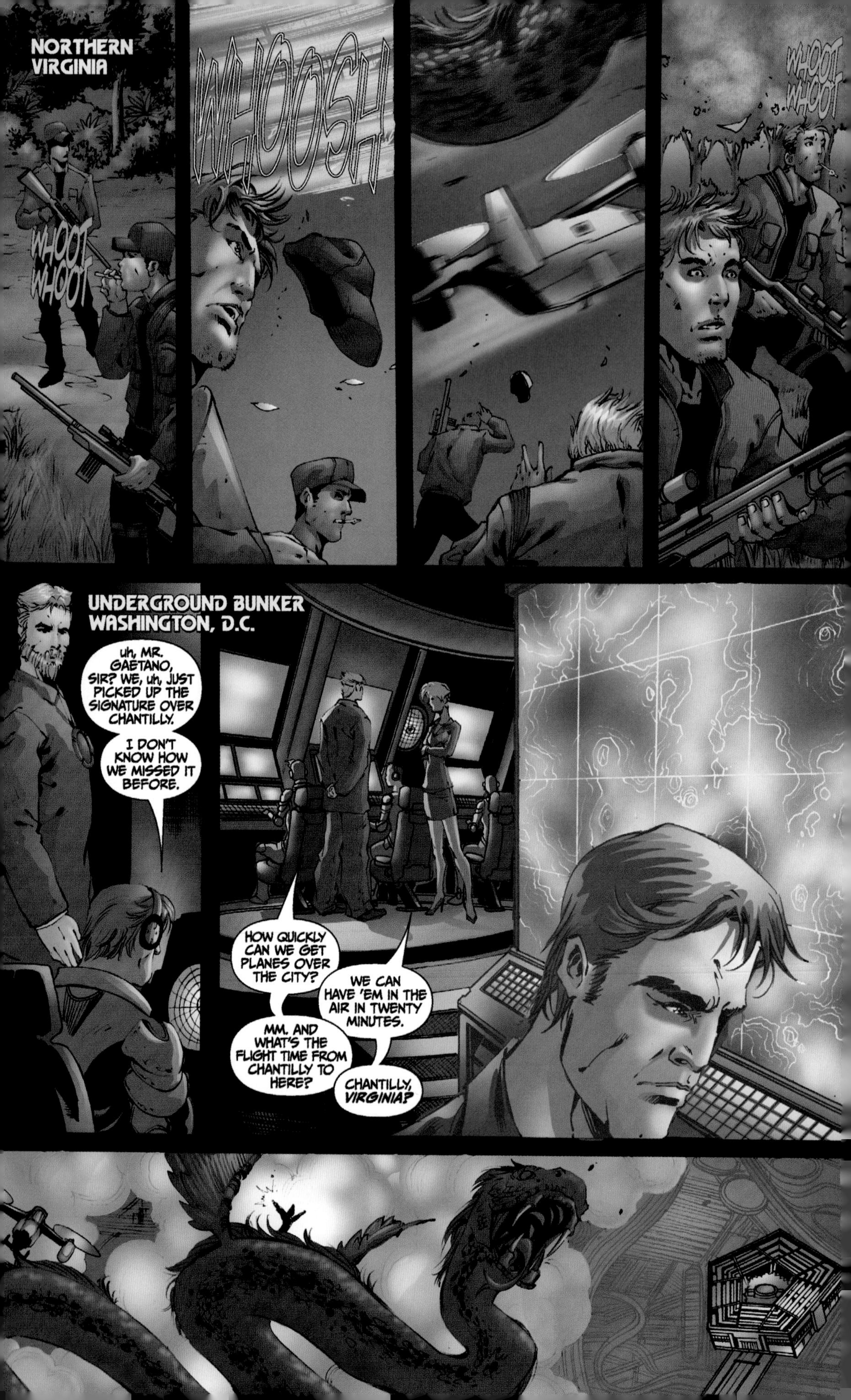
NORTHERN VIRGINIA
WHOOT WHOOT
WHOOSH
WHOOT WHOOT
UNDERGROUND BUNKER WASHINGTON, D.C.
uh, MR. GAETANO, SIR? WE, uh, JUST PICKED UP THE SIGNATURE OVER CHANTILLY.
I DON'T KNOW HOW WE MISSED IT BEFORE.
HOW QUICKLY CAN WE GET PLANES OVER THE CITY?
WE CAN HAVE 'EM IN THE AIR IN TWENTY MINUTES.
MM. AND WHAT'S THE FLIGHT TIME FROM CHANTILLY TO HERE?
CHANTILLY, *VIRGINIA?*

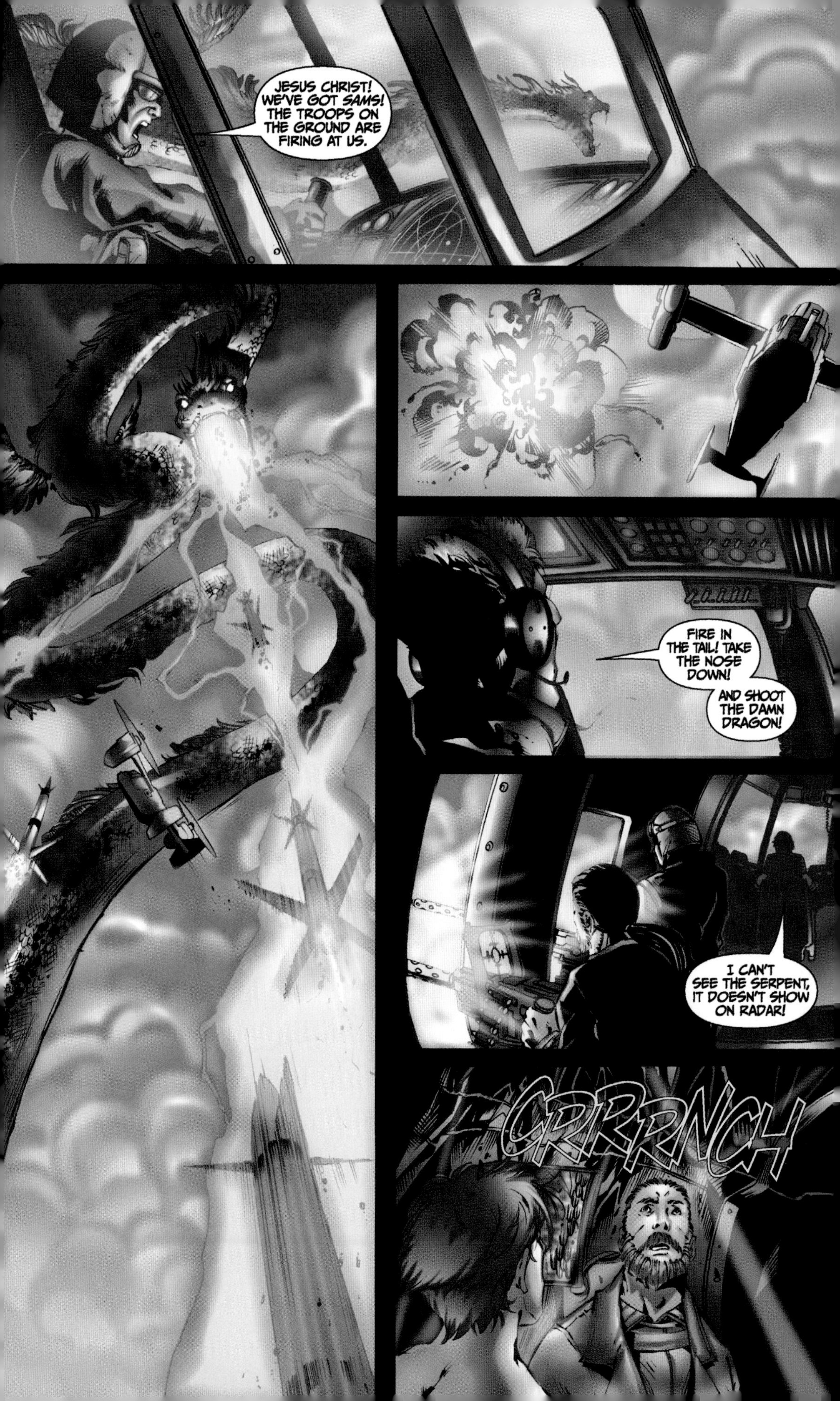

JESUS CHRIST! WE'VE GOT SAMS! THE TROOPS ON THE GROUND ARE FIRING AT US.
FIRE IN THE TAIL! TAKE THE NOSE DOWN!
AND SHOOT THE DAMN DRAGON!
I CAN'T SEE THE SERPENT, IT DOESN'T SHOW ON RADAR!
CRRRNCH

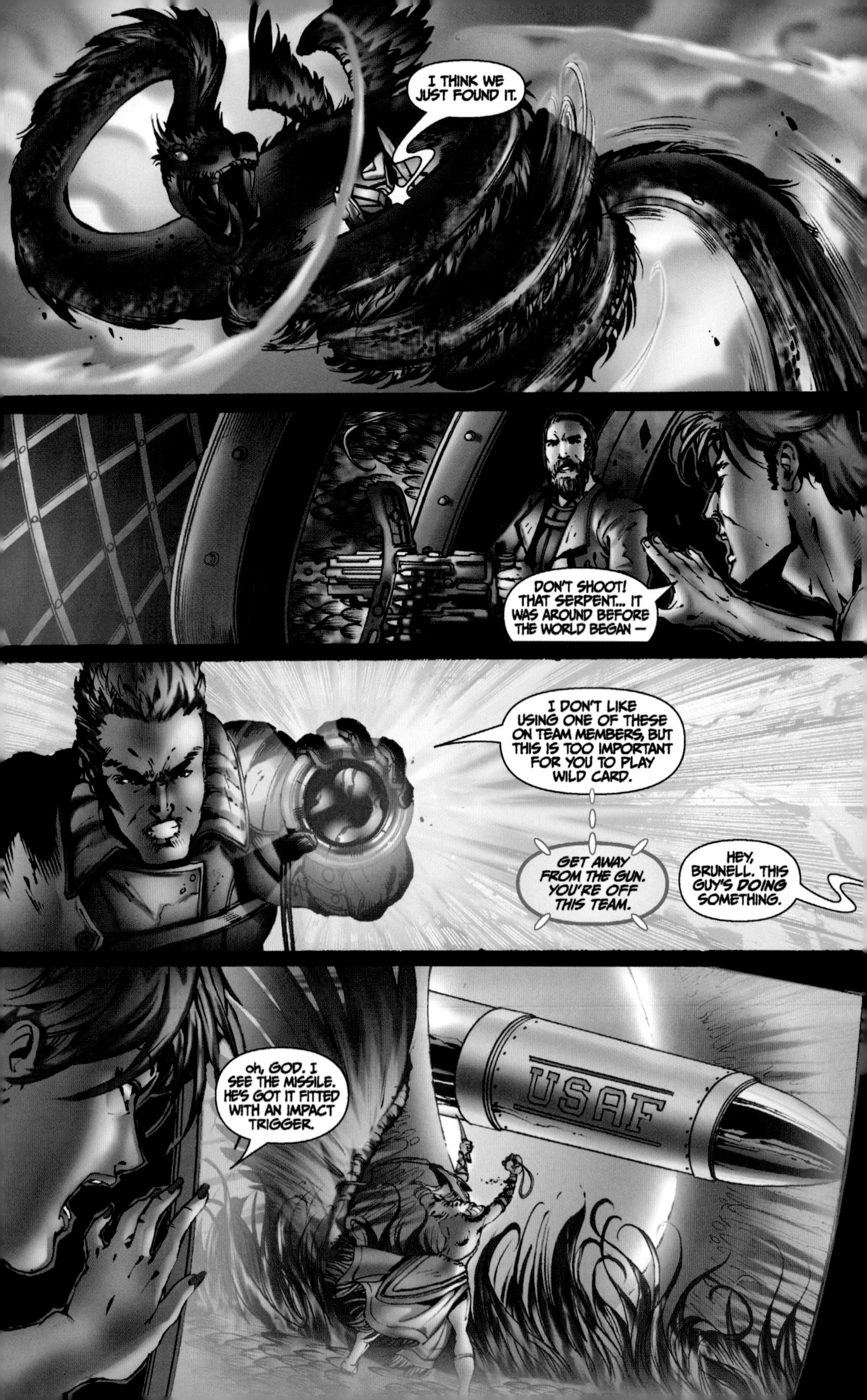
I THINK WE JUST FOUND IT.
DON'T SHOOT! THAT SERPENT... IT WAS AROUND BEFORE THE WORLD BEGAN —
I DON'T LIKE USING ONE OF THESE ON TEAM MEMBERS, BUT THIS IS TOO IMPORTANT FOR YOU TO PLAY WILD CARD.
GET AWAY FROM THE GUN. YOU'RE OFF THIS TEAM.
HEY, BRUNELL. THIS GUY'S DOING SOMETHING.
oh, GOD. I SEE THE MISSILE. HE'S GOT IT FITTED WITH AN IMPACT TRIGGER.
USAF

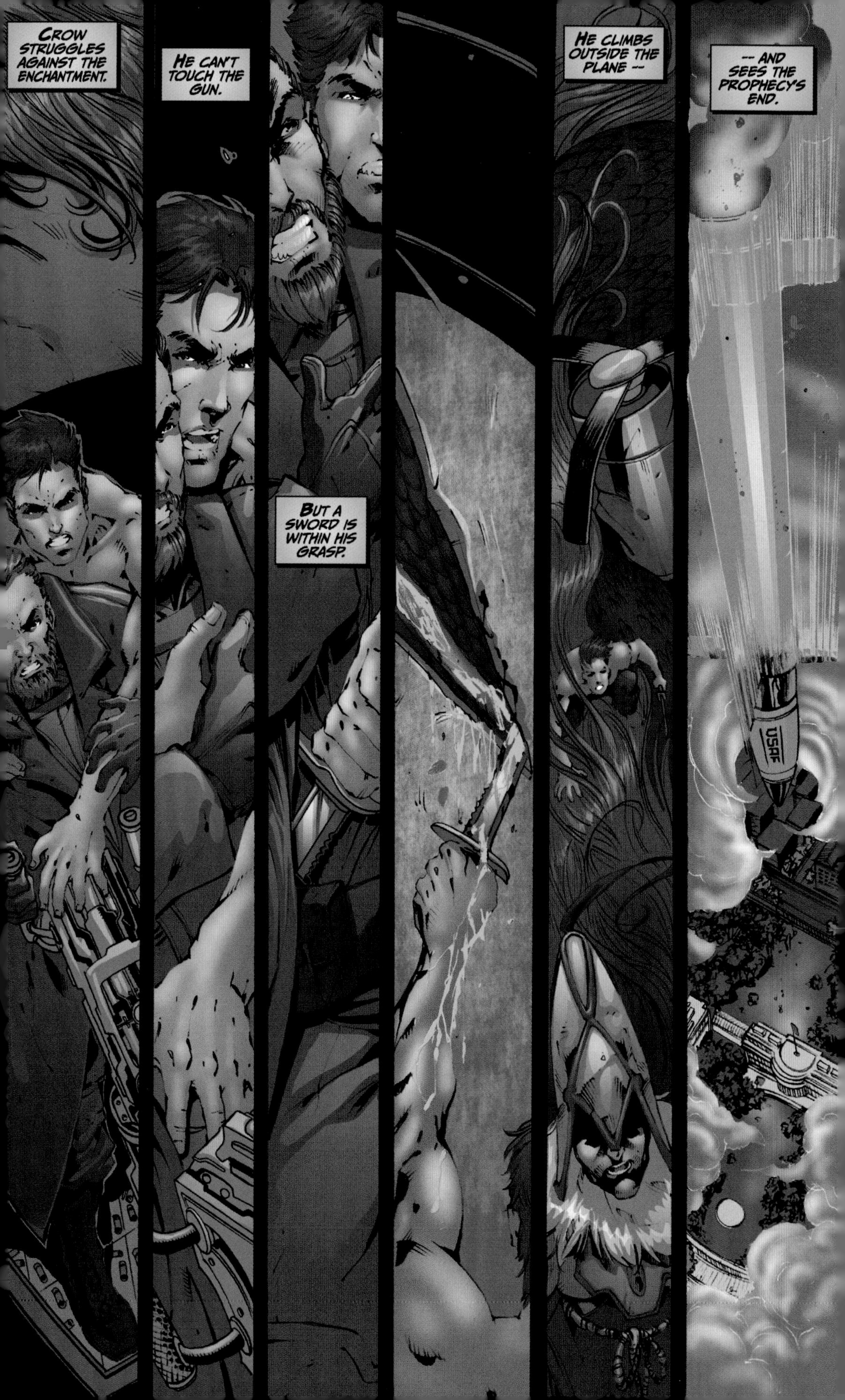
CROW STRUGGLES AGAINST THE ENCHANTMENT.
HE CAN'T TOUCH THE GUN.
BUT A SWORD IS WITHIN HIS GRASP.
HE CLIMBS OUTSIDE THE PLANE --
-- AND SEES THE PROPHECY'S END.
USAF

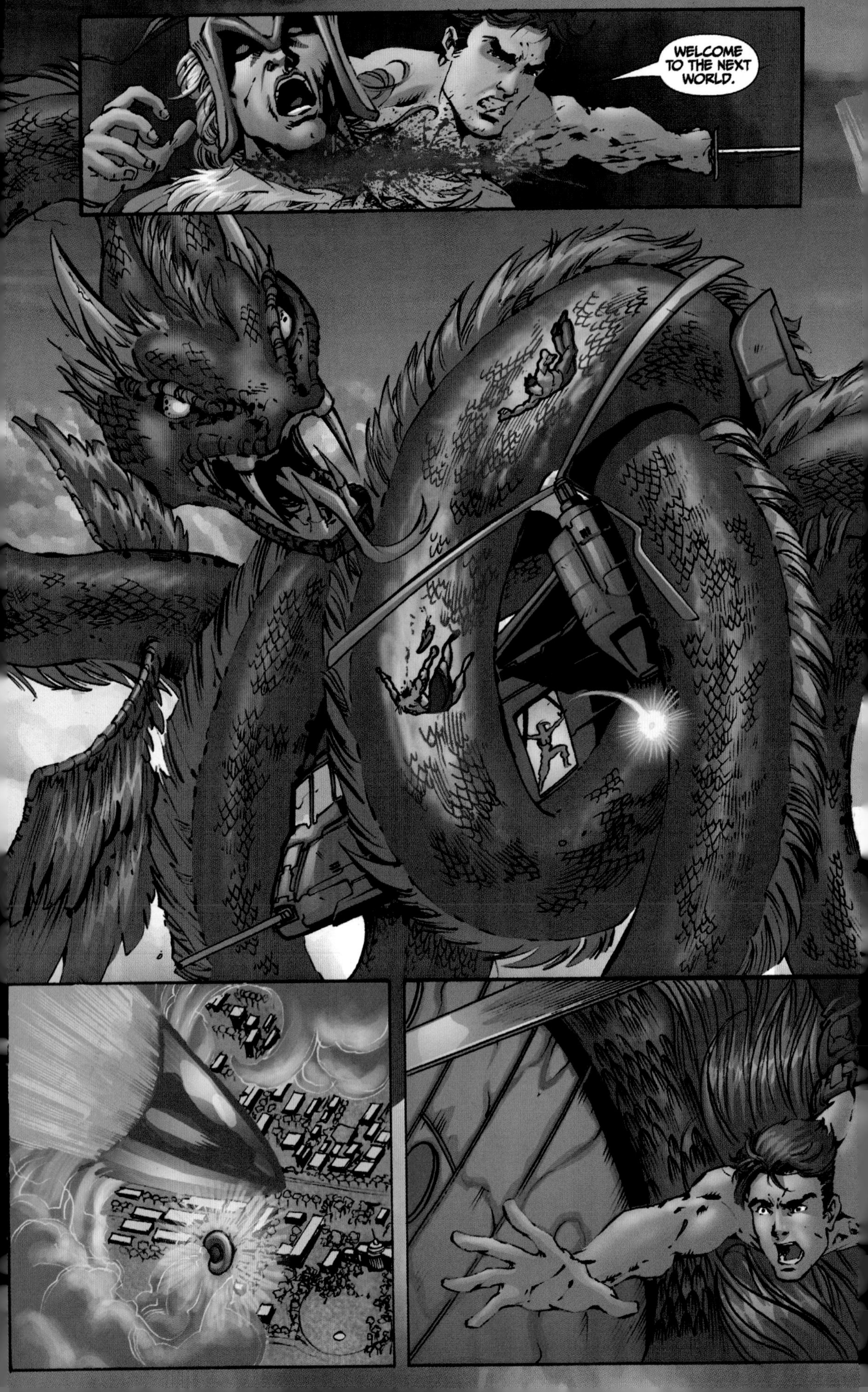
WELCOME TO THE NEXT WORLD.

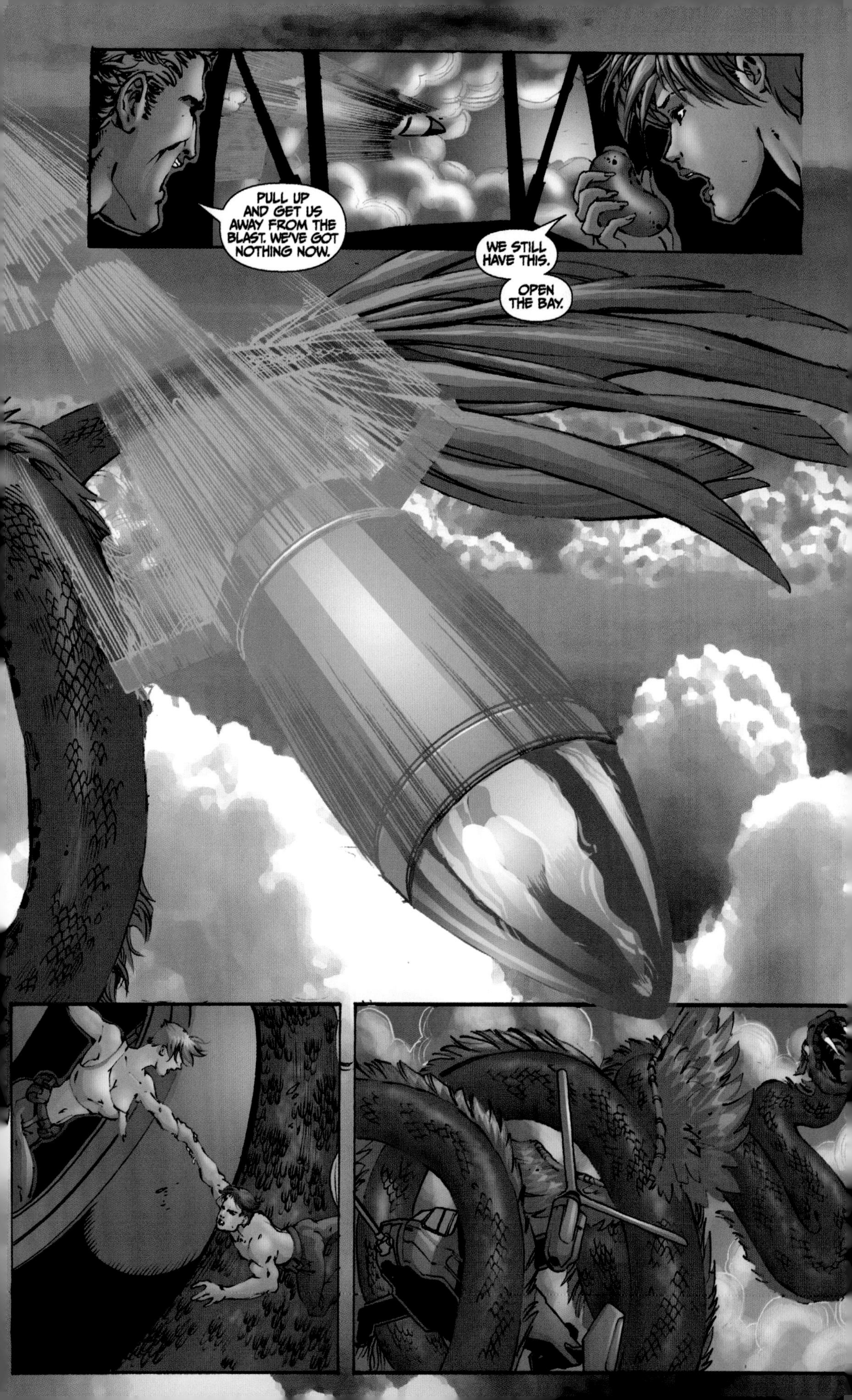
PULL UP AND GET US AWAY FROM THE BLAST. WE'VE GOT NOTHING NOW.
WE STILL HAVE THIS.
OPEN THE BAY.

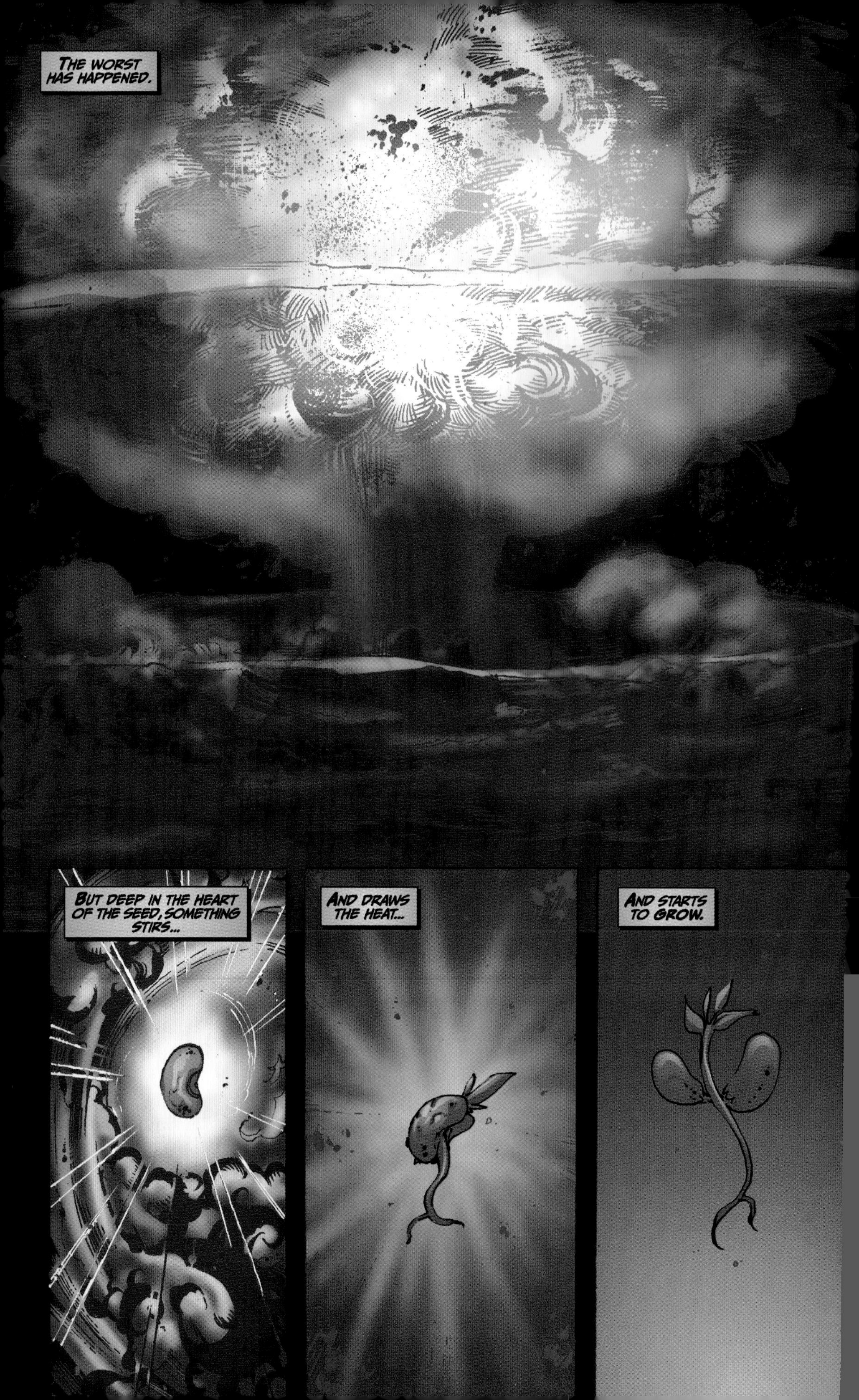
THE WORST HAS HAPPENED.
BUT DEEP IN THE HEART OF THE SEED, SOMETHING STIRS...
AND DRAWS THE HEAT...
AND STARTS TO GROW.

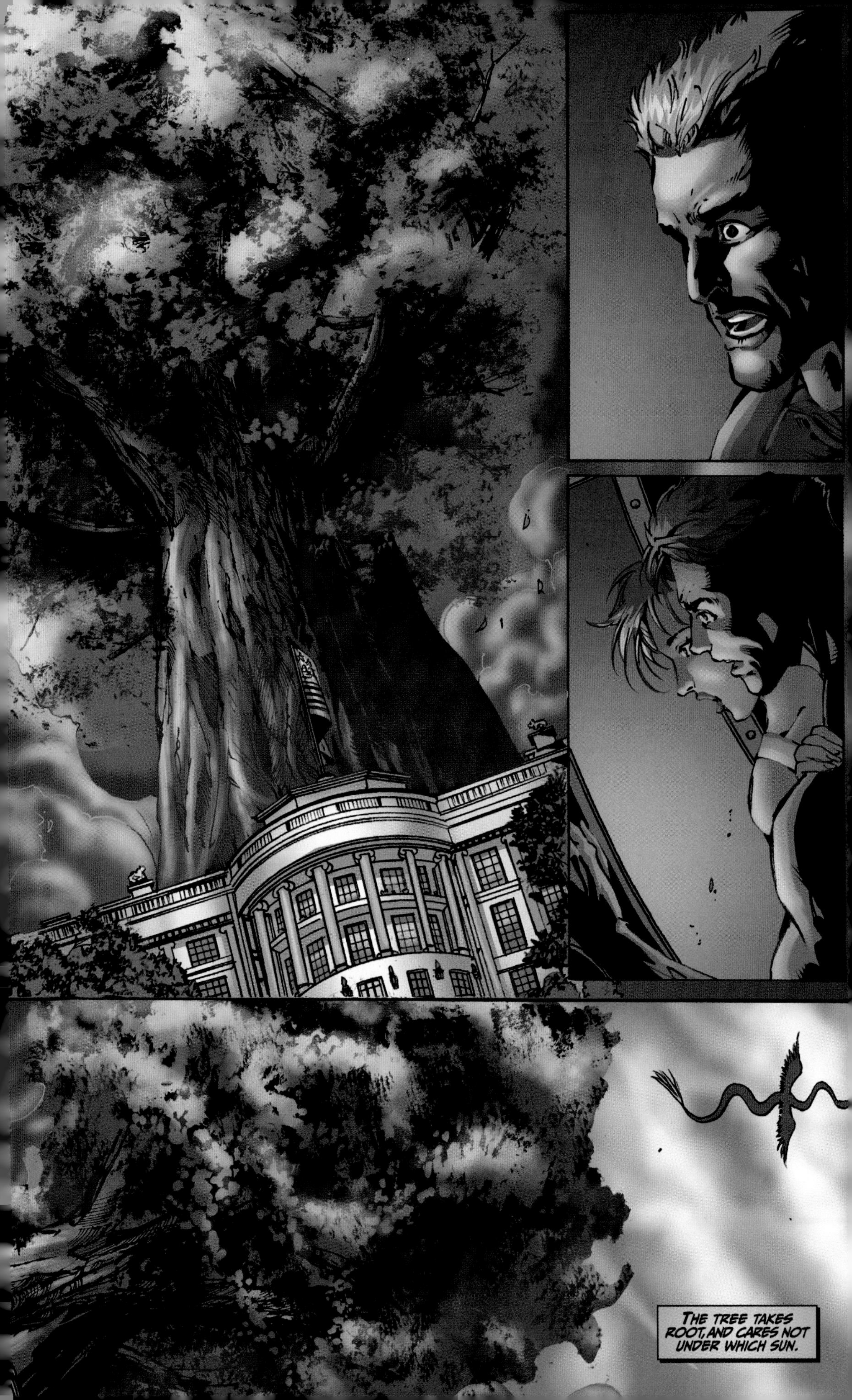
THE TREE TAKES ROOT, AND CARES NOT UNDER WHICH SUN.

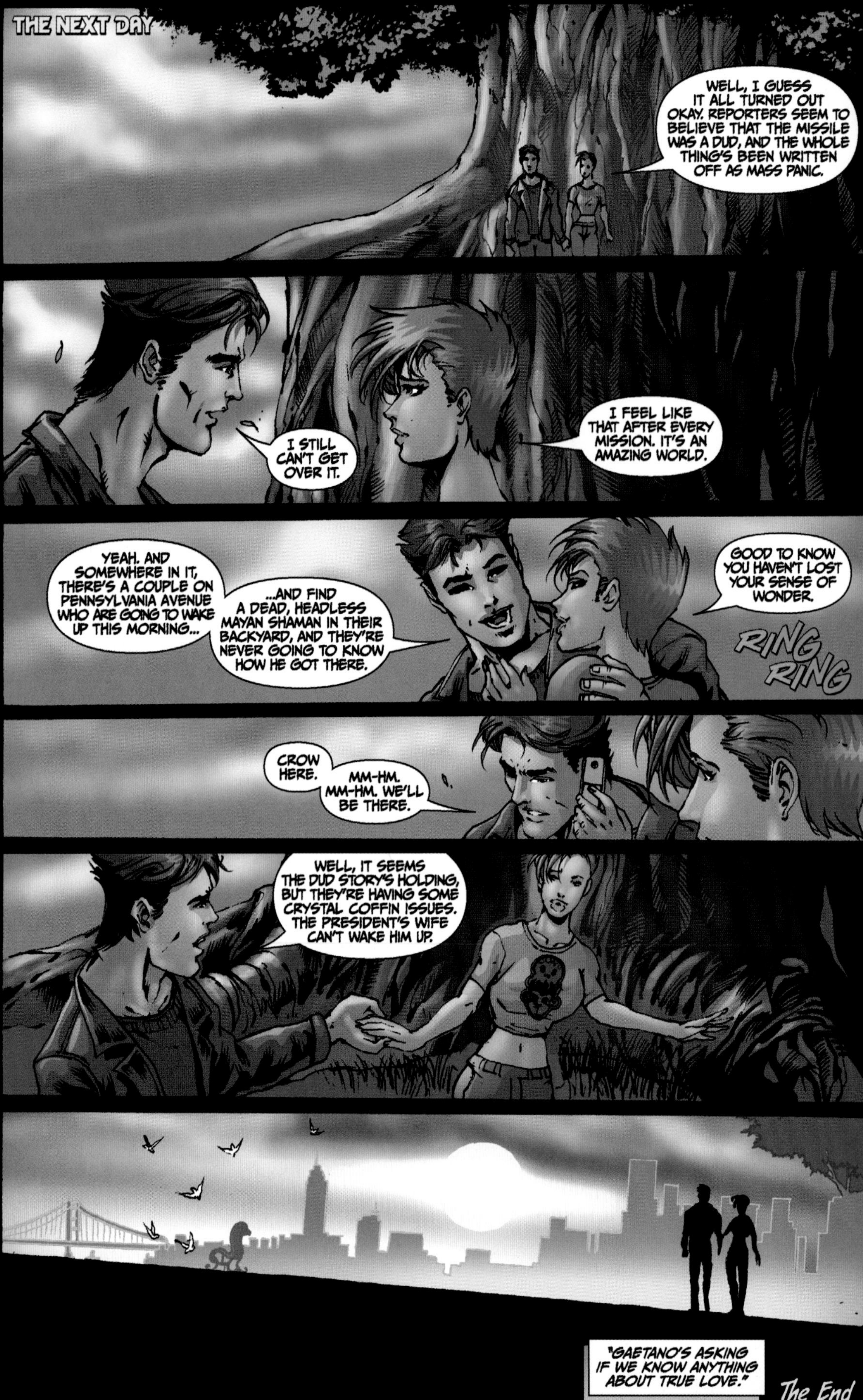
THE NEXT DAY
WELL, I GUESS IT ALL TURNED OUT OKAY. REPORTERS SEEM TO BELIEVE THAT THE MISSILE WAS A DUD, AND THE WHOLE THING'S BEEN WRITTEN OFF AS MASS PANIC.
I STILL CAN'T GET OVER IT.
I FEEL LIKE THAT AFTER EVERY MISSION. IT'S AN AMAZING WORLD.
YEAH. AND SOMEWHERE IN IT, THERE'S A COUPLE ON PENNSYLVANIA AVENUE WHO ARE GOING TO WAKE UP THIS MORNING...
...AND FIND A DEAD, HEADLESS MAYAN SHAMAN IN THEIR BACKYARD, AND THEY'RE NEVER GOING TO KNOW HOW HE GOT THERE.
GOOD TO KNOW YOU HAVEN'T LOST YOUR SENSE OF WONDER.
RING RING
CROW HERE.
MM-HM. MM-HM. WE'LL BE THERE.
WELL, IT SEEMS THE DUD STORY'S HOLDING, BUT THEY'RE HAVING SOME CRYSTAL COFFIN ISSUES. THE PRESIDENT'S WIFE CAN'T WAKE HIM UP.
"GAETANO'S ASKING IF WE KNOW ANYTHING ABOUT TRUE LOVE."
The End

M.I.T.H.™

> "Man will occasionally stumble over the truth, but most of the time he will pick himself up and continue on as if nothing had ever happened."
>
> -- Winston Churchill

THE END.

The D.C.

July 29, 2005

.75 cents

Gardener At White House Begins "Extensive Changes"

by Carrie Winter

WASHINGTON - The Rose Garden has been a fixture of the White House since 1913, when Ellen Wilson, first wife of Woodrow Wilson, replaced Eleanor Roosevelt's colonial West Garden with one that grew roses.

But the current White House gardener, Yomato Iku, has decided to bring the garden up to date for the twenty-first century, beginning with a commemorative tree that was a gift from the government of Guatemala. Commemorative trees have been added to the White House grounds before, but never one of such size. The tree, known as a holds-up-sky, measures thirty-two feet in circumference and is approximately one hundred and forty feet tall.

Iku says the tree is "merely one of many new, extensive changes," he has planned. "This enormous tree was no accident," he proclaimed. "It is a symbolic representation of our long-standing relationship with the people of Guatemala. Tourists will be fascinated to notice how the ground around the tree is hardly disturbed, as if the tree has been there for centuries. That was quite a trick, let me tell you."

According to White House spokesmen, the choice of tree was reached by popular consensus among U.S. and Guatemalan ambassadors. "We debated over whether or not a tree this size would be an eyesore," says one White House staffer, "but in the end, we fully support the gardener's decision."

Other White House staff complain that

MISSILE

Army Officials Call Exercise "Great Success"

by Max Whitsunday

WASHINGTON - A large, multi-part terrorism alert exercise took place Monday, in what experts are calling a "highly successful" venture.

The Public Panic Media Crisis Response Scenario Exercise involved combined air and land operations as central as the Mall and as far away as the Gulf of Mexico. In a unique twist on traditional readiness exercises, false information about the theft of a nuclear warhead was disseminated through major media outlets in order to observe how print, television, and Web journalists reacted to the dire emergency. The test even went so far as to release a disarmed warhead into the D.C. area, to be found by scrambled National Guard units.

UPDATE

SCARE!

The White House responded swiftly to questions about the hazy moral and legal grounds of such an act. "This is a normal and ethical procedure," said White House spokesman Victor Gaetano. "It would be remiss of us not to include the media for the sake of verisimilitude. There was never any danger. Please repeat that and then go about your business."

However frightening such a specter might be, it was a normal and ethical procedure, and in this reporter's opinion, it would be remiss of the exercise's planners to not include the media in such events, if only for the sake of verisimilitude. After all, there was never any danger.

The exercise revealed minor coordination issues at the local level, but overall, says one Army official, "It was so successful that you can expect to see many more in the immediate future."

Beheaded Party-Goer Found in Yard
by Horace Gelder

WASHINGTON - Police are trying to piece together how a headless body ended up in the back yard of a rowhouse on Constitution Avenue and 19th Street. No autopsy results have been released, but witnesses say that the headless body was found dressed in a colorful outfit, including a cape of feathers.

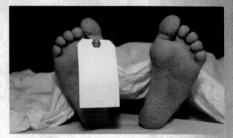

"It looks like he was going to Mardis Gras," says one unnamed source. "Except he didn't bring his head, and someone broke every bone in his body."

Property-owner Russ Yalen says he has no idea how the body appeared in his yard. "It's a mystery to me," he says. "The gate was locked and there were no footprints. It's like he just fell out of the sky."

The body, male and in its late 30s, carried no identification on it, or even a wallet, says Yalen. "His arms were scarred, like he'd survived a lot of cuts. Maybe he was really clumsy in the kitchen," he conjectures.

Yalen says he was instructed by police not to talk to the media, but felt the need to speak out. "I just wish I knew who to contact," he says. "Somewhere, there's a sky-diving costume party wondering where their friend is. It's really sad."

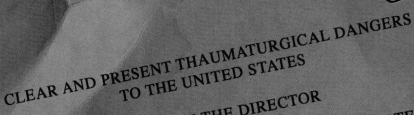

CLEAR AND PRESENT THAUMATURGICAL DANGERS
TO THE UNITED STATES

OFFICE OF THE DIRECTOR

MAGICAL INTELLIGENCE TACTICAL HEADQUARTERS

JANUARY 2004-JUNE 2005

MAGICAL INTELLIGENCE TACTICAL HEADQUARTERS

M.I.T.H.

11 JULY 2005

NRSPACE

WARNING: HANDLE VIA M.I.T.H. CONTROL CHANNELS ONLY

VITAL RECORDS COPY

THIS DOCUMENT CONTAINS INFORMATION USABLE ONLY WITHIN THE M.I.T.H. CONTROL SYSTEM. IT IS TO BE SEEN ON A MUST-KNOW BASIS ONLY BY PERSONNEL ESPECIALLY INDOCTRINATED AND AUTHORIZED. REPRODUCTION IS PROHIBITED UNLESS APPROVED BY THE ORIGINATOR.

...ECTIVELY AS "MAGIC." WHILE NO FORMAL ... D DUE TO THE NEED TO PRESERVE THE TOP SECR... , IN TWO YEARS IN THE FIELD THERE HAS BEEN NO ... OR REPORT OF THE COLLECTED THAUMATURGICAL ... VER ONE HUNDRED AND TWENTY NATIONS INVESTIG... OR HAVE ANY OF THE NATIONS INVESTIGATED ENGAGED IN SIGNIFICANT EXPLORATION OF VALUABLE ANTIQUITIES SITES, OR STOCKPILING OF SO-CALLED "WEAPONS OF MAGICAL DESTRUCTION."

All succeeding reports concur. We are alone in our possession of a significant store of thaumaturgically active items, recovered from archaeological digs throughout the world. To all evidence, no other national government has discovered the powers of these items yet. We credit this to Genie #15139, who claims to have granted President Nixon's wish that this be so. -- VG

UNFORTUNATELY, NEITHER HAVE WE. DESPITE OUR BEST EFFORTS, WE HAVE MADE LITTLE HEADWAY IN ATTEMPT... TO CREATE MAGIC OF OUR OWN AND MUST STILL RELY ... THOSE ITEMS ALREADY RECOVERED. ONE OF OUR FEW BREAKTHROUGHS IN THIS AREA HAS BEEN TO DEVELO... CAMERA USING LENSES OF CRYSTAL BALL GLASS, WHI... ENABLES US TO PRODUCE PHOTO DOCUMENTATION ... OUR RESEARCH. FORTUNATELY FOR THE CONTINUE... SECRECY OF THIS PROGRAM, MAGICAL EFFECTS DO... OTHERWISE SHOW UP ON VIDEO OR FILM. -- V...

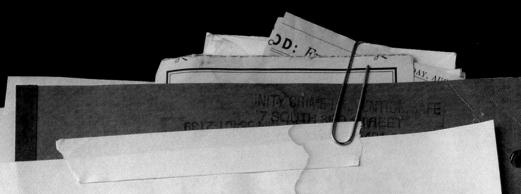

THAUMATURGICAL BRIEF
16/06/05

I. Summary

During the period of January 2004 to June of 2005, the number of suspected non-governmental sorcerous organizations (NGSOs) increased considerably, from an estimated 38 to 112. These NGSOs are believed to be made up primarily of indigenous peoples who have preserved their ancient magical traditions through a lack of external influences. This makes them a primary threat to the United States, as they are able to work magical spells and use powerful artifacts with no additional training.

Of these, 14 accomplished their stated goal of stealing nuclear weapons from United States and other sources; of these, all 14 threats were located and neutralized before completion of a successful terror act. Such acts have decreased in frequency by 12.5% from the previous period of July 2002 to December 2004. The remaining groups resorted to thaumaturgically-assisted activities on a lesser scale, as shown below.

Suicide/Animated corpse bombings: 16%
Assaults on ground transport: 28%
Assaults on air transport: 5%
Assaults on shipping: 14%
Oil-refinery-to-wine transformations: 11%
Zombification: 8%
Mind control: 2%
Kidnappings: 5%
Curses: 11%

As much of M.I.T.H.'s collection work was done before we became aware of these groups' existence, the majority of our current stockpile was taken from sites which these groups consider to be their "holy places" or "capital cities." This has led to a certain resentment of Americans on their part, and we believe that at least thirty-two of these groups have called down so-called "blood curses" upon the so-called "godless heathen American pig-dogs." -- VG

Supplemental Transmutational Resource 1A (hereafter STR-1A) has the outw ap-pearance of a common female Branta canadensis, or Canadian goose. STR-1A me res 6 feet (1.82m) wing tip to wing tip, 40 inches (0.98m) beak to tail and masses pounds 8 ounces (6.13 kilos), though weight fluctuates when gravid.

STR-1A's reproductive organs are possessed of a profound generative/ transmutational dweomer that allows for the refinement of precious metals and/or currencies of small value. This process was first discovered by Franklin Machise, owner of the Mill Valley golf course in Greenwich, Connecticut, who has since been relieved of this information. No other geese collected from the Mill Valley golf course have paralleled STR-1A's ability, nor have any other transmutational abilities been reported amongst the geese population of Connecticut.

STR-1A's ability was at first believed to solely consist of laying eggs with a gold content of 94% purity or better. This was later disproved, however, by a serendipitous occasion when STR-1A, presumably believing the greenish paper to be some kind of vegetation, ate a five-dollar bill, and has been laying crumpled counterfeit notes ever since. Such notes are distinguished from the genuine article by their imprecise watermark and lack of detail on Lincoln's head. However, as the five-dollar bills seem to provide STR-1A with an easier gestation and laying experience, STR-1A preferentially lays them rather than gold eggs at a ratio of approximately 3 to 1. Attempts to feed currency of higher denominations to STR-1A or to refine her forgery abilities have so far proven unsuccessful.

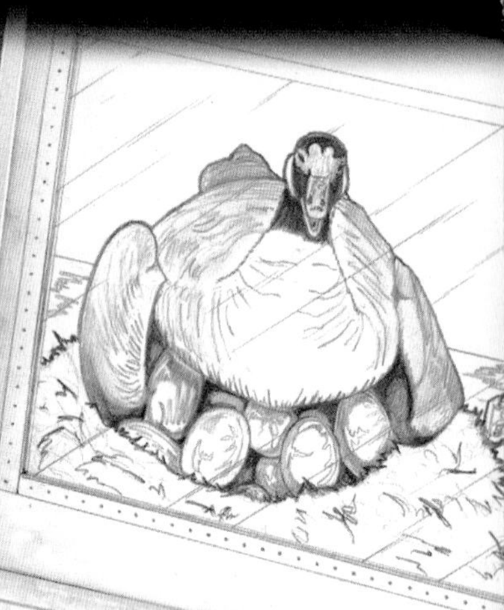

Item: Supplemental Transmutational Resource 1A
Colloquial Nomenclature: "Black Budget"
Office: Budgetary Oversight and Transmutational Resources

The POEND #4 consists of a series of two interlocking bronze rings with a third silver ring between them, w weight of 77-16/100 grains (5 grams). On the inside of the rings are a series of prayers written in colloquial seventeenth-century Tagalog, asking God to write His words on the hearts of men, so that they might obey brought out of wickedness. Molecular analysis has confirmed traces of human blood within the grooves of prayer, classifying POEND #4 as an anting-anting, or personal religious charm.

POEND #4 amplifies the suggestive power of its bearer's voice, allowing him to make any suggestion, tion, or comment, with which his listener is then compelled to agree. This has led to strategic recalculation number of departments (see "Disappearance of the Middleman," M.I.T.H. Quarterly #238) and no end of a staff and private contractor alike (see "The Ethics of Ultimate Power," M.I.T.H. Quarterly #280, for a mas articles reporting abuses, including but not limited to M.I.T.H. funding, inter-office fraternizing, and forc agement to wear underclothes on their head and chant "Who's the Big Man Now?"). Staffers should be al symptoms of past abuse, such as speaking in a slow monotone, repetitious answers to complex question dance machine music, and mimicking the haircuts of popular television stars.

Although M.I.T.H. researchers have yet to determine the precise method of construction for POEND have managed to replicate it several times by the expedient step of wearing the amulet and ordering oth "go make me one of these." There are currently twelve known, and five rumored, amulets in stock.

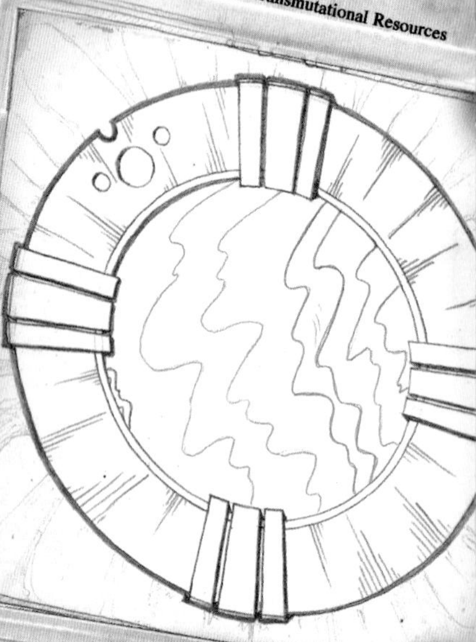

Item: Primary Obedience Enforcement Negotiating Device #4
Colloquial Nomenclature: "Command and Control"
Office: RESTRICTED ACCESS
Commi
Serial

The LITRSEM is a thi that alters its own length, ranging from 12 to 150 feet (3.67 to 45.73m) but rem always at 1.3 inches (33.02mm) in width and apparently zero thickness. An optical effect surrounds the chain in a slight nimbus, creating a prismatic aura. The fetter is highly resistant to temperature differentials or attempts to break, cut, or pierce it.

The creation of the LITRSEM dates to the tenth century A.D., in the region of Uppsala on the Swedish peninsula. After being exiled there for the practice of female magics (also known as seid or "black magic"), a magician named Corvander (more properly, Korvandr) attempted to recreate Gleipnir, the silken ribbon that bound Fenrir, the devouring wolf of Norse mythology. Gleipnir's strength came from its impossible ingredients, such as the roots of a mountains, a bird's spittle, the noise of a cat's footfall and a hair from a woman's beard.

Unable to acquire these ingredients, Corvander substituted the roots of a tree, the tongue of a chicken, the paw of a cat, and a hair from the chin of the demonic witch Jezi Baba. The resultant fetter appears to have retained Jezi Baba's predatory instincts: it is self-aware and self-mobile. It will lengthen or shrink as directed, and has been observed to wag or nod in response to questions, though its intellect is limited. When left unsupervised, the LITRSEM will conceal itself in the highest point in a room and entangle anyone who enters the area. Attempts to train the LITRSEM to restrain only those with proper identification have met with great success, and the LITRSEM has been employed at a number of high-clearance facilities.

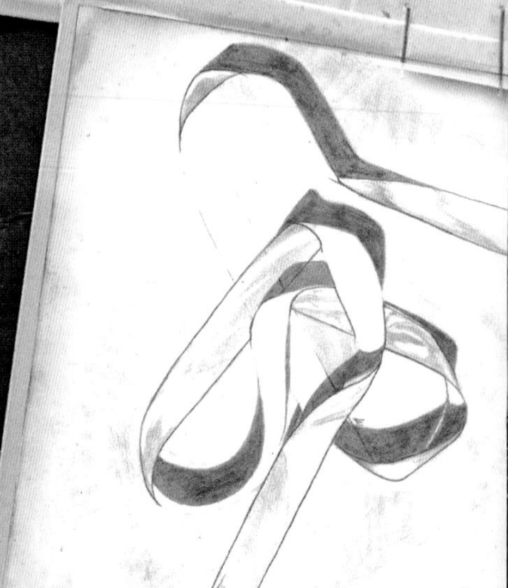

Item: Lightweight Thaumaturgical Restraint, Self-Mobile
Colloquial Nomenclature: "The Slithering Chains of Corvander the Black
Office: Security
Committee: Nuclear, Biological, and Chemical Secu
Serial Number: 0239-2899-3927

M.I.T.H.

II. Suitable and Priority Areas

group seeking Greek control for
rved their knowledge of ancient
henian-age Olympian religion,
of many of the surviving
ology, but also the abilities
igned by the ancient scholar

e mythological beings who
eus was hidden -- and raised,
protected by the Dactyli.
e Dactyli were Ida's chil-
nst this second explanation
descendants of Zeus, who

modern-
lt's

day
symbol,
sacred ge
medium i
the case o
many nota

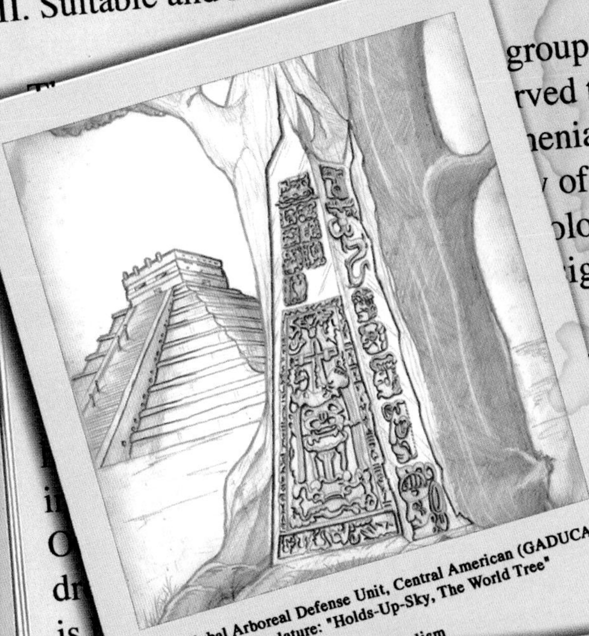

Item: Global Arboreal Defense Unit, Central American (GADUCA)
Colloquial Nomenclature: "Holds-Up-Sky, The World Tree"
...tegic Defense
...fense, Herbalism

The GADUCA, to all ordinary appearances, is a tree of no known genus or species, singular in nature, of ever-increasing height and circumference, with an average bough length of 25 feet. While there have been several "World Trees" from various cultures (such as Yggdrasil of Norse mythology), the individual plant of the Maya is prominent in the attention of the OSD due to its unique properties.

First and foremost is the legend that the tree is capable of surviving the death of repeated "suns," presumably cataclysmic explosions of apocalyptic magnitude. Second is its new and fortuitous location on the Ellipse in the District of Columbia (see the after-action report, "Operation Smoking Jaguar" for those with Epsilon Theta clearance), and third are the GADUCA's derivative enchantments, or DEs.

Bark from the GADUCA may be extracted with some effort, and the resulting wood product has proven exceptionally resistant to heat, failing to burn at 4500 degrees Celsius. Possible applications of this DE are attached in Appendix A, "Materials Science and the World Tree." Experiments are currently underway to construct bark-based vehicular armor.

The leaves of the GADUCA are oblanceolate in shape and number three to a stem. Similar to the bark, they do not burn under laboratory conditions and are not poisonous if fed to rabbits, mice, or rats. Indeed, rabbits that have ingested leaves from the GADUCA appear to have increased resistance to heat (see attached file, "Heat Prostration in GADUCA-Enhanced Oryctolagus cuniculus) and radiation (see attached file, "Cancer, Tumors, and Irradiation Immunity in GADUCA-Enhanced Oryctolagus cuniculus"). Human trials are eagerly anticipated due to their battlefield potential, but a double-blind test is still pending as of this writing.

...ng pages are samples of the art of M.I.T.H.

Illustrations this spread by: **Jacques David**

M.I.T.H. Pin ups
Art by **Jason Badower** pg 110 and 111

On the final page the complete M.I.T.H Cover
by **Tyler Kirkham** and **John Starr**, pg. 112

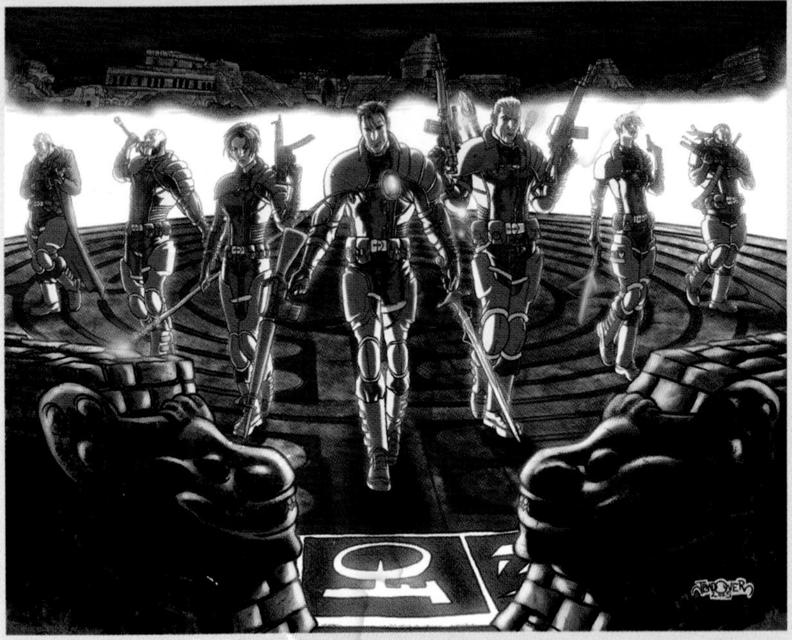

M.I.T.H. File number 0239-2899-3978

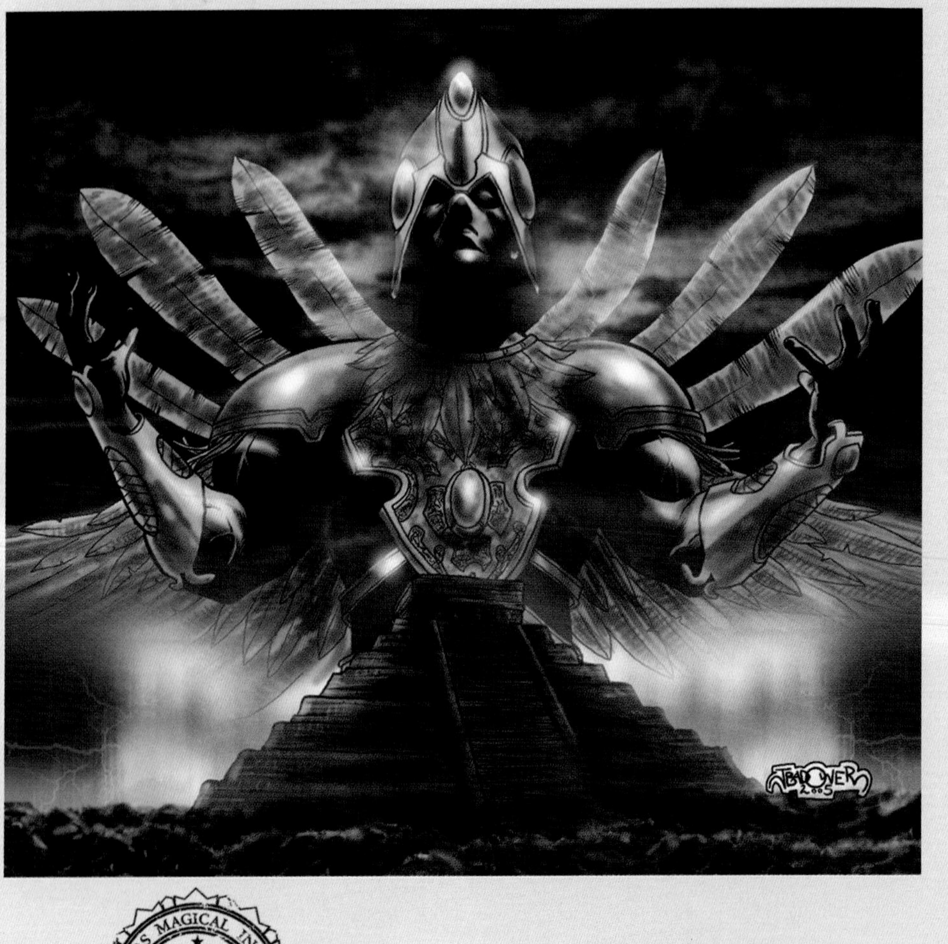

M.I.T.H. File number 0239-2899-3979